Four-coupled Tank Locomotive Classes Absorbed by the Great Western Railway

Front cover photo:
South Devon Railway 4-4-0ST 2122 Gorgon built in 1866 and which lasted to the end of the broad gauge in 1892, seen here c1890. (GW Trust)

Back cover photos:
Upper left: 4-4-4T, No.17 in lined M&SWJR livery at Swindon Town, April 1921. (A.W.Croughton/MLS Collection)

Upper right: Barry Railway 'G' class 0-4-4T, 68, renumbered 4 by the GWR, at Swindon, c1923. (Real Photographs/MLS Collection)

Lower: Ex-Monmouthshire Canal Co. 1870 built No. 14, rebuilt by the GWR in 1893, renumbered 1304 by the GWR at Gloucester, June 1903. (W.Beckerlegge/MLS Collection)

Four-coupled Tank Locomotive Classes Absorbed by the Great Western Railway

DAVID MAIDMENT

AN IMPRINT OF PEN & SWORD BOOKS LTD.
YORKSHIRE – PHILADELPHIA

First published in Great Britain in 2023 by
Pen & Sword Transport
An imprint of Pen & Sword Books Ltd
Yorkshire - Philadelphia

Copyright © David Maidment, 2023

ISBN 978 1 39909 543 3

The right of David Maidment to be identified as author of this work has been asserted by him in accordance with the Copyright, Designs and Patents Act 1988.

A CIP catalogue record for this book is available from the British Library.

All rights reserved. No part of this book may be reproduced or transmitted in any form or by any means, electronic or mechanical including photocopying, recording or by any information storage and retrieval system, without permission from the Publisher in writing.

Typeset in Palatino by SJmagic DESIGN SERVICES, India.
Printed and bound in India by Replika Press Pvt. Ltd.

Pen & Sword Books Ltd incorporates the Imprints of Pen & Sword Books Archaeology, Atlas, Aviation, Battleground, Discovery, Family History, History, Maritime, Military, Naval, Politics, Railways, Select, Transport, True Crime, Fiction, Frontline Books, Leo Cooper, Praetorian Press, Seaforth Publishing, Wharncliffe and White Owl.

For a complete list of Pen & Sword titles please contact:

PEN & SWORD BOOKS LIMITED
47 Church Street, Barnsley, South Yorkshire, S70 2AS, England
E-mail: enquiries@pen-and-sword.co.uk
Website: www.pen-and-sword.co.uk

Or

PEN AND SWORD BOOKS
1950 Lawrence Rd, Havertown, PA 19083, USA
E-mail: Uspen-and-sword@casematepublishers.com
Website: www.penandswordbooks.com

All royalties from this book will be donated to the Railway Children charity [reg. no. 1058991] [www.railwaychildren.org.uk]

Other books by David Maidment:
Novels (Religious historical fiction)
The Child Madonna, Melrose Books, 2009
The Missing Madonna, PublishNation, 2012
The Madonna and her Sons, PublishNation, 2015
The Reluctant Traitor, PublishNation, 2021

Novels (Railway fiction)
Lives on the Line, Max Books, 2013
Steamy Stories, PublishNation, 2021 (Short stories)

Non-fiction (Railways)
The Toss of a Coin, PublishNation, 2014
A Privileged Journey, Pen & Sword, 2015
An Indian Summer of Steam, Pen & Sword, 2015
Great Western Eight-Coupled Heavy Freight Locomotives,
    Pen & Sword, 2015
Great Western Moguls and Prairies, Pen & Sword, 2016
Southern Urie and Maunsell 2-cylinder 4-6-0s, Pen & Sword, 2016
Great Western Small-Wheeled Double-Framed 4-4-0s, Pen & Sword, 2017
The Development of the German Pacific Locomotive, Pen & Sword, 2017
Great Western Large-Wheeled Double-Framed 4-4-0s, Pen & Sword, 2017
Great Western Counties, 4-4-0s, 4-4-2Ts & 4-6-0s, Pen & Sword, 2018
Southern Maunsell Moguls and Tank Engines, Pen & Sword, 2018
Southern Maunsell 4-4-0s, Pen & Sword, 2019
Great Western Granges, Pen & Sword, 2019
Cambrian Railways Gallery, Pen & Sword, 2019
Great Western Panniers, Pen & Sword, 2019
Great Western Kings, Pen & Sword, 2020
Great Western & Absorbed Railway 0-6-2Ts, Pen & Sword, 2020
Drummond's L&SWR Passenger & Mixed Traffic Locomotives,
    Pen & Sword, 2020
Southern 0-6-0 Tender Locomotives, Pen & Sword, 2021
LNER 4-6-0 Locomotives, Pen & Sword, 2021
Midland & LMS 4-4-0s, Pen & Sword, 2021
Great Western Castle 4-6-0 Locomotives, 1923-1959, Pen & Sword, 2022
Great Western Castle 4-6-0 Locomotives, The Final Years, 1960-1965,
    Pen & Sword, 2022
Great Western Castle 4-6-0 Locomotives in the Preservation Era,
    Pen & Sword, 2023
Four-coupled Tank Locomotives built by the Great Western Railway,
    Pen & Sword, 2023

Non-fiction (Street Children)
The Other Railway Children, PublishNation, 2012
Nobody ever listened to me, PublishNation, 2012

CONTENTS

	Acknowledgements	7
	Introduction	8
Chapter 1	**The Engineers**	10
Chapter 2	**The Broad Gauge Locomotives**	14
	Bristol & Exeter Railway	14
	Carmarthen & Cardigan Railway	16
	Llynvi & Ogmore Railway	17
	South Devon Railway	17
	South Wales Mineral Railway	21
	Torbay & Brixham Railway	22
	Vale of Neath Railway	23
Chapter 3	**Standard Gauge Locomotives absorbed by the GWR before 1914**	24
	Birkenhead Railway	24
	Bristol & Exeter Railway	26
	Bristol Port Railway	28
	Festiniog & Blaenau Railway	29
	Liskeard & Looe Railway	29
	Llanelly Railway & Dock Company	31
	Llynvi & Ogmore Railway	32
	Manchester & Milford Railway	32
	Monmouthshire Canal Co.	34
	Newport, Abergavenny & Hereford Railway	37
	Oxford, Worcester & Wolverhampton Railway	38
	Severn & Wye and Severn Bridge Railway	39
	South Devon Railway	40
	Shrewsbury & Chester Railway	43
	Shrewsbury & Birmingham Railway	44
	Shrewsbury & Hereford and Tenbury Railways	45
	Watlington & Princes Risborough Railway	46
	West Cornwall Railway	48
	West Midland Railway	48

Chapter 4	**Locomotives absorbed by the GWR 1914–23**	50
	Alexandra Dock Railway	50
	Barry Railway	54
	Brecon & Merthyr Railway	61
	Burry Port & Gwendreath Valley Railway	66
	Cambrian Railways	67
	Cardiff Railway	79
	Midland & South Western Junction Railway	83
	Swindon, Marlborough & Andover Railway	84
	The Midland & South Western Junction Railway	86
	Neath & Brecon Railway	91
	Port Talbot Railway	94
	Rhymney Railway	97
	Swansea Harbour Trust Railway	103
	SHT - Powlesland & Mason Engines	110
	Vale of Rheidol Railway	128
Chapter 5	**Locomotives acquired by the GWR after 1923**	130
	Weston, Cleveland & Portishead Railway	130
	Ystalavera Tin Mine	131
	Corris Railway	132
	Wantage Tramway	134
Chapter 6	**Preservation**	135
	Appendix	140
	Bibliography	179
	Index	180

ACKNOWLEDGEMENTS

I could not have written this book without access to the details of the large variety of four-coupled tank engines that belonged at one time or another to the Great Western Railway or its constituent parts without the use of the comprehensive collection of books and photographs held by the Manchester Locomotive Society at their clubrooms on Stockport railway station. I am particularly grateful to the copies of the RCTS research on Great Western locomotives held in the MLS library and the archive of photographs made available to me, free of any publication fee, by their photo archivist, Paul Shackcloth, as once again I'm donating all royalties from this book to the Railway Children charity (www.railwaychildren.org.uk) which I founded in 1995. The charity supports street children living on the railway and bus stations of India and East Africa and works with the British Transport Police to protect and counsel runaway children picked up on the railway stations of our own country. I also acknowledge the help given to me by a colleague for many years in the railway industry, John Hodge, who has made a large number of photographs available to me from the F.K. Davies collection which he owns. As is often the case with collections, it is not always possible to identify the original photographer and if I have missed giving credit to the copyright holder, please contact the publisher. I also acknowledge the interest and research of Denis Lewis and Tess Walker of the Railway Studies Collection at Newton Abbot who were inspired to research the gaps in my knowledge about the South Wales engineers that I admitted in my earlier book on the GW 0-6-2 tanks. By chasing up census data and old newspaper cuttings, they have unearthed new details I have used in this book for which I'm grateful.

I also thank the Pen & Sword company staff for their usual helpful and very competent way in which they have brought this book to publication – my editor, Carol Trow, Commissioning Editor and friend, John Scott-Morgan, Transport Production Manager, Janet Brookes and the design and marketing staff at the company headquarters at Barnsley during the difficult periods of lockdown due to the Covid pandemic, working from home.

David Maidment
March 2023

INTRODUCTION

I didn't realise when I agreed to tackle the story of the Great Western Railway's four-coupled tank engines just how many there were. My immediate thought and inspiration was to tell the history of the GW's classic branch line engines, the 14XX 0-4-2 tank engines and their predecessors, the Wolverhampton built '517' class 0-4-2Ts and the Swindon built 2-4-0Ts – the 'Met Tanks'. Then as I began to research in the library and photo archives of the Manchester Locomotive Society in their clubrooms on Stockport station, the scale of the work that I had committed myself to in signing the contract with Pen & Sword Books began to dawn on me.

Delving back into the nineteenth century, the number of small railway companies that existed in the West of England, the West Midlands and South Wales that struggled and were taken over by the Great Western surprised me and their stories were complex. All had four-coupled locomotives within their fleets almost from the beginning and many had comparatively short routes, so tank engines were appropriate for nearly all of them. Most of these companies were taken over by the Great Western towards the end of the nineteenth century, a few retained their nominal existence but their operations were carried out by the GWR, and others, most notably the majority in South Wales and the Midland & South Western Junction Railway, were not absorbed by the GWR until 1922-3.

On lines in South Wales and South Devon and Cornwall and in the London suburban area, four-coupled tank engines became for decades the main passenger engines and only as traffic levels grew towards the turn of the century did the need for larger locomotives relegate the four-coupled varieties to secondary and branch line work. As well as the passenger activity, local freight trip work and shunting operations also became the domain of four-coupled tank engines, many remaining to near the end of steam in industrial sidings, collieries and docks. And on the country branches many engines, some dating from the 1850s and 1860s, though often much modified or rebuilt, lived on to a great age – at least until the 1920s and 30s, when Charles Collett in his drive for cost reduction replaced many by the simple, but very similar 48XX (later 14XX) 0-4-2 tank engines which remained the staple power of Great Western branch lines along with the 0-6-0 pannier tanks until the lines were closed or steam power was replaced by diesel multiple units. The Great Western and its absorbed companies were also among the railways that pioneered the use of railmotor vehicles incorporating a steam engine and carriage on the same chassis and as the locomotive part of the railmotor was of the 0-4-0T wheel arrangement, I have included the designs of the constituent companies.

I therefore tackle a comprehensive review of all the Great Western's four-coupled tank engines from the main company itself (in the first volume entitled *Four-coupled tank locomotives built by the Great Western Railway*) and all its constituent companies that merged or were taken over by it. I start with a chapter about the Broad Gauge engines, with following chapters on engines taken over from its constituent companies before the 1923 Grouping. Because most of these locomotives were withdrawn before I was born, I regret that I cannot include my normal practice of recounting my own experience with these engines – apart from one journey in the late 1950s to Swansea Docks when I surprised the foremen at Swansea East Dock and Danygraig by turning up with a shed permit before 6am and seeing some of the former Swansea

Harbour Trust and Powlesland & Mason shunting 0-4-0STs set off for their morning shift on the docks. I conclude with a description of preserved locomotives.

There is inevitably some duplication with earlier books that I have written for Pen & Sword. The description of the Cambrian engines was included in the book I co-wrote with Paul Carpenter, *The Cambrian Railways Gallery,* and a few of the engines described in this book were rebuilt with pannier tanks and were included in my Pen & Sword's *Great Western Pannier Tank Classes.* I repeat the text describing the design, construction and operation of these classes, and have included a few photos for completeness.

Chapter 1
THE ENGINEERS

Nearly all the locomotives constructed for the railway companies that were absorbed by the Great Western Railway between the 1870s and 1923 were purchased from contractors to their design. The locomotive construction companies identified as builders of these engines were, in alphabetical order:

Andrew Barclay
Avonside Engineering Co.
Beyer, Peacock
Brush Electrical Co.
Dodds & Co.
Dübs
E.B.Wilson
Fairlie Engine & Rolling Stock Co.
Falcon Engineering & Car Co.
Fox, Walker & Co.
Haigh Foundry
Hawthorn, Leslie
Henry Hughes & Co. (Loughborough)
Hopkins, Gilkes & Co. (Middlesbrough)
Hudswell Clarke
Hunslet
Ince Forge Co.
James Cross (St Helen's)
Jones & Son (Liverpool)
Kerr, Stewart & Co.
Kitson & Co.
Longridge & Co.
Manning, Wardle
Nasmyth, Wilson & Co.
North British Loco Co.
Peckett
R.Stephenson & Co.
Rothwell & Co.
Sharp Bros.
Sharp, Stewart
Slaughter, Gruning & Co.
Stothert & Slaughter
Vulcan Foundry
W.Sissons & Co. (Gloucester)
William Fairbairn & Sons
Yorkshire Engine Co.

The number of companies offering locomotive building capability in the second half of the nineteenth century is astonishing as is the wide variety utilised by the companies in the West of England and South Wales. Some companies acquired Daniel Gooch designed engines from the Great Western or had engines built for their use to his design.

Only in South Wales, with its profitable coal and steel industries, were companies large and financially secure enough to appoint their own locomotive superintendents designing and constructing engines at their own workshops. However, it has been extremely difficult to research the lives and personalities of the engineers who were the designers and drivers of locomotive policy in South Wales in the nineteenth and early part of the twentieth century. Despite searches of society libraries and enquiries of the National Railway Museum, the Institute of Mechanical Engineers and the Welsh Railway Research Circle, and past volumes of *The Engineer* and *Railway Magazine*, it has been hard to find other than the bare appointment dates with the honourable exception of Tom Hurry Riches of the Taff Vale and Cornelius Lundie of the Rhymney Railway, both of whom were large personalities who dominated their companies for very long periods of time. Some additional information about the Barry Railway's officers in the November 2020 *Welsh Railways Archive* added a little about H.F. Golding and his successor John Auld. Other than that, nearly all references have been to their work – the locomotives and rolling stock they designed, had constructed and maintained – especially from the comprehensive books of the Railway Correspondence and Travel Society (RCTS). However, on reading my efforts in the book I wrote about 0-6-2T locomotives in South Wales, Denis Lewis and Tess Walker of the Railway Studies Collection at Newton Abbot contacted me and were able to provide me with some additional material, much from newspaper cuttings and census data of the day.

Sir Daniel Gooch

Daniel Gooch was born in 1816 in Bebington, Northumberland, the son of an ironfounder. His family moved to Tredegar in 1831. He trained under Thomas Ellis who worked with Samuel Homfray and Richard Trevithick to pioneer steam locomotion. At the age of twenty he was recruited by Brunel as Superintendent of Locomotive Engines, starting in 1837. In 1840 he found the site for Swindon Works and in 1846 designed the prototype of the 'Iron Duke' broad gauge 4-2-2, *Great Western*, the first engine constructed at the new Works. Although he was mainly involved in the design and construction of broad gauge engines at Swindon, between 1854 and 1864 he designed a number of standard gauge engines for the GWR's Northern Division at Wolverhampton. He resigned in 1864 when he entered politics as a Conservative MP but continued as a member of the GWR Board, a post he retained until 1889. He died on 15 October 1889.

Tom Hurry Riches, Taff Vale Railway, 1873-1911

Tom Hurry Riches was born in Cardiff on 24 November 1846, the son of Charles, educated at Trices' Academy in the city and was apprenticed in the locomotive works of the Taff Vale Railway at the age of seventeen. After serving five years, he gained a scholarship to the Royal School of Mines. Before taking that up, he spent several months at sea as second engineer on the SS *Camilla*. After completing his scholarship course, he became manager of Bute Iron Works, designing and building iron roofs, bridges and engines of all types that belonged to the Marquis of Bute Trust.

In 1872, he became Chief Locomotive Foreman of the Taff Vale Railway and less than a year later was appointed as Locomotive Superintendent – at twenty-seven years of age, the youngest in the United Kingdom, following five previous superintendents appointed and let go in quick succession. He then held this post for thirty-eight years, dying in the post of heart failure on 4 September 1911. During his period of office, he doubled the locomotive stock of the company and extended his responsibility to cover carriages and wagons, dock and harbour machinery and coaling appliances. His reputation amongst his fellow engineers was high, despite only belonging to a relatively small railway. He was at various times President of the UK Association of Locomotive, Carriage & Wagon Superintendents, and Member of the Institute of Civil Engineers and the Iron & Steel Institute. He was a Council Member of the South Wales Institute of Engineers from 1885 and its President in 1907/8.

In 1877 he was presented at the Mansion House in London with a piece of silver plate in recognition of his bravery in rescuing 240 miners entombed during a flood at the Tynewydd Colliery, and wrote several highly regarded papers to the various professional bodies on a number of engineering topics throughout his career. He was reporter to the International Railway Congress in both 1900 and 1910 on 'Express Passenger Engines' and 'Railway Motor-Carriages'.

He took great interest in the education and training of young people and was for nine years a member of the elected Cardiff City Council, being Chairman of the Technical Committee of the County Borough of Cardiff. He was also a Justice of the Peace, a Governor of the National Museum of Wales and a Council Member of the University College of South Wales & Monmouthshire.

His health deteriorated in the last few months and he had to ease back on some of his many commitments, but he died on 4 September 1911 whilst still in office and active to the end.

John Cameron, Taff Vale Railway, 1911-22

John Cameron was born in Wigtonshire, Scotland and was educated at Inverness. He was apprenticed to Stroudley at Brighton and afterwards became Foreman of the Carriage & Wagon activity there. In 1885 he was appointed as Rolling Stock Inspector of the London & South Western Railway and, later that year, as Works Manager at Cardiff for the Taff Vale Railway. He was appointed as assistant to the Locomotive Superintendent in 1894 and became the Locomotive Superintendent himself after Tom Hurry Riches' death in 1911. He continued the TVR locomotive policy of building 0-6-2Ts for the Cardiff Valleys coal and passenger traffic and designed the class 'A' tanks which, rebuilt by Swindon with taper boilers, lasted well into the British Railways era. He retired when the Great Western Railway absorbed the Taff Vale Railway in 1922. He died on 17 March 1938.

Cornelius Lundie, Rhymney Railway 1872-1905

A Scot, born in Kelso in May 1918, he was educated privately and then attended science classes at both Glasgow and Edinburgh universities. His father died in 1832 and he began work at Broomielaw Bridge on the Clyde. In 1836, he moved to Durham in charge of the Clarence Railway (subsequently part of the North Eastern Railway). In 1839 he emigrated to Australia, undertaking various roles in engineering, returning to Britain in 1847. He then worked for the famous engineering contractor, Mr Brassey, and from 1855-61 was manager of the Blyth & Tyne Railway (also later absorbed by the North Eastern).

In 1861, he was appointed manager of the Rhymney Railway, then still in the early stages of its existence, and retained that role for over forty years. He helped it through the early years of financial difficulty and developed its expansion throughout the Rhymney Valley and Cardiff Docks area and the building of Caerphilly Works. Mr Ahrons, in his book on locomotive and train working in the nineteenth century, describes him by 1872 as the 'Pooh-Bah' of the Rhymney Railway, encompassing – using the same metaphor – Lord High Executioner, Mikado, Lord High Everything Else, Chorus and Band! He was the RR's General Manager, Traffic Manager, Superintendent of the Line, Chief Engineer and Chief Locomotive Superintendent, all rolled into one. (Mr Ahrons ironically stated that when visiting Cardiff station, he was disappointed to find that Lundie – in his presumed role of Chief Ticket Inspector – was off duty!)

Although there were so-called locomotive engineers under him, it was his influence and control that drove the company's locomotive policies, wedded to double-framed 0-6-0 and 0-6-2 saddle tanks throughout his career (many later converted to pannier tanks in the Churchward and Collett GW eras). He was eventually persuaded to retire in 1905 when he was 89 years old, but he was then appointed as a consulting director of the company and did not take a back seat, being seen in the Head Office only two days before he died, aged 93, on 12 February 1908. Richard Jenkins was nominally Locomotive Superintendent from 1884, but only took full control after Lundie's retirement in February 1905 and retired himself in December of the same year.

Lundie had one son and several grandchildren and was a man of strong religious principles applied strictly in his professional life, and more informally in his private life, where he was known as genial and good-hearted. He was a cultured man and was proud of personally knowing Sir Walter Scott and other writers of the time.

C.T. Hurry Riches, Rhymney Railway, 1906-22

He was the son of the Taff Vale's Tom Hurry Riches and was appointed to the role of Locomotive Superintendent of the Rhymney Railway on 1 January 1906 after the lengthy reign of Cornelius Lundie in that role in 1905, though for the first few years, Lundie's views still held considerable sway. Previously he had been Assistant Works Manager at Gorton (Manchester).

Charles Long, Brecon & Merthyr Railway, 1872-88

Charles Abraham Long was born on 28 May 1829 at Bitton in Gloucestershire in a community that included fitters and other men engaged in engineering. By 1851, he was employed as a fitter by the Great Western Railway in Bristol. He married Ann Knight there in 1855 and between 1856 and 1874 had four sons and three daughters, two of the sons dying in childhood. By 1871 he was Foreman, Engine Fitter of the Brecon & Merthyr Railway living at Newport and in 1872 was appointed as Locomotive Superintendent of the Brecon & Merthyr Railway. He retired in 1888 and died on 9 February 1890 aged 60.

George C. Owen, Brecon & Merthyr Railway, 1888-1909

George Charles Mickleburgh Owen was born in 1857, the son of George Owen, a Civil Engineer employed by the Cambrian Railways at Oswestry. In the 1881 census he was described as a mechanical engineer at Oswestry and in 1882 he married Marion Davies in South Kensington. He was appointed as Locomotive Superintendent of the Brecon & Merthyr Railway in 1888 and had two sons and a daughter. The family lived near the B&M Works at Machen and he was killed in 1909 while crossing the line to visit a signal box. He had been decapitated by a train running towards Newport and the verdict of accidental death was passed by the coroner. He was 52. He is buried at Llangattock Juxta, Caerleon. He left £10,000 to his widow.

James Dunbar, Brecon & Merthyr Railway, 1909-22

James Dunbar was born in 1862 in Grantham, the son of Andrew, a Chelsea Pensioner innkeeping in the town, and his wife, Mary. He was the second of eleven children and by 1891 he was a Foreman, Engine fitter of the Midland & Great Northern Railway based at Melton Constable.

He married Isabella in Portsmouth in 1891 and they had three sons and four daughters. He was appointed Locomotive Superintendent of the Brecon & Merthyr Railway in 1909 and moved to Machen near the B&M Works. He died on 26 February 1922 before he could take up his new post of Works Manager at Oswestry in February 1922 when the GWR absorbed the Brecon & Merthyr and other Welsh railways. He left £1,666 to his widow.

J.H. Hosgood, Barry Railway, 1884-1905

John Howell Hosgood was born in October 1860 in Cardiff, son of William, an engine fitter of the Taff Vale Railway, and Ellen. He became Chief Draughtsman of the Taff Vale Railway and in 1881 was made a member of the Institute of Mechanical Engineers. In 1884 he became a member of the Bute Lodge of the Freemasons and the same year was appointed as Locomotive Superintendent and Hydraulics Engineer of the Barry Railway. He married Florence Sainsbury of Thornbury in Gloucestershire in 1891 and they had two sons, the family living in Barry. He left the Barry Railway when it was incorporated in July 1905 and is recorded as leaving Liverpool for New York in December 1906. He returned to Wales on an unspecified date and died in Roath, Cardiff on 28 January 1910, aged 50, leaving £19,753 to his widow. He designed and was responsible for the construction of all bar ten of the Company's 150 locomotives.

Henry Frederick Golding, Barry Railway, 1905-09

Henry (Harry) Frederick Golding was born in 1868 at Weybridge, Surrey, the son of Edwin, a bricklayer/builder, and Anne Walpole of Loughborough. He started as a printer's apprentice but by the age of 15 became a draughtsman on the London & South Western Railway, spending four years in the drawing office before moving to the engineering shops at Nine Elms. In 1892 he married Helen Walker of New Pitsligo in Aberdeenshire in Portsea Island, Hants and they had five children. In 1893, aged 26, he became chief draughtsman of the Taff Vale Railway and then was assistant locomotive superintendent at Penarth Dock steam sheds under John Cameron. He was involved in the design of engines on that railway before moving to the Barry Railway as Locomotive Superintendent in 1905. Although well thought of on the Taff Vale Railway, his career on the Barry Railway seems to have been controversial and somewhat chequered involving disputes with the Trade Unions and allegations about the state of the engines involving a visit from inspectors from the Board of Trade. His management style was abrasive, and he was accused in particular of his tyrannical treatment of his drivers and firemen and his excessively strict disciplinarian style, notable even in that period. He resigned in 1909 with relationships with the company somewhat strained and left the country in 1913 for a senior position on the Northern Railway of Nigeria. He returned to Wales in 1915, but whether for a visit or permanently is unknown.

John Auld, Barry Railway, 1909-1922

John Auld was born in Kilmarnock on 8 March 1871, the son of David Auld, an engineer, and Sarah Manson. They were living in Bootle in Lancashire in 1881 but by 1891 the twenty-year-old John, after a five year apprenticeship, was an engine fitter for the Glasgow & South Western Railway in Glasgow. His marital situation seems confusing as he was recorded as marrying a Katherine Griffiths on an unknown date but by 1901 he was married to Agnes who came from Feald in Scotland. In 1895 he was a draughtsman on the Great North of Scotland Railway at Aberdeen and then moved south in 1898 to become Assistant to the Locomotive Superintendent of the London, Tilbury & Southend Railway at Plaistow, living at West Ham. In 1902 he returned to Scotland as Chief Locomotive Foreman of the G&SWR. John Auld came to the Barry Railway to replace Henry Golding in 1909. He became a member of the Institute of Mechanical Engineers in 1910. He was Locomotive Superintendent of the Barry Railway until its absorption by the GWR and clearly mended relationships after the forceful and abrasive Golding. In June 1922, he was appointed by the GWR as Mechanical Engineer to Barry Docks and Divisional Locomotive Superintendent of the Cardiff Valleys Division. Two months later, in August 1922, he moved to become Docks Assistant to the GWR Chief Mechanical Engineer (Charles Collett). In 1924 to 1932 he was designated as a Principal Assistant to the GWR C.M.E. By 1939 he was widowed and living with his sister and two housekeepers in Swindon, where he died on 17 May 1947, aged 76, leaving £30,994.

Chapter 2
THE BROAD GAUGE LOCOMOTIVES

The Great Western main lines constructed from 1835 onwards on Brunel's 7ft broad gauge were copied by a number of smaller companies in the same geographical area. The first GW broad gauge four-coupled tank locomotives were 2-4-0 tank locomotives converted from 2-4-0 tender engines and appeared as early as 1841 and similar designs to the GW engines were purchased or built by engineering companies for the South Devon, Bristol & Exeter and Torbay & Brixham railways in the West of England and the Vale of Neath, Llynvi & Ogmore and South Wales Mineral railways in Wales. Information about some of the earliest locomotives is sketchy and I have been very reliant on information unearthed by the Railway Correspondence & Travel Society and documented in their comprehensive reviews of Great Western locomotives published in the early 1950s.

Bristol & Exeter Railway
The Bristol & Exeter Railway was built to the broad gauge in 1844 and was leased to the Great Western Railway until 1849 when the B&E took over responsibility for motive power which were initially 4-2-2 express locomotives and a steam rail car. The latter though had only a single driving wheel under the locomotive and therefore does not qualify to be included in this book. The motive power was the responsibility of C.H. Gregory as Engineer until 1850 when James Pearson from the South Devon Railway took charge, although the early engines acquired were to Daniel Gooch's design. The company's own works and erecting shops were opened in 1854 at Bristol and the first engines built there appeared in 1859. The B&E built both broad and standard gauge engines. Early expresses were hauled by Gooch 4-2-2 tender engines and a remarkable group of 4-2-4 tank engines with a 9ft flangeless driving wheel and were capable of high speed (credited with at least one '80mph'), although they were converted to tender engines after a derailment of one in 1876.

47-52, 61-74, 85-90 (GW 2028 -2053) class 4-4-0ST, 1855
A batch of six 4-4-0 saddle tanks were built by Rothwell & Co. in 1855 and were numbered 47-52. Their key dimensions were:

Coupled wheels: 5ft 6in
Bogie wheels: 3ft 6in
Cylinders: 17in x 24in
Tank capacity: 1,100 gallons

A further four constructed by Beyer, Peacock & Co., (61-64) and ten by Vulcan Foundry (65-74) were larger, the Beyer, Peacock engines being built in 1862 and the Vulcan machines in 1867. Their dimensions were additionally:

Heating surface: 1,208sqft
Grate area: 20.7sqft
Weight: 44 tons 16 cwt
Tank capacity: 1,280 gallons

A final batch of six 4-4-0STs were built by the Avonside Engine Co. in 1872/3 and numbered 85-90. They differed only by having a smaller heating surface – 1,064sqft and a larger tank capacity – 1,440 gallons. When taken into GWR stock in 1876 they were renumbered 2028-2033 (the Rothwell engines), 2034-2037 (Beyer, Peacock), 2038-2047 (Vulcan) and 2048-2053 (Avonside).

Most broad gauge engines seemed ugly though impressive because of their size to those used only to standard gauge engines and these 4-4-0 saddle tanks looked badly proportioned and unprepossessing, but in fact they were successful, initially hauling passenger and freight services between Bristol and Exeter and then, after being absorbed into GWR stock, spending their last years in Devon and Cornwall.

2051 (Avonside B&E 88) was involved in a fatal collision at Norton Fitzwarren in 1890 and was withdrawn immediately in November, the other Avonside engines all remaining until the abolition of the broad gauge. The Rothwell engines were withdrawn between 1879 and 1884, the Beyer, Peacock engines between 1880 and 1886 and most of the Vulcan engines, like the Avonside ones, staying until May 1892. 2038 (B&E 65) and 2041 (68) were withdrawn early in 1880, 2044 in 1882, and three (2040, 2043 and 2046) in 1888/9.

110 (GW 2058) class 0-4-2ST, 1874

Two engines were purchased from contractors, Brotherhood of Chippenham, one of which was an 0-4-2 saddle tank engine used on the South Wales Mineral Railway – a Manning Wardle engine of 1864 (see later chapter on engines absorbed by the GW from the South Wales Mineral Railway). It was purchased by the Bristol & Exeter Railway in 1874 and numbered 110 (later GWR 2058). Its known dimensions were:

- Coupled wheels: 4ft 0in
- Trailing wheels: 3ft 6in
- Cylinders: 14in x 20in

Bristol & Exeter broad gauge 4-4-0T, No.71, built by Vulcan, 1867 and withdrawn in 1882. (F.K. Davies/John Hodge Collections)

Bristol & Exeter broad gauge 4-4-0T, No.74, built by Vulcan, 1867, at work on the docks at Watchet in north Somerset, an early photograph thought to be at the end of the 1860s or early 1870s. (F.K. Davies/John Hodge Collections)

Its use is not known, and it was withdrawn in 1881.

91 & 92 (GW 2094 -2095) class 0-4-0WT, 1872

91 and 92 were two well tanks built in the Bristol & Exeter Railway workshops at Bristol, the first in 1872 and the second two years later. Their only known dimensions were:

- Coupled wheels: 3ft 6in
- Outside cylinders: 14in x 18in
- Tank capacity: 800 gallons

They were built for shunting, were renumbered by the GWR as 2094 and 2095 and were withdrawn in 1880 and 1881 respectively, after only 7-8 years' service which suggests that they were not adequate for the task and were replaced by more suitable GW classes after the B & E's amalgamation with the GWR.

Carmarthen & Cardigan Railway

The Carmarthen and Cardigan Railway was an impecunious broad gauge system that started in 1860 building from Carmarthen towards Pencader, the first section opened in 1861. They hired two 4-4-0 tank engines and when the line reached Llandyssil in 1864, purchased two more. The line converted to standard gauge in 1872 to reduce costs and they sold their remaining broad gauge engines to the South Devon Railway. The line was sold to the GWR in 1882 and that company extended the branch to Newcastle Emlyn and never reached Cardigan (which was linked via Whitland).

Heron & Magpie 4-4-0T, 1861

Heron and *Magpie* were two 4-4-0 side tank locomotives hired by the Carmarthen & Cardigan Railway in 1861. They were built by Sharp, Stewart & Co. and their known dimensions were:

Coupled wheels:	5ft 2in (later 5ft 3in)
Bogie wheels:	3ft 3in
Cylinders:	17in x 24in
Heating surface:	1,312sqft
Grate area:	20sqft
Tank capacity:	900 gallons

On conversion of the line to standard gauge in 1872, they were sold to the South Devon Railway who immediately replaced the side tanks with saddle tanks. They were numbered by the GWR 2134 and 2135. They both survived until the end of the broad gauge and 2134 (*Heron*) pulled the last broad gauge train from Tavistock to Plymouth Millbay on 20 May 1892 before taking itself and the empty stock to Swindon for scrapping.

Etna & Hecla, 4-4-0ST, 1864

Etna and *Hecla* were built in 1864 by Rothwell & Co. and were 4-4-0 saddle tanks. Their known dimensions were:

Coupled wheels:	5ft 3in (later 5ft 6in)
Bogie wheels:	3ft 6in
Cylinders:	17in x 24in
Heating surface:	1,223sqft (new Avonside boiler for *Hecla* 1875)
Grate area:	15.5sqft (ditto)

The 4-4-0 side tank built by Sharp, Stewart & Co. in 1861 for the Carmarthen & Cardigan Railway and sold to the South Devon Railway and rebuilt as a saddle tank in 1872. Photo as built in 1861. (LPC/F.K. Davies/John Hodge Collection)

Tank capacity: 700 gallons (*Etna*), 1,000 gallons (*Hecla*)

Etna was sold to the South Devon Railway in 1868 and *Hecla* in 1872. *Hecla* received a new boiler and tank from the Avonside Engineering Co. in 1875. They were numbered 2132 and 2133 by the GWR after acquisition of the South Devon Railway in 1872. Both lasted until the end of the broad gauge in 1892.

Llynvi & Ogmore Railway

The Llynvi Valley Railway from Bridgend to Maesteg had three broad gauge engines, two 0-6-0 goods tank engines and a 4-4-0 saddle tank named *Rosa*. When it amalgamated with the Ogmore Valley Railway from Tondu to Ogmore Vale in 1868, it opted for the standard gauge and exchanged its three broad gauge engines for four standard gauge locomotives from the West Cornwall Railway, which had become part of the South Devon Railway in 1866.

Rosa 4-4-0ST, 1863

Rosa was constructed by Slaughter, Gruning & Co. in 1863 as a 4-4-0 saddle tank with the following known dimensions:

Coupled wheels: 5ft 6in
Cylinders: 16½in x 24in

It was acquired as part of the locomotive exchange by the South Devon Railway in 1868 and altered to the 0-6-0ST wheel arrangement in 1874 and given the number 2145 when that railway was amalgamated with the GWR in 1876. It was withdrawn in October 1885.

South Devon Railway

The South Devon Railway adopted in 1844 the 'atmospheric' system of traction and it took three years to get it running after any fashion. The first section between Exeter and Teignmouth was opened in 1846 and GW engines were used instead. The abandoned atmospheric section through to Plymouth with its gradients of around 1 in 40 was too much for the early GW engines and Gooch supplied the two 1849 'Corsair' 4-4-0STs to operate the line. Further tender engines were supplied by the GW in 1851 and in 1851, a contract with Evans & Geach was agreed to supply the motive power for ten years – twelve 4-4-0 saddle tanks and four 0-6-0 saddle tanks, built under the supervision of Gooch. The West Cornwall standard gauge railway was acquired in 1866 and converted to broad gauge and Evans, Walker and Gooch supplied further 4-4-0 and 0-6-0 saddle tanks, before the Great Western took over the South Devon Railway, along with the Bristol & Exeter, in 1876.

2096- 2105 4-4-0ST, 1851

The first five 4-4-0 saddle tanks acquired from the contractors in 1851 were built by Longridge & Co. of Bedlington and were named:

Comet Lance Rocket Meteor Aurora

The second batch of four engines were built by Haigh Foundry of Wigan between 1851 and 1853 and were named:

Priam Damon Falcon Orion

Just one was built by William Fairbairn and Sons of Manchester in 1852, named *Ostrich*, and the final two by Stothert and Slaughter of Bristol in 1853 named *Ixion* and *Osiris*.

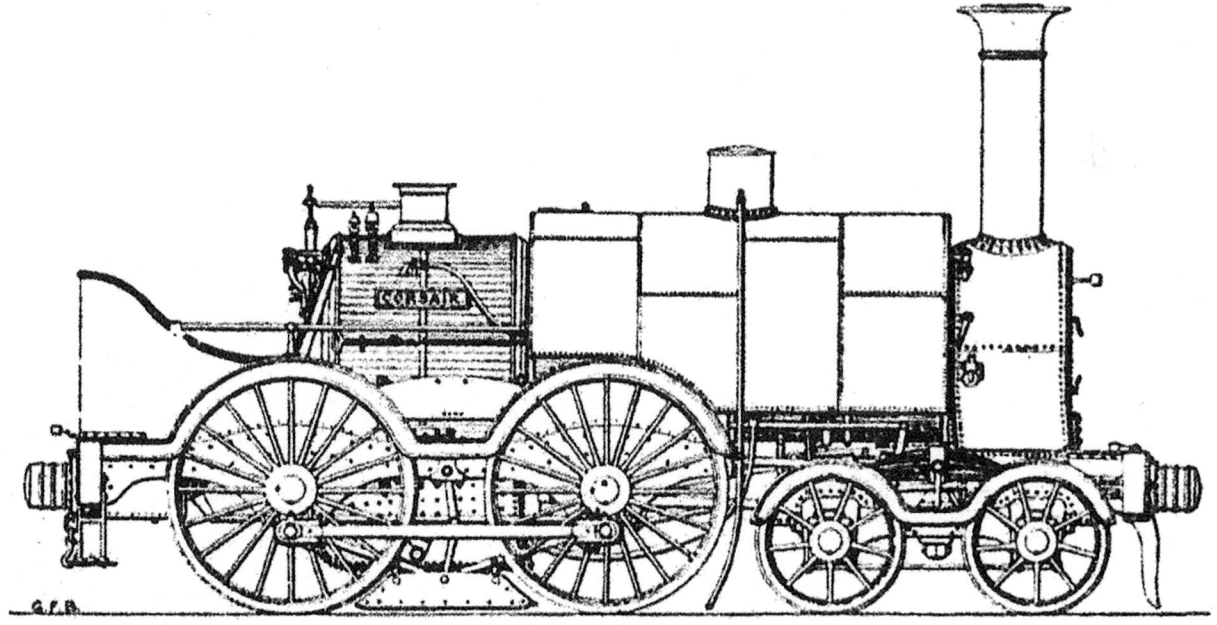

A drawing of the GW 'Corsair' class, examples of which were supplied by the GWR to the Bristol & Exeter Railway in 1849. (G.F. Bird/LCGB)

They were all similar to the GW 'Corsair' design, key dimensions being:

Coupled wheels:	5ft 9in
Bogie wheels:	3ft 6in
Cylinders:	17in x 24in
Boiler pressure:	60lb psi
Heating surface:	1,323sqft
Grate area:	22sqft
Tank capacity:	800 gallons

They were all operational in Devon and Cornwall, though many of them hardly survived the transfer to GW stock. The company struggled to keep them running and it was reported in October 1854 that only four of the twelve were operational, one of those in very poor condition, even though they were scarcely two or three years old. To keep the service running the South Devon Railway had to borrow a locomotive from the GWR. *Lance* was destroyed in a collision of goods trains at Menheniot in 1873 and *Osiris* was used as a stationary engine in 1873 for the Portreath Incline. The remaining ten locomotives were numbered 2096-2105 by the GWR in 1876. *Priam* and *Damon* were withdrawn the same year and all except *Comet* and *Meteor* had gone by 1878. These two were withdrawn in 1884 and 1881 respectively.

2106- 2121 4-4-0ST, 1859

A second batch of twelve 4-4-0 saddle tanks were supplied under contract in 1859/60 and a further four between 1863 and 1865, very similar in design although the saddle tanks were lengthened to 1,100 gallon capacity. Their key dimensions were:

Coupled wheels:	5ft 6in (the last four had 5ft 9in, later reduced to 5ft 6in)
Bogie wheels:	3ft 6in
Cylinders:	16½in x 24in
Heating surface:	1,195sqft
Grate area:	20sqft
Weight:	38 tons 18 cwt
Axleload:	13½ tons

They were named:

Eagle	*Elk*	*Hawk*	*Lynx*	*Gazelle*
Mazeppa	*Giraffe*	*Lion*	*Antelope*	*Wolf*
Tiger	*Hector*	*Cato*	*Dart*	*Pollux*
Castor				

They all operated west of Exeter and when that railway was acquired by the GWR in 1876 they were numbered 2106-2121. Two (2106 and 2109) were condemned immediately and a further three went in 1877. The last survivors were 2108, 2110, 2111, and 2119 withdrawn in 1885 and 2117 (*Hector*) which was the only one to last until the end of the broad gauge in 1892.

2122-2127 4-4-0ST, 1866

The company ordered six further 4-4-0 saddle tanks in 1866, delivered from the Avonside Engineering Company (formerly Slaughter & Gruning). These had inside plate frames and were named:

Gorgon	*Pluto*	*Sedley*
Sol	*Titan*	*Zebra*

4-4-0ST 2122 *Gorgon* built in 1866 and which lasted to the end of the broad gauge in 1892, seen here c1890. (GW Trust)

4-4-0ST 2125 *Sol* also built in 1866. This one also lasted to the end of the broad gauge in 1892. (GW Trust)

Their key dimensions were:

Coupled wheels:	5ft 8in
Bogie wheels:	3ft 4in
Cylinders:	17in x 24in
Heating surface:	1,365sqft
Grate area:	22sqft
Tank capacity:	1,100 gallons

They were numbered by the GWR in 1875 2122-2127 and operated like the other South Devon engines between Exeter and Penzance, including west of Truro after a third rail had been added to the West Cornwall standard gauge lines after 1866. 2124 was withdrawn in 1885 and 2126 at the end of 1886 but the other four lasted to the end of the broad gauge.

2128 – 2131 4-4-0ST, 1872

The last four 4-4-0 saddle tanks built for the South Devon Railway were built by Avonside Engine Co. in 1872 (two) and 1875 (two more as replacements for the withdrawn *Lance* and *Osiris* whose names they took. The first two were named *Leopard* and *Stag*. They had similar dimensions to the 1866 batch apart from the diameter of the coupled wheels, marginally larger at 5ft 9in. The GWR numbered them 2128-2131. All four lasted to the end of the broad gauge and *Lance* and *Osiris* (2130 and 2131) were used shunting broad gauge stock at Swindon until the work there was completed in June 1893 when they were both cut up.

2132-2135, 2145 4-4-0ST, Secondhand Locomotives

The South Devon Railway acquired four 4-4-0 saddle tanks from the Carmarthen and Cardigan Railway in 1868 (*Etna*) and 1872 (*Hecla, Heron, Magpie*). They were numbered 2132-2135 by the GWR. These were described earlier on page 16. *Magpie* was withdrawn in 1889 and the other three lasted until the end of the broad gauge. *Rosa* was part of an exchange for standard gauge

2132 built in 1864 by Rothwell & Co. for the Carmarthen and Cardigan Railway as *Etna*. It was purchased by the Bristol and Exeter Railway in 1868 and numbered 2132 by the GWR. (GW Trust)

engines with the Llynvi and Ogmore Railway in 1868. She was numbered 2145 by the GWR and was withdrawn in 1885 (see description on page 17).

Penwith 2136, 2-4-0ST, Secondhand Locomotive

Penwith was a 2-4-0 standard gauge tender locomotive built for the West Cornwall Railway in 1853 and rebuilt as a 2-4-0 saddle tank at Newton Abbot in 1872 after the company's acquisition by the SDR and conversion of the Cornish lines to broad gauge. It had 5ft coupled wheels and 15in x 22in cylinders and ran morning and evening local services to and from Liskeard and was used during the day as a passenger shunting engine at Plymouth Millbay. The GWR numbered it 2136 and it was withdrawn in 1888.

Prince 2137, 2-4-0ST, 1871

Prince was built by the Ince Forge Company in 1871 and was a small 2-4-0 saddle tank with 4ft coupled wheels, 3ft leading wheels, 12in x 17in cylinders, heating surface of 589sqft and a small grate area of just 9.3sqft. It was numbered 2137 by the GWR and converted to standard gauge in 1893, renumbered 1316 and was withdrawn in 1899 before being used as a stationary boiler at Swindon until 1935 (see page 40).

King 2-4-0T, 1871 (GW 2171)

King was an even smaller 2-4-0 side tank built by the Avonside Engine Co. in 1871 with 3ft coupled wheels, 2ft 6in leading wheels, 218.8sq ft of heating surface and a tiny grate area of just 4.84sqft. Its tank capacity was shown as only 80 gallons, possibly an

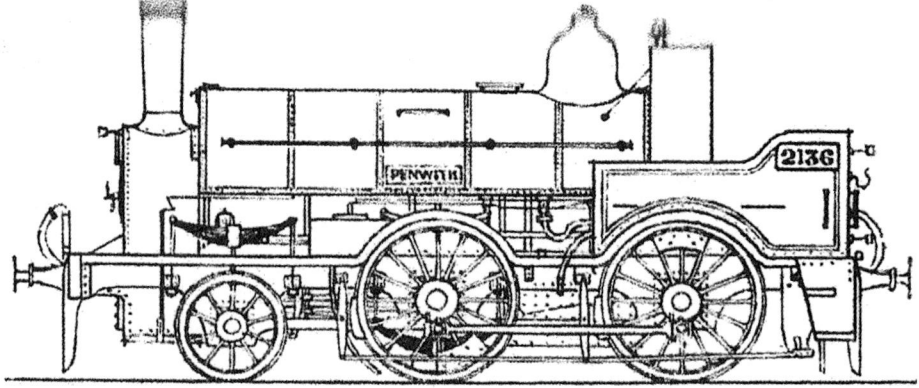

Drawing of the South Devon Railway's 2-4-0ST *Penwith*, formerly of the West Cornwall Railway as renumbered 2136 by the GWR. (J.B.N. Ashford/RCTS)

error as a crude drawing of the tank seems larger, possibly 800 gallons. It had been ordered by the Torbay & Brixham Railway, but they had been unable to pay for it, so it was bought by the SDR and the GWR numbered it 2171 and converted it to standard gauge in 1878. The GWR renumbered it No.2 and withdrew it in 1907, selling it on to the Bute Works Supply Company (see page 20).

2172-2179 class 0-4-0WT & ST, 1873
Eight 0-4-0 shunting tanks were built by the South Devon Railway, three well tanks in 1873 and five saddle tanks in 1874/5. The well tanks were named *Owl*, *Goat* and *Weasel* and had the following dimensions:

Coupled wheels:	3ft 0in
Cylinders:	10in x 16in (later 11in x 16in)
Heating surface:	357.9sqft
Grate area:	6.7sqft
Tank capacity:	150 gallons

The saddle tanks were named *Raven*, *Rook*, *Crow*, *Lark* and *Jay* and had these dimensions:

Coupled wheels:	3ft 0in
Cylinders (outside):	14in x 18in
Heating surface:	565.3sqft
Grate area:	9.28sqft
Tank capacity:	450 gallons

Initially the engines worked on Plymouth Docks. 2173 (*Weasel*) was withdrawn in 1882 and became a works engine of the Engineering Department. 2172 (*Owl*) and 2174 (*Goat*) were withdrawn in 1889 and 1885 respectively and sold to Pearson & Son (a quarry near Ivybridge). 2175 (*Raven*) was sold to the Torbay & Brixham Railway in 1877 and returned to the GWR when that line was absorbed in 1883. The GWR bought 2172 and 2174 back in 1893, converted them all to standard gauge in 1893 and renumbered them (apart from 2173) 1327-1333, when they continued to work on the docks, those lines now converted to standard gauge. 1329 (*Raven*) went to the Wantage Tramway between 1906 and 1910 and was scrapped after a collision in 1919. The others went to Powlesland & Mason at Swansea Docks and one, 1330 (*Rook*), was returned to the GWR in 1924 and renumbered 925, being scrapped as late as 1929 (see later, page 115).

2180 *Tiny*, 0-4-0WT, 1868
Tiny was a vertically boilered 0-4-0 well tank holding just 80 gallons with 3ft coupled wheels, 9in x 12in cylinders and grate area of 6.1sqft. It was built for the Sutton Harbour branch to replace horses, was numbered 2180 by the GWR and was withdrawn in 1883 and retained as a stationary boiler in Newton Abbot Works until 1927 when it was overhauled and placed on display on Newton Abbot station platform, until moved to Buckfastleigh for display in the South Devon Railway Museum (see further details in Chapter 6, pages 138-139). Its dimensions are:

Coupled wheels:	3ft 0in
Cylinders:	9in x 12in
Vertical boiler	
Grate area:	6.1sqft
Tank capacity:	80 gallons

South Wales Mineral Railway
The 12¾ mile railway from Briton Ferry to Gyncorrwg Colliery was incorporated in 1853 and opened in 1861 and was leased to and worked by the Glyncorrwg Coal Co. until 1870. It was built to the broad gauge and was converted to standard gauge in 1872. It fell out

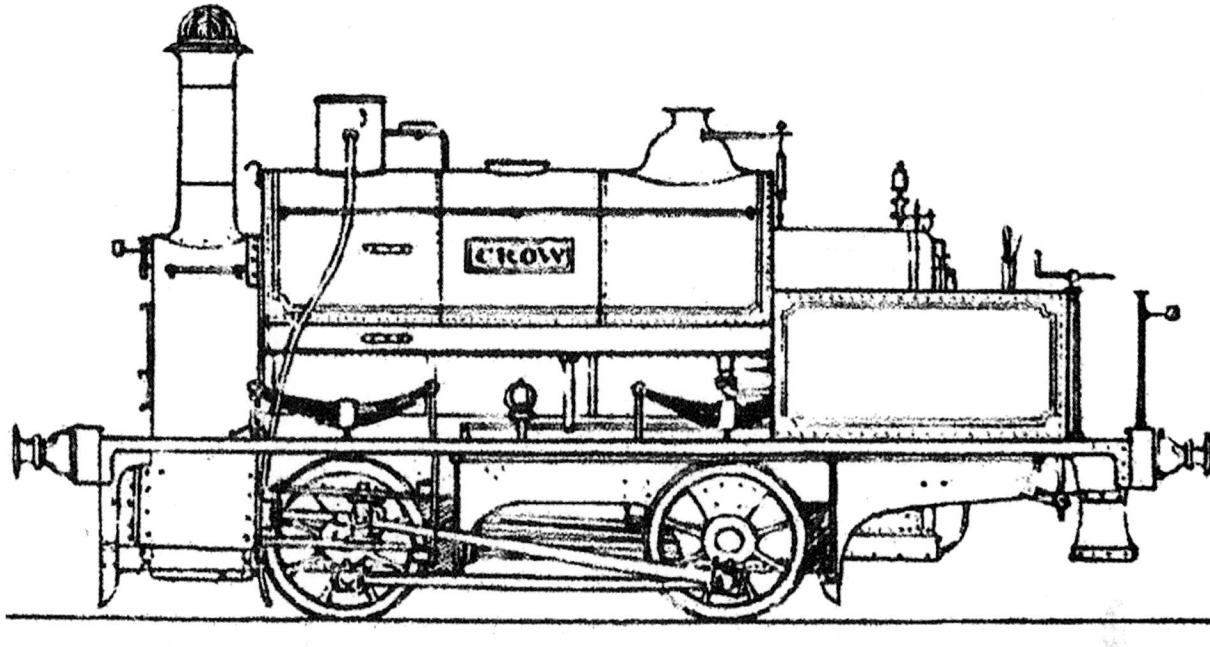

Drawing of South Devon Railway 0-4-0ST *Crow* as a standard gauge locomotive.

2180 *Tiny* as a stationary boiler at Newton Abbot Works, c1900. (GW Trust)

of use apart from the section from Cymmer Afan to Glyncorrwg in 1898 when an alternative route via the Port Talbot Railway provided direct facilities. The GWR took over the remaining route and the PTR in 1908. The line worked with contractors' engines until 1863.

Princess & *Glyncorrwg* 0-4-0ST & 0-4-2ST, 1863

Princess was built by Manning, Wardle in 1863 as an 0-4-0 saddle tank and was rebuilt later with trailing wheels as an 0-4-2ST. *Glyncorrwg* was built in 1864 by the same company as an 0-4-2 saddle tank. Both had 14in x 20in cylinders but little else is known of them. In 1872, when broad gauge on the SWMR ceased, *Princess* was rebuilt as an 0-6-0ST to standard gauge and survived until 1901 when it was sold – possibly to Baldwin's Landore steelworks. *Glyncorrwg* was sold to the Brotherhood of Chippenham in 1872 and on to the Bristol & Exeter Railway in 1874 where it was numbered 110 and later GW 2058 (see reference in Bristol & Exeter locomotives earlier, page 15).

Torbay & Brixham Railway

The Torbay & Brixham Railway was opened in 1868 and consisted of just two miles of track from Churston to Brixham. It was initially operated by the South Devon Railway, but owned two engines for part of its existence before being taken over by the GWR in 1883.

Queen 0-4-0WT, 1852

Queen was an 0-4-0 well tank built in 1852 by E.B. Wilson for the construction of Portland breakwater. It was purchased in 1868. Its key dimensions were:

Coupled wheels:	4ft 0in
Cylinders:	10½in x 17in
Boiler pressure:	120lb psi
Heating surface:	329sqft

Grate area: 7sqft
Tank capacity: 150 gallons

Although it operated the branch from 1870, it was included in South Devon Railway stock and was taken over by the GWR in 1876 and withdrawn in 1877.

Raven (GW 2175) class 0-4-0ST, 1874

Raven was a South Devon Railway 0-4-0 saddle tank built in 1874, taken into GWR stock in 1876, and sold to the Torbay & Brixham Railway in 1877 to replace *Queen*, before being absorbed back into GW stock in 1883. For further details see description in South Devon Railway 2175-2179 class, page 21.

Vale of Neath Railway

The Vale of Neath Railway was a broad gauge exception to the majority of railways in South Wales which were built to the standard gauge. It opened 44 miles between Merthyr, Aberdare and Neath in 1851 with the purpose of taking iron products from Merthyr and coal from the Aberdare area to Swansea Docks. Its first locomotives were 4-4-0 passenger saddle tanks built by R. Stephenson & Co., followed by 0-6-0 saddle tanks built by Vulcan Foundry and Slaughter, Gruning and Co. When the Newport, Abergavenny and Hereford standard gauge railway linked up in 1864, the V of N laid a third rail to enable mixed gauge working. The Great Western absorbed the Vale of Neath Railway in 1866 and converted it to standard gauge only in 1872.

1-6 4-4-0ST, 1851

The company's first locomotives were six 4-4-0 saddle tanks built by R. Stephenson & Co. in 1851 and resembled the Gooch 'Corsair' class in many ways. They were numbered 1-6 and their key dimensions were:

Coupled wheels: 5ft 6in
Bogie wheels: 3ft 6in
Cylinders: 17in x 24in
Heating surface: 1,232.6sqft

As well as the saddle tank, they had a small rear tank under the footplate. They were painted in the Vale of Neath livery of dark green with a brass numberplate between the letters V and N on the tank side. They were transferred to GWR stock in 1866 and were all withdrawn in 1872 on the conversion of the line to standard gauge. Nos. 1, 3 and 5 were then sold.

7-9 4-4-0ST, 1854

A further three 4-4-0 saddle tanks were constructed in 1854 by the same manufacturer and numbered 7-9. They were more powerful, with 5ft coupled wheels and enlarged diameter cylinders, 17½in x 24in. However, by 1858 they had been converted to 0-6-0STs and were transferred to the GWR stock in that condition. In 1872, on conversion of the line to standard gauge, they were moved to other parts of the GW system that had still retained broad gauge. They were scrapped between 1874 and 1880 – the last survivor was No.8.

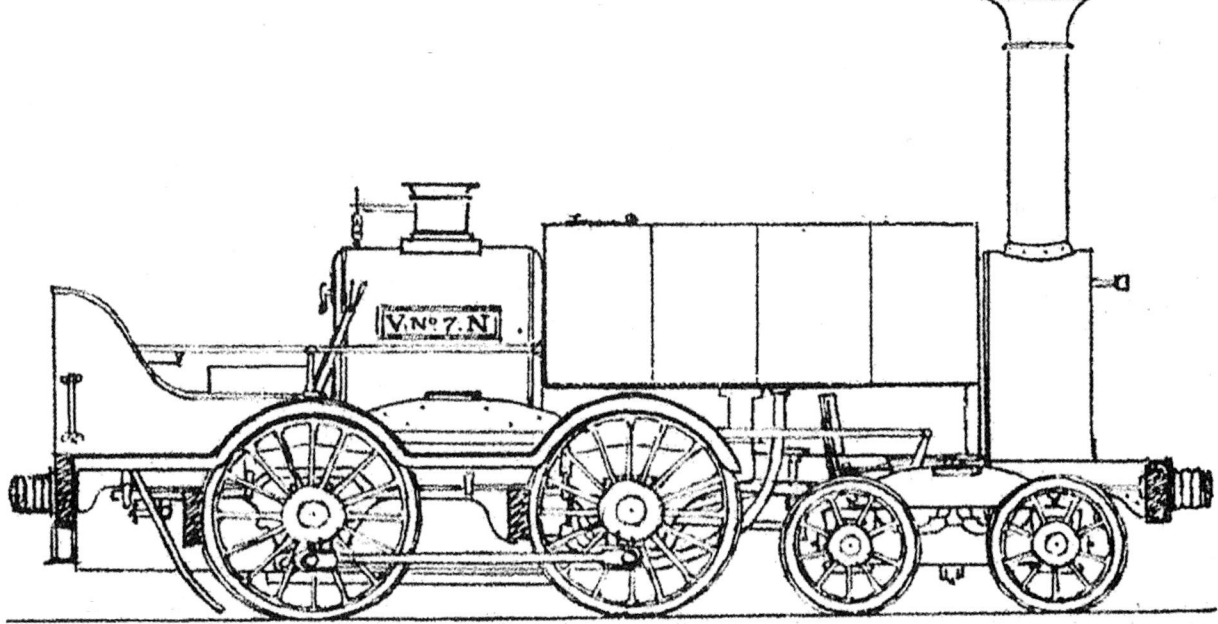

Drawing of Vale of Neath 4-4-0ST No.7. (R.A.S. Abbott/RCTS)

Chapter 3
STANDARD GAUGE LOCOMOTIVES ABSORBED BY THE GWR BEFORE 1914

The Great Western Railway amalgamated with – in effect took over – a number of broad gauge and standard gauge railways in the West of England, South Wales and West Midlands from the mid-1860s to 1914. It converted many of these lines to mixed or standard gauge around 1872 and removed the remaining broad gauge tracks of the Devon and Cornish lines in 1892. In addition to building its own standard gauge engines, it took many standard gauge four-coupled tank engines onto its booked stock during this period, often in very small numbers and these will be described in this chapter.

Birkenhead Railway

The Chester & Birkenhead Railway was opened in 1840 and amalgamated in 1847 with the Birkenhead, Lancashire and Cheshire Junction Railway, changing its name to the Birkenhead Railway in 1859. It was vested jointly in the GWR and LNWR in 1860. Its locomotives were split between the two companies and those four-coupled tank engines taken into GWR stock are described below.

32 & 33 (GW 97-98) 2-4-0T, 1856

Two 2-4-0 side tanks named *Volante* and *Voltigeur* and numbered 32 and 33 were built by R. Stephenson & Co. in 1856. Their key dimensions were:

Coupled wheels:	5ft 3in
Leading wheels:	3ft 8in
Cylinders:	14in x 20in
Heating surface:	788.35sqft
Grate area:	10.2sqft
Weight:	29 tons 11 cwt
Axleload:	10½ tons
Tank capacity:	600 gallons

They retained their names for a number of years but were renumbered 97 and 98. The GWR moved them for a while to the London area to work between Victoria and Southall, before returning them to Birkenhead and Shrewsbury. They were withdrawn in 1878 and 1880 respectively.

39 & 6 (GW 95-96), 0-4-0ST, 1856

Sharp, Stewart built two 0-4-0 saddle tanks in 1856/7 and the Birkenhead Railway named them *Cricket* and *Grasshopper*. Their key dimensions were:

Coupled wheels:	4ft 0in
Cylinders:	14in x 18in
Heating surface:	605sqft
Weight:	19 tons 7 cwt
Axleload:	13½ tons

No.6, built second, was given the number of a withdrawn early Chester & Birkenhead Railway 2-2-2 tender engine. 6 was renumbered by the GWR as 95 and 39 as 96. 96 received new 14½in x 18in cylinders in 1871 and received a new boiler with the following dimensions in 1888:

Heating surface:	889sqft
Grate area:	9.4sqft
Boiler pressure:	140lb psi
Weight:	25 tons 17 cwt
Axleload:	15¾ tons
Tank capacity:	490 gallons

Standard Gauge Locomotives absorbed by the GWR before 1914 • 25

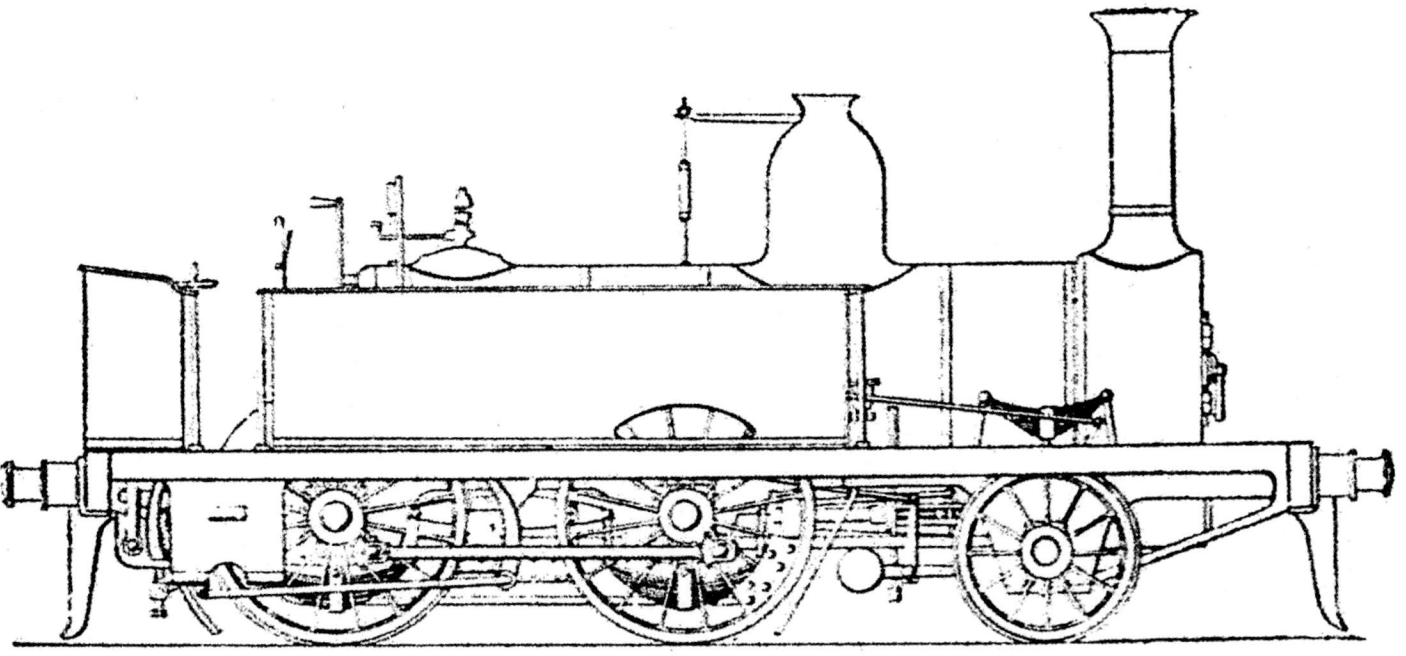

Drawing of 2-4-0T 32 (GWR 97). (R.A.S. Abbott/RCTS)

GW 96, formerly Birkenhead Railway No.39 of 1856, as rebuilt in 1888, c1930. (W. Potter/MLS Collection)

FOUR-COUPLED TANK LOCOMOTIVE CLASSES ABSORBED BY THE GREAT WESTERN RAILWAY

GW 96, formerly Birkenhead Railway No.39 of 1856, as rebuilt in 1888, reverse side, c1930. (MLS Collection)

Heating surface:	950sqft
Grate area:	24sqft
Tank capacity:	1,000 gallons

Although they entered GW stock in 1876 and were renumbered 1353 and 1354, they survived little more than a year, both being withdrawn in November 1877.

Nos. 30 & 33 (GW 1358-1359) 2-4-0T, 1875

Two 2-4-0 side tanks were under construction at the B&E's Bristol workshop in 1875 just before absorption by the GW and entered service in 1876 as GW 1358 and 1359. Their dimensions were:

Coupled wheels:	5ft 0in
Leading wheels:	3ft 6in
Cylinders:	16in x 24in
Boiler pressure:	130lb psi
Heating Surface:	862.5sqft
Grate area:	24sqft
Tank capacity:	800 gallons

They were both based at Bristol and were withdrawn in 1888 and 1890 respectively after a short life of only twelve and fourteen years.

Nos. 93-95 (GW 1378-1380), 0-4-0T, 1875

Three shunting 0-4-0 side tanks were constructed at the Bristol Works in 1875 numbered 93-95. Their known dimensions were:

Coupled wheels:	4ft 0in
Cylinders:	14in x 18in
Tanks capacity:	750 gallons

They were renumbered 1378-1380 by the GWR and had extremely short lives, being all withdrawn in 1880.

95 was similarly rebuilt with new cylinders in 1872 and new boiler in 1890. Its chimney, dome and roof were cut down and it was refitted with 3ft 6in coupled wheels to enable it to operate through a low tunnel in the Croes Newydd area (it later had the height of chimney and cab restored). 95 left the Chester area in 1899 and worked in South Wales until 1902 when it returned to the Chester area again until 1922 when it was allocated to Bristol St Philip's March and was withdrawn in 1924. 96 survived until 1935, all in the GW's Northern Division.

Bristol & Exeter Railway

The Bristol & Exeter Railway was converted to a mixed gauge line in 1875 and became part of the GWR in 1876 and 95 of its 119 broad gauge locomotives were taken into the GW stock and were numbered 2001-2095 and were described in Chapter 2. Thirty standard gauge engines also became GWR stock and were renumbered 1353-1382.

83-84, (GW 1353-1354) 2-4-2T, 1868

The oldest standard gauge B&E engines received by the GWR were two 2-4-2 passenger well and back tank engines, numbered 83 and 84, which were built by the Worcester Engine Co. in 1868. They shared similar boilers to six 0-6-0 goods tender engines built in the preceding months. Their key dimensions were:

Coupled wheels:	6ft 4in
Front and rear wheels:	3ft 6in
Cylinders:	16in x 24in

Standard Gauge Locomotives absorbed by the GWR before 1914 • 27

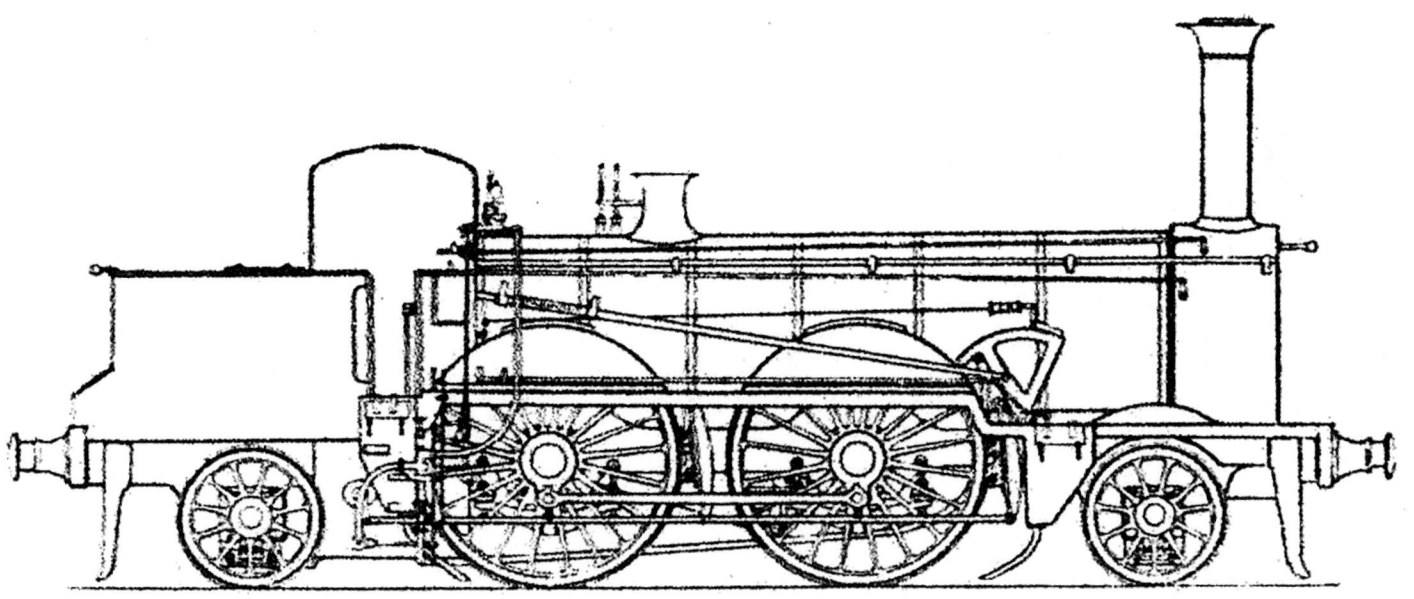

Drawing of Bristol & Exeter Railway 2-4-2T No. 83 (GW 1353). (G.F. Bird/LCGB)

1358 (formerly 30), one of the Bristol & Exeter 2-4-0Ts built in 1875 seen c1885. (MLS Collection)

Corporation Rivers Dept. and named *Bear*, being sold for scrap eventually in 1914.

Bristol Port Railway

The Bristol Port and Pier Railway was opened in 1865 and operated jointly with the Midland Railway between Clifton and Avonmouth.

Nos. 1 & 2, 0-4-2T, 1854

It appears to have acquired two LNWR 0-4-2s, that company's 1370 and 1389, and had them converted by J. Cross & Co. to 0-4-2 side tanks. They were painted green and had their numbers, 1 and 2, displayed on the bufferbeam. The tender engines had been built in 1854-1856 for the St Helens Railway. Known dimensions were:

Coupled wheels:	4ft 6in
Trailing wheels:	3ft 6in
Cylinders:	14½in x 22in
Weight:	26 tons

3ft gauge well tank 1381 (formerly B&E 112) at Westleigh Quarry with a stone train for Burlescombe, c1890. (GW Trust)

Nos. 112 & 113 (GW 1381-1382), 0-4-0WT, 1874

Two narrow 3ft gauge 0-4-0 well tanks were built at the Bristol workshop for operating the tramway from Burlescombe station to Westleigh Quarry under a twenty-five year lease. Their dimensions were:

Coupled wheels:	2ft 0in
Cylinders:	8in x 12in
Boiler pressure:	100lb psi
Heating surface:	130.9sqft
Grate area:	4.6sqft
Tank capacity:	76 gallons

The lease expired in 1898 and the two engines were sold to Bute Works Supply Co. 1382 is traced to movement to the Manchester

Bristol Port Railway No.1, formerly *Hercules*, a 2-4-0 of the St Helens Railway and later L&NWR, and rebuilt as an 0-4-2 side tank in 1865, photographed in the 1880s before sale on acquisition of the line by the GW and Midland railways in 1890. (Bob Miller/MLS Collections)

The line was purchased by the Midland and Great Western railways in 1890 and the BPR's two locomotives were immediately sold without going into either the Midland or GW stock. No.2 appears to have gone to the Shropshire & Montgomery Railway and been converted to a saddle tank and survived until the early 1930s. No.1 is reported to have gone to Yorkshire and nothing further is known about it.

Festiniog & Blaenau Railway

The 3½ mile Festiniog & Blaenau narrow gauge railway (1ft 11½in) was opened in 1868 and purchased by the GWR in 1883 and converted to standard gauge as an extension to the Bala branch.

Nos. 1 & 2, 0-4-2ST NG, 1868

The company had two narrow gauge 0-4-2 saddle tanks, numbers 1 and 2, built by Manning, Wardle & Co. in 1868. Their dimensions were:

Coupled wheels:	2ft 3in
Trailing wheels:	1ft 6in
Cylinders (outside):	8½in x 14in
Boiler pressure:	80lb psi
Heating surface:	284.5sqft
Grate area:	4.75sqft
Weight:	11 tons
Tank capacity:	300 gallons

They were both sold in 1883 when the gauge was widened without coming into GW stock.

Liskeard & Looe Railway

The Liskeard & Caradon Railway was opened from Moorswater to Caradon mines in 1844 and was worked by horses until 1862. The line was extended by the Liskeard & Looe Union Canal Co. in 1860 from Moorswater through Liskeard to Looe. The Looe section started passenger working in 1879. The Liskeard & Caradon Railway was taken over by the Liskeard & Looe Railway in 1901 and remained until operated by the GWR in 1909.

Narrow gauge No.2 of the Festiniog & Blaenau Railway photographed around 1880 before the line was widened and the narrow gauge engines sold. (LGRP/F.K. Davies/John Hodge Collections)

Liskeard & Looe Railway 2-4-0 side tank *Lady Margaret,* on the day it became GWR property and was given its new GW number, 1308, 1 January 1909. (Bob Miller/ MLS Collections)

Liskeard & Looe Railway 2-4-0 side tank *Lady Margaret,* GW 1308, after its 1929 rebuilding and ex-works at Oswestry. (L.B. Lapper/ MLS Collection)

Lady Margaret, GW 1308, at Oswestry in 1936.
(Loco & General Railway Photos/ MLS Collection)

Lady Margaret (GW1308), 2-4-0T, 1902

Lady Margaret was a 2-4-0 side tank locomotive built by Andrew Barclay in 1902 to replace 1901 built 0-6-0 saddle tank *Looe* which had proved unsuitable and had been sold. Its key dimensions were:

Coupled wheels:	4ft 0in
Leading wheels:	2ft 7½in
Cylinders:	14½in x 22in
Boiler pressure:	160lb psi
Heating surface:	650.5sqft
Grate area:	11.6sqft
Weight:	28 tons
Tank capacity:	560 gallons

It became GW 1308 and received a boiler with reduced pressure (140lb psi) and very slightly reduced heating surface and grate area. It was further rebuilt in 1929 with a boiler having a heating surface of 632.5sqft and grate area of 11.5sqft. and now weighed 32 tons with an 11½ ton axleload. Its livery was light green with black and red lining, black frames and yellow lining. Its nameplates were in the centre of the tanks. After repainting in GW green livery, the words 'GREAT WESTERN' were in the tank centres with the nameplates above.

After spending its life in the West of England, much of the time on the Liskeard-Looe branch, it was transferred in 1920 to Oswestry where it remained until withdrawal in 1948, apart from a short period after the 1929 rebuilding when it worked from Exeter on the Culm Valley branch.

Llanelly Railway & Dock Company

The Llanelly Railway & Dock Company opened a short horse-worked branch in 1833 and the first main line section to Pontardulais was opened in 1839. The line reached Llandilo in 1857 and was taken over by the GWR in 1873. The first steam locomotives were six-coupled tender engines.

Loughor 2-4-0T class, 1865

The first tank engines were two 2-4-0 saddle tanks built by Hopkins,

Gilkes & Co. of Middlesbrough and in 1867 they were named *Lougher* and *Amman*. In 1871 *Amman* was rebuilt as a tender engine. Their known dimensions were:

Coupled wheels: 5ft 0in
Cylinders: 14in x 20in

The GW numbered *Lougher* 901 and the tender engine *Amman* 900. The tender 2-4-0 was withdrawn in 1884 and *Lougher* in 1886.

Llynvi & Ogmore Railway

It had been a broad gauge railway (see the previous chapter, page 17) but when it amalgamated with the Ogmore Valley Railway from Tondu to Ogmore Vale in 1868, it opted for the standard gauge and exchanged its three broad gauge engines for four standard gauge locomotives from the West Cornwall Railway, which had became part of the South Devon Railway in 1866. The GWR took over the railway in 1873.

Nos. 7-9 class 2-4-0ST, 1855

The four standard gauge engines were 2-4-0 passenger engines originally built between 1853 and 1860, named *Mounts Bay, Penzance, Helston* and *St Ives*, and they lost their names and were numbered 6-9 by the L & O railway. Three of the four, 7-9, were rebuilt as 2-4-0 saddle tanks before the GWR received them into their stock and although they were renumbered GW 915 (6) and 916-918 (7-9) the tender engine was withdrawn in 1874 and the three tank engines the following year. The known dimensions of the rebuilt tank engines were:

Coupled wheels: 5ft 0in
Leading wheels: 3ft 6in
Cylinders: 15in x 24in
Heating surface: 978.5sqft

Manchester & Milford Railway

The Manchester & Milford Railway was linked up with the Carmarthen & Cardigan Railway in 1866 and opened the stretch from Pencader to Strata Florida that year and on to Aberystwyth in 1867. Manchester could be reached (eventually!) via the various companies that formed the Cambrian Railways and the L&NWR. The company was in the hands of the receiver by 1880 and was leased to the GWR in 1906.

Nos. 2, 6 (GW 1304, 1306) 2-4-2T, 1891

A 2-4-2 side tank engine was built by the Sharp, Stewart Company in 1891 and identified as No.2 *Plynlimmon*. Its dimensions were:

Coupled wheels: 5ft 6in
Leading &
  trailing wheels: 3ft 6in
Cylinders: 17in x 22in
Boiler pressure: 140lb psi
Heating surface: 948.6sqft
Grate area: 12.9sqft
Weight: 43 tons 6 cwt
Axleload: 12½ tons
Tank capacity: 1,000 gallons

A second 2-4-2T, No.6 *Cader Idris*, was built by the same company in 1896 but was larger and its dimensions varied from No.2 in the following ways:

Coupled wheels: 5ft 2in
Heating surface: 1,014.5sqft
Grate area: 15.25sqft

Manchester & Milford Railway No.2 *Plynlimmon*, c1900. (Real Photographs/MLS Collection)

Standard Gauge Locomotives absorbed by the GWR before 1914 • 33

The 1896 built No.6 *Cader Idris*, c1900.
(Real Photographs/ MLS Collection)

GWR 1306 *Cader Idris* on a passenger train at Newcastle Emlyn, 1911.
(L&GRP/MLS Collection)

Weight:	47 tons 8 cwt
Axleload:	15 tons
Tank capacity:	1,290 gallons

Both locomotives were retained by the GWR in 1906 and were numbered 1304 and 1306. 1304 was withdrawn in 1916 and 1306 in 1919.

Monmouthshire Canal Co.

The Monmouthshire Canal Company originated in 1792 and connected various collieries in the early nineteenth century with tramways, some horse and some locomotive hauled. A railway from Newport to Pontypool was authorised in 1845 and the company was renamed the Monmouthshire Railway & Canal Company in 1848. The line was standardised at 4ft 8½in by 1849 and all lines were complete to this gauge by 1855. The company built workshops at Newport Dock Street in the late 1850s. The Great Western Railway assumed control in 1875.

Nos. 9-10 (GW 1301-1302), 2-4-0T, 1849

Two 2-4-0 well tanks were ordered from Sharp Brothers in 1849 and were constructed with inside frames and outside cylinders. Their dimensions were:

Coupled wheels:	5ft 0in
Leading wheels:	3ft 2in
Cylinders:	13in x 18in
Heating surface:	759.7sqft
Grate area:	10.8sqft
Tank capacity:	450 gallons

They were offered unsuccessfully for sale in 1873 and in 1875 No.9 (then renumbered 9A) was rebuilt at Dock Street and became GW 1302, No. 10 becoming 1301. The latter was withdrawn in 1877, but 1302 survived until 1884.

No. 16 (GW 1303) 4-4-0ST, 1850

No.16 appears to have started as a 4-4-0 tender engine built in 1850 by Stothert, Slaughter & Co. In 1854, it was fitted with saddle and back tanks for use on the Western Valley lines and had then the following dimensions:

The 1849 Sharp Bros. 2-4-0T No.9, rebuilt in 1875 and taken over by the GWR as 1302, c1880 before withdrawal in 1884. (Bob Miller/MLS Collections)

Coupled wheels:	4ft 6in
Bogie wheels:	2ft 5½in
Cylinders:	15½in x 22in
Heating surface:	749.8sqft
Grate area:	13.75sqft
Weight:	32 tons 2 cwt
Axleload:	10 tons 18 cwt
Tank capacity:	2 gallons

It was renumbered 1303 by the GWR in 1875 and was withdrawn in 1882.

Nos. 10A, 14, 15 & 41 (GW 1304-1307), 4-4-0T, 1870
Four 4-4-0 passenger side tanks were built at Newport Dock Street between 1870 and 1875. They were rebuilt at Swindon in the mid-1890s, and their dimensions before and after rebuilding were:

	As built	After rebuilding
Coupled wheels:	5ft 0in	5ft 2in
Bogie wheels:	2ft 8in	2ft 8in
Cylinders:	16in x 24in	16in x 24in
Boiler pressure:		150lb psi
Heating surface:	913.4sqft	1,128.7sqft
Grate area:	14sqft	16.44sqft
Weight:	41 tons 3 cwt	42 tons 4 cwt
Axleload:	14½ tons	15 tons 4 cwt
Tank capacity:	750 gallons	650 gallons

Ex-Monmouthshire Canal Co. 1870 built No. 14, rebuilt by the GWR in 1893 at Gloucester, June 1903. (W. Beckerlegge/MLS Collection)

Monmouthshire Canal Co. No.10A, built in 1875, rebuilt 1898 by the GWR, as 1307 in the West of England when it was Truro based, 1904. (L&GRP/MLS Collection)

They worked Eastern and Western Valley passenger services above Newport until around 1890 but after rebuilding they were dispersed to the Gloucester, Swindon and Weymouth areas. Just before withdrawal in 1904 and 1905 two, 1304 and 1307, were in the West of England, 1307 based at Truro.

Nos. 42-50 (GW 1345 - 52) 0-6-0ST 1871, reb.0-4-4T, reb.1891/2
Avonside built five 0-6-0 saddle tanks numbered 42-46 between 1871

Cylinders:	17in x 24in
Boiler pressure:	150lb psi
Heating Surface:	1,241.9sqft
Grate area:	17.2sqft
Weight:	48 tons
Axleload:	14 tons 13 cwt
Tank capacity:	1,300 gallons

After operation in the Eastern and Western Valleys and rebuilding, most stayed in South Wales, several going to Tondu. One, 1346, spent a short time in South Devon. The first examples were withdrawn in 1906, 1346 was sold in 1910, and the last pair – 1350 and 1351 – were withdrawn in 1913.

Nos. 47, 5 & 51 (GW 1308-1310) 0-4-4T, 1873

Three 0-4-4 tank engines were built by the Avonside Company in 1873-5. They were numbered 47 (built in 1873), 5 (in 1874) and 51 (in 1875). They had outside bearings to the coupled wheels and inside

The rebuilt 0-4-4ST 1351 (ex-Monmouthshire Canal Co. No.49) after withdrawal at Swindon in 1913. (Bob Miller/MLS Collection)

and 1873, and Dübs built a further three (48-50) in 1875. The GWR renumbered them 1345-1352. All were rebuilt at Swindon in 1891/2 and converted to the 0-4-4ST wheel arrangement. As well as saddle tanks, they had back tanks. The dimensions of the rebuilt engines were:

Coupled wheels:	4ft 1½in
Trailing bogie wheels:	3ft 8in

The first of the Monmouthshire Canal Company 0-4-4Ts, 1308 (formerly 47) with back tank only, before rebuilding, c1895. (Bob Miller/MLS Collections)

for the bogie. 47 only had a back tank, but 5 and 51 had a smaller back tank and a saddle tank over the boiler barrel. They were rebuilt at Swindon between 1897 and 1899 with new boiler and full length saddle tanks and their dimensions before and after the rebuilding were:

	As built	After rebuilding
Coupled wheels:	5ft 0in	5ft 2in
Bogie wheels:	2ft 8in	2ft 8in
Cylinders:	17in x 24in	17in x 24in
Boiler pressure:	150lb psi	
Heating surface:	1,222.2sqft	
Grate area:	17.33sqft	
Weight:	49 tons 18 cwt	49 tons 11 cwt
Axleload:	17 tons 6 cwt	16¾ tons
Tank capacity:	900 gallons (47), 1,000 gallons (5, 51)	1,366 gallons

They were renumbered 1308-1310 by the GWR and 1307 was withdrawn in 1903, 1308 in 1904 and 1310 in 1908. They left the Newport area in the 1880s and spent most of their later years at Weymouth working the Bridport branch.

Newport, Abergavenny & Hereford Railway
Nos. 20-22 (WMR 90-92, GW 194, 195 & 227) 0-4-2 1854, reb. 0-4-2T, 0-4-0T, 1872

The Newport, Abergavenny & Hereford Railway was opened in 1854 between Hereford and Pontypool, joining up with the Monmouthshire Canal Company Railway at the latter place. It was initially worked by L&NWR locomotives, then Thomas Brassey, the contractor for the line, took on the responsibility, with the NA&H railway taking on its own responsibility in 1855.

The West Midland Railway was formed in 1860 and took over the railway and its twenty-six locomotives, numbering them 71-96 in its stock list. Most of the early locomotives were six-coupled tender goods engines, but in December 1854, Thomas Brassey had purchased three 0-4-2 tender engines from Dodds & Co. of Rotherham. They were numbered 20-22 and renumbered 90-92 by the West Midland Railway. The West Midland Railway was then taken over by the Great Western in 1863 and the former NA&H Railway engines were again renumbered – 194, 195 and 227. In their original form, the 0-4-2 tender engines had 4ft 6in coupled wheels and 14in x 20in cylinders.

Already by 1863, 92 (GW 227) had been rebuilt into an 0-4-2 side tank with the following dimensions:

Coupled wheels:	4ft 6in
Trailing wheels:	3ft 4in
Cylinders:	14½in x 22in
Heating surface:	688sqft

Drawing of the rebuilt GW 227 (former WMR 92) as an 0-4-2 side tank locomotive. (RCTS)

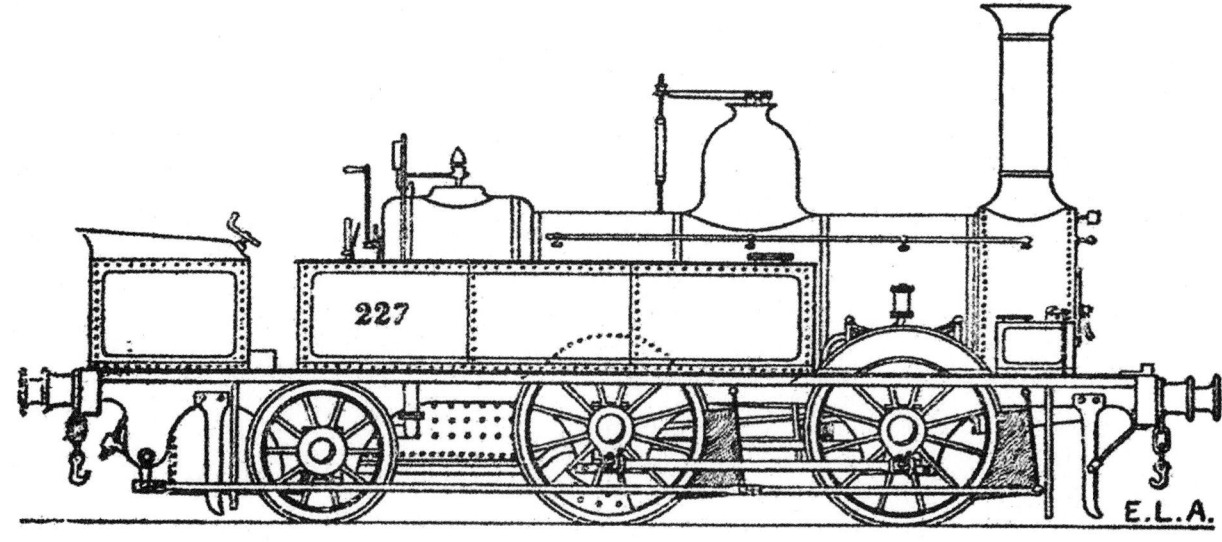

Drawing of the rebuilt GW 195 (former WMR 91) as an 0-4-0 saddle tank locomotive. (RCTS)

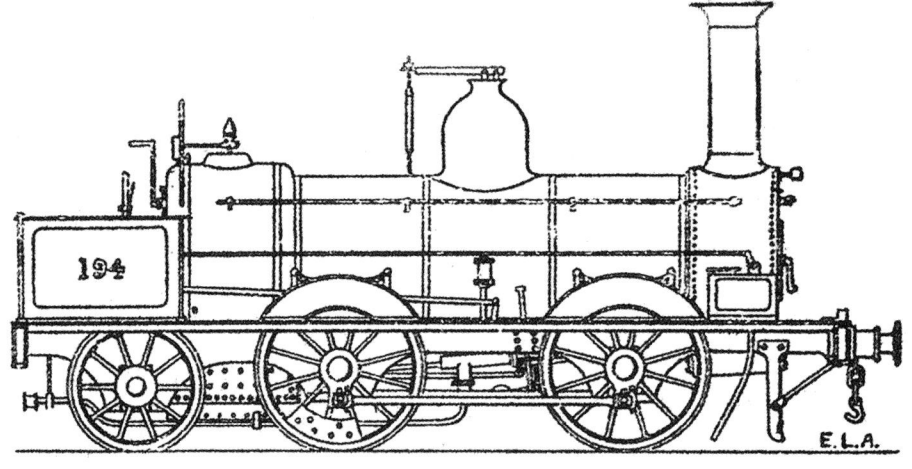

Drawing of the 0-4-2 tender engine GW 194 (former NA&H Railway 20, WMR 90) and also an official sketch of 194 in its rebuilt 0-4-2ST form. (RCTS)

Grate area: 10sqft
Weight: 28 tons 12 cwt
Axleload: 10 tons

In 1865, the second 0-4-2, WMR No. 91, by now GW 195, was rebuilt as an 0-4-0 saddle tank. The tank was short just over the boiler barrel and its weight has been quoted as both 24 tons and 21¾ tons. Little else appears to be known about it but a drawing exists.

The first 0-4-2, now GW 194 (ex-NA&H Railway 20, WMR 90), was rebuilt at Wolverhampton in 1872 as an 0-4-2 saddle tank. It received new link motion and reversing gear and weighed 27 tons 14 cwt, with an axleweight of 11 tons.

194 and 195 were active in the Birkenhead area before their withdrawal in 1881 and 1879 respectively. 227 was already in rebuilt form when taken into GWR stock and it was sold in 1870 to the Bishop's Castle Railway where it was named *Perseverence*. In 1887 on that company's bankruptcy, it was transferred to the Wrexham, Mold & Connah's Quay Railway, numbered 14 and was then sold again in 1895 to the Brynkinallt Colliery in Chirk.

Oxford, Worcester & Wolverhampton Railway
Nos. 35 & 36 (GW 221-222), 0-4-2ST, 1853

The Oxford, Worcester & Wolverhampton Railway was another component of the West Midland Railway formed in 1860 and amalgamated with the GWR in 1863. The OW&W Railway commenced operations in 1850 between Worcester and Abbot's Wood Junction and was worked by the Midland Railway until 1852. The OW&W

Standard Gauge Locomotives absorbed by the GWR before 1914

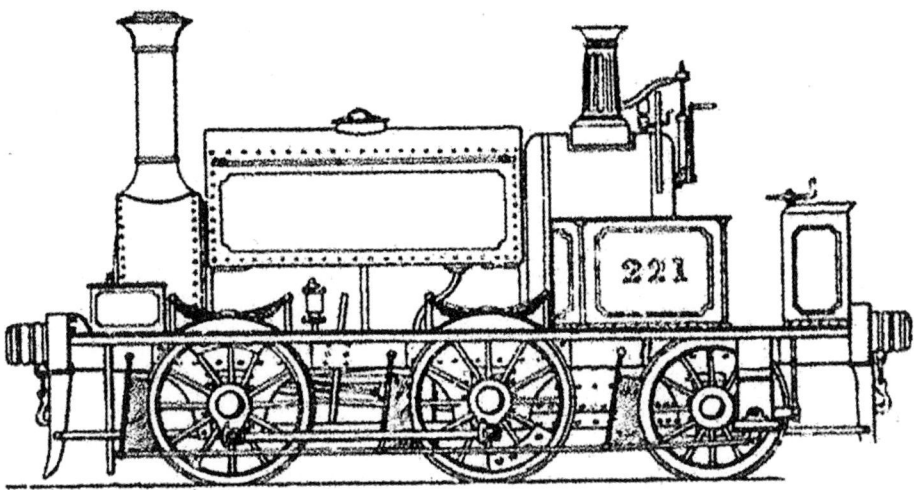

Drawing of 0-4-2 saddle tank GW 221 (former O.W.&W. Railway No.35). (RCTS)

was completed by 1854, including its main line from Wolverhampton to Oxford. The railway was purchasing locomotives from the L&NWR. Workshops were opened at Worcester in 1854. The OW&W engines retained their numbers (1-59) on the WMR. The early locomotives were tender engines, mainly 0-6-0s, 2-4-0s and 0-4-2s.

However, two small 0-4-2 saddle tanks were constructed by E.B. Wilson in 1853 and 1855 which were numbered 35 and 36. They retained these numbers when taken over by the West Midland Railway and were renumbered in 1863 by the GWR as 221 and 222. Their dimensions were:

Coupled wheels:	3ft 5in
Trailing wheels:	3ft 0in
Cylinders:	9¼in x 14in
Heating surface:	263.3sqft
Grate area:	6.7sqft
Weight:	13 tons 16 cwt
Axleload:	5 tons

221 was withdrawn in 1872 and sold to Woodall & Co. in the West Midlands and 222 was withdrawn the following year and sold to Bryndu Colliery in South Wales. The latter appears to have resurfaced as one of the engines received when the Port Talbot Railway & Docks Company purchased the Cefn & Pyle Branch Railway in 1897, though little is heard of it after that.

Severn & Wye and Severn Bridge Railway

The Lydney and Lydbrook Railway was incorporated as early as 1809, changing its name to the Severn & Wye Railway and Canal Company the following year. Several light railways were constructed in the Forest of Dean, horse drawn until 1853 when locomotives were authorised. By 1864 there were thirty miles of 3ft 8in track with still mostly horse drawn traffic, but in 1865 its engineer obtained five steam locomotives. The lines began to be converted to broad gauge in 1867 and by 1869 enough of the line had been widened to engage three broad gauge locomotives. However, by 1872, seeing many of the other railways changing to standard gauge, the Severn & Wye Railway also reverted, and the three broad gauge engines were reconfigured to the standard gauge and two new locomotives were built. The Severn Bridge was opened in 1879 and the two railways formed the Severn & Wye and Severn Bridge Railway although it was in financial trouble by 1883. It was jointly purchased by the Midland and Great Western railways in 1894 and the company's locomotives were shared between them in 1895. The first locomotives were 0-4-0 tender engines, followed by 0-6-0 tank engines.

The only four-coupled tank engine was *Wye*, an 0-4-0 small side tank engine built by Fletcher, Jennings in 1876 which had been sold to the contractors of the Severn Bridge Railway and came into the stock of the joint company in 1879. Its key dimensions were:

Wye (GW 1359) 0-4-0T, 1876

Coupled wheels:	3ft 5in (later 3ft 3in)
Cylinders (outside):	10in x 20in
Boiler pressure:	120lb psi
Heating surface:	389sqft
Grate area:	5.6sqft
Weight:	17 tons 3 cwt
Axleload:	9 tons 4 cwt
Tank capacity:	330 gallons (later 400 gallons)

It was repaired in 1892 with new firebox and tanks and in 1895 was numbered by the GWR as 1359. It spent time then in the Wolverhampton area, then was tried for a while on the Wantage Tramway before being withdrawn in 1910.

South Devon Railway

King 2-4-0T, 1871 reb. 1878 (GW 2)

The South Devon Railway had predominantly broad gauge locomotives but after the GWR take over in 1876 they converted broad gauge 2-4-0T *King* (GW 2171) to standard gauge in 1878 and renumbered it 2. It was withdrawn in 1907 and sold to the Bute Works Supply Company (see pages 20-21).

Prince, 2-4-0ST, 1871 reb. 1893, (GW 1316)

Prince was also a broad gauge engine converted to standard gauge by the GWR in 1893. (see page 20 for history as a broad gauge locomotive). It was renumbered 1316 and was withdrawn in 1899 before being used as a stationary boiler at Swindon until 1935.

Saturn (GW 1298-1300) 2-4-0T, 1878

Three 2-4-0 saddle tank locomotives were under construction at Newton Abbot at the time that the South Devon Railway was taken over by the GWR. They were transferred to Swindon Works where they were completed as standard gauge side tanks and numbered 1298-1300.

Their dimensions in the new format were:

Coupled wheels:	4ft 0in
Leading wheels:	3ft 0in
Cylinders:	11½in x 17in (1300, 12¼in x 17in)
Boiler pressure:	140lb psi
Heating surface	481.54sqft (1300, 541.56sqft)
Grate area:	8.5sqft
Weight:	22 tons 12 cwt
Axleload:	8 tons 12 cwt
Tank capacity:	324 gallons

GW 1316, formerly South Devon Railway Broad Gauge 2-4-0ST, No.14 *Prince*, built in 1871, acting as a stationary boiler at Swindon before its withdrawal in 1935. (MLS Collection)

The crane engine 1299, the former *Jupiter*, at Swindon, c1929, before its return to Departmental stock. (MLS Collection)

1300 was rebuilt in 1905 with slightly enlarged cylinders and a new boiler with increased heating surface. 1299 was fitted with a crane in 1881 and transferred to the Engineering Department until 1893 when it returned to the Traffic Department. The crane engine had 12in diameter cylinders and an increased weight of 28 tons 12 cwt. In 1925 it was also rebuilt with a new boiler similar to 1300. 1299 was transferred back to Departmental stock in 1929 until its withdrawal in 1936. Both 1298 and 1300 spent their days in the West of England working from Exeter on the Culm Valley (Hemyock branch). 1298 was withdrawn in 1926 and 1300 in 1934.

The former South Devon *Mercury*, GW 1300, at Exeter, c1930. (F. Moore/MLS Collection)

1300 at Hemyock on the Culm Valley branch train, 25 May 1929. (H.C. Casserley/MLS Collection)

A rear view of 1300 stored at Exeter, 1933. (L.B. Lapper/F.K. Davies/ John Hodge Collections)

Shrewsbury & Chester Railway

The Shrewsbury and Chester Railway was formed in 1846 and together with the Shrewsbury and Birmingham Railway, was taken over by the GWR in 1854. At that time, the S&C had thirty-four locomotives numbered 1-32 and 34, 35 and these numbers were retained by the GW. Joseph Armstrong was appointed the S&C's Engineer in 1853, and then moved to Wolverhampton to take charge of the locomotives of both the Shrewsbury companies. These were the first standard gauge locomotives owned by the GWR.

No.2 (GW 2) 2-4-0T, 1846, reb.1868

A 2-4-0 tender engine was built at Longridge of Bedlington in 1846 and was rebuilt as a 2-4-0 saddle tank in 1868 by the GWR. It was No.2 of the S&C and also of the GW. Its dimensions as a 2-4-0ST were:

Coupled wheels:	4ft 9in
Leading wheels:	3ft 6in
Heating surface:	491sqft
Grate area:	17.4sqft
Weight:	24 tons 14 cwt
Axleload:	8 tons 8 cwt

It was withdrawn from service in 1873.

No.15 (GW 15) 0-4-0ST, 1847

Two branch line engines were ordered and one was an 0-4-0 saddle tank constructed by Bury, Curtis & Kennedy in 1847. Its initial dimensions were:

Coupled wheels:	4ft 0in
Cylinders:	15in x 20in
Heating surface:	755.4sqft
Grate area:	11.53sqft
Weight:	20 tons 4 cwt
Axleload:	12 tons 6 cwt

Above: **Drawing of** Shrewsbury & Chester Railway No.2 rebuilt as a 2-4-0T in 1868. (RCTS)

Below: **Former Shrewsbury** & Chester Railway 0-4-0ST No.15 in its final form after the rebuilding in 1890. Note the lack of protection given to the train crew. (F. Moore/MLS Collection)

44 • FOUR-COUPLED TANK LOCOMOTIVE CLASSES ABSORBED BY THE GREAT WESTERN RAILWAY

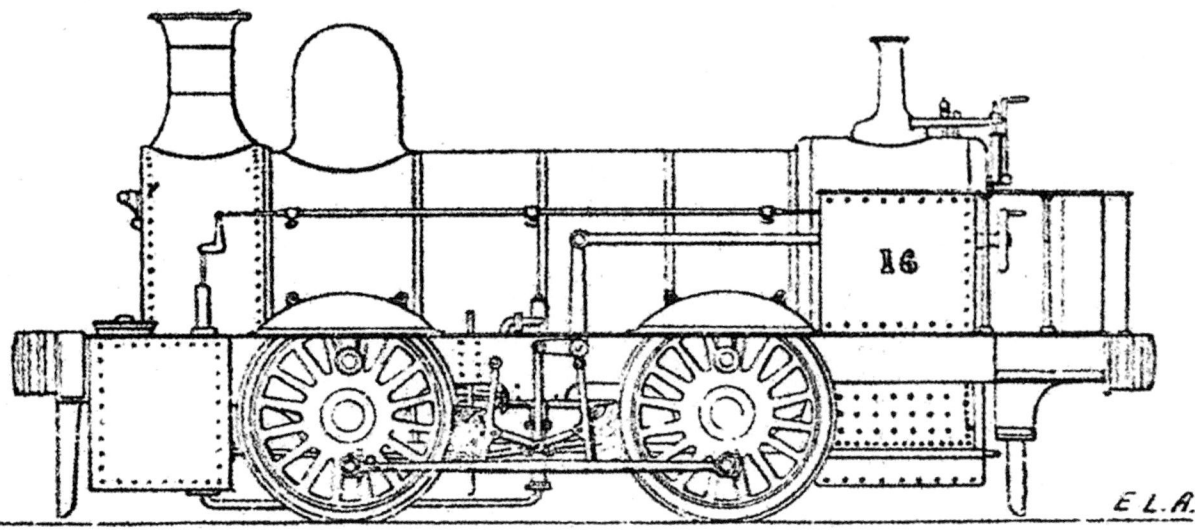

Drawing of Shrewsbury & Chester Railway 0-4-0 well tank No.16. (RCTS)

It was rebuilt in 1866 with 4ft 2in coupled wheels, 15in x 24in cylinders and boiler with 130lb psi pressure. Its cylinders were renewed again in 1881 and another boiler in 1888. Its tank capacity was extended to 640 gallons capacity. It had its frames replaced in 1890 and its heating surface was then 699.6sqft, grate area 9.9sqft and boiler pressure had been reduced to 120lb psi. This much renewed engine was clearly useful and had cut down mountings for clearance in the colliery sidings. It was finally withdrawn in 1904.

No.16 (GW 16) 0-4-0WT, 1849
The second branch engine was an 0-4-0 well tank built by Sharp Brothers in 1849. Its dimensions were:

Coupled wheels:	4ft 6in
Cylinders:	15in x 22in
Heating surface:	944.16sqft
Grate area:	10.97sqft
Tank capacity:	470 gallons

It was rebuilt as a saddle tank in 1872 and spent its later career in the Birkenhead area. It was withdrawn in 1879.

Shrewsbury & Birmingham Railway

The Shrewsbury & Birmingham Railway was opened between Shrewsbury and Wolverhampton in 1849 and to Birmingham in 1854. It was a standard gauge railway and was taken over along with the Shrewsbury and Chester Railway by the GWR in 1854. Two four-coupled tank engines were inherited by the GWR that are of interest in this book.

No. 6 (GW 40) 0-4-2T, 1849, reb.1862
The first was an 0-4-2 passenger tender engine, that was delivered from Longridge in 1849, the first of five engines numbered 6-10. It was a problem in traffic and frequently out of use requiring adjustments and at first the GWR tried to sell it (unsuccessfully). It was taken out of stock in 1858 and was being rebuilt at Wolverhampton over the next four years, emerging in 1862 as an 0-4-2 saddle tank. Its new dimensions were:

Coupled wheels:	4ft 4in
Trailing wheels:	3ft 6in
Cylinders:	14½in x 22in
Boiler pressure:	110lb psi
Heating surface:	763.85sqft
Grate area:	11.2sqft
Weight:	25 tons 2 cwt
Axleload:	9½ tons

It was numbered 40 by the GWR and subjected to further rebuilding. In 1873 it received 16in x 22in cylinders and a GW '850' class boiler and a saddle tank with a 568 gallon capacity. The new boiler was pressed at 140lb psi and had a heating surface of 927sqft and grate area of 12.33sqft. It weighed 27¾ tons. It was rebuilt again in 1897 and again had new cylinders at 15in x 22in and boiler with a revised heating surface of 911.2sqft and grate area of 11.17sqft.

It worked the Oldbury branch for many years and was withdrawn in 1904.

No.11 (GW 45) 0-4-0WT, 1853
The other four-coupled tank engine was an 0-4-0 well tank built by Sharp, Stewart in 1853 and delivered a month before the GW takeover. It had been allotted the number 11 after an earlier engine of that number had been sold but was immediately numbered 45 by the GWR. Its dimensions were:

Coupled wheels:	3ft 9in
Cylinders:	15in x 22in
Heating surface:	866.25sqft
Grate area:	10.66sqft

In 1862 it was rebuilt to an 0-4-2 wheel arrangement with a saddle

Shrewsbury & Birmingham Railway 0-4-2T GW 40 (former B&H No.6) as rebuilt by the GWR in 1897 and operating the Oldbury branch service. (Loco Publishing Co/MLS Collection)

Drawing of the Shrewsbury & Birmingham 0-4-0ST No.11 as GWR No.45, c1875. (RCTS)

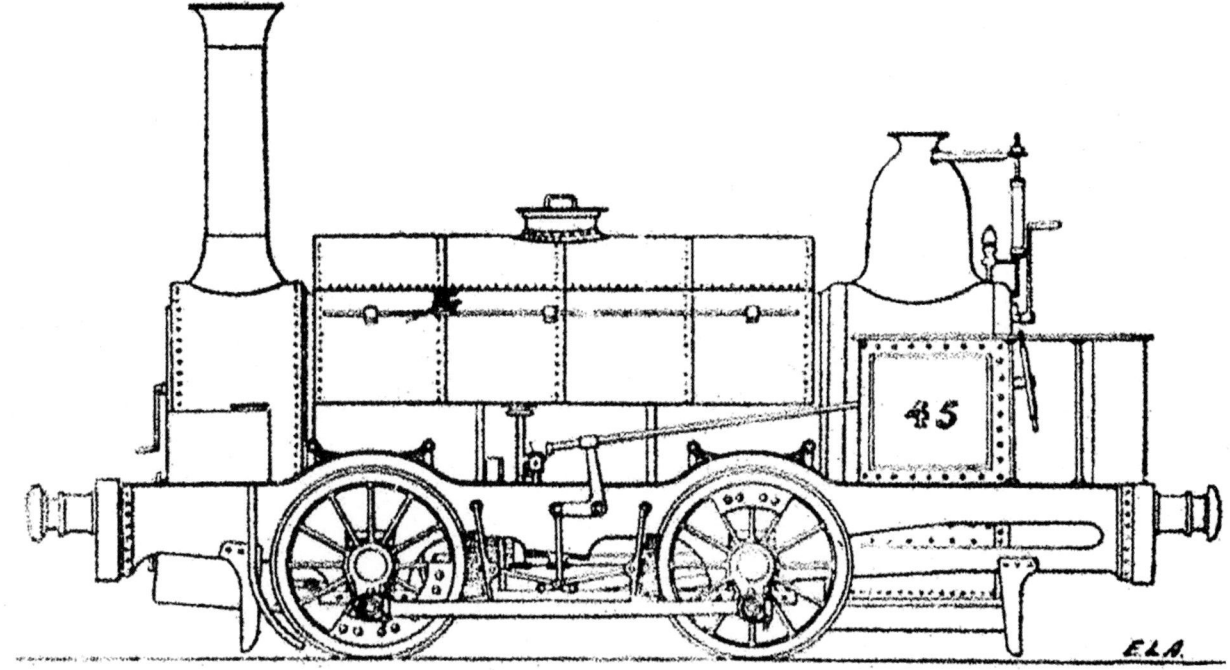

tank replacing the well tank. It was later rumoured to have been converted back to an 0-4-0 saddle tank. It was withdrawn in 1877.

Shrewsbury & Hereford and Tenbury Railways

The Shrewsbury & Hereford and Tenbury Railways were opened between Shrewsbury and Ludlow in 1852 and on to Hereford by 1853. It became part of the West Midlands Railway in 1860. The Tenbury Railway was built in 1861 and the whole system was leased jointly to the L&NWR and the GWR from 1862. The Leominster & Kington Railway opened in 1857 and was also taken over by the West Midland and then the joint companies in 1862.

Drawing of Shrewsbury & Hereford Railway 2-4-0 well tank, West Midlands Railway 121, GW 228. (RCTS)

121, 130 & 131, 2-4-0WT, 1856

121 was a 2-4-0 outside cylinder well tank built by Jones & Son of Liverpool in 1856. It became GW 228 in 1863 and had the following dimensions:

Coupled wheels:	5ft 6in
Leading wheels:	3ft 6in
Cylinders (outside)	15in x 20in
Heating surface:	882sqft
Grate area:	12.25sqft
Weight:	26 tons 17 cwt

Two similar 2-4-0WTs, 130 and 131, were built for the Leominster & Kington Railway by the same company in 1857 and became GW 229 and 230. The only dimensional difference was the cylinder diameter of 14in x 20in.

228 was withdrawn in 1872, but the other two lasted longer. 229 was operating in the Paddington area and 230 at Oxford until both were withdrawn for sale in 1874 but as no sale was accomplished, both were scrapped in 1878.

Watlington & Princes Risborough Railway

The Watlington & Princes Risborough Railway opened in 1872 as a standard gauge railway. The line was vested in the GWR in 1883.

No.2 (GW 1384) 2-4-0T, 1876

Initially motive power was hired from the GWR but the company acquired two locomotives, a 2-2-2WT and a 2-4-0 side tank built by Sharp, Stewart & Co. in 1876. The latter's dimensions were:

Coupled wheels:	4ft 0in
Leading wheels:	2ft 9in
Cylinders:	12in x 17in
Boiler pressure:	120lb psi
Heating surface:	570sqft
Grate area:	8.25sqft
Tank capacity:	480 gallons

It was renumbered 1384 in 1883 and rebuilt with a Belpaire boiler in 1899 with a heating surface of 620.9sqft and a grate area of 8.77sqft. The tank was enlarged to 640 gallons capacity. Weight was 24 tons 7 cwt and the wheel dimensions had been slightly increased to 4ft 2in and 2ft 10½in.

Watlington & Princes Risborough 2-4-0 side tank No.2 after acquisition by the GWR in 1883. (MLS Collection)

Standard Gauge Locomotives absorbed by the GWR before 1914 • 47

1384 working a Wrington Vale train between Congresbury and Blagdon in North Somerset, c1900. (MLS Collection)

1384 at Hemyock, c1908. (Bob Miller/ MLS Collections)

The GWR used 1384 in the construction of the Bodmin branch in 1886, lent it to the Lambourne Valley Railway in 1898, then on the Wrington Vale light railway in the Cheddar Valley and later it was active on the Hemyock branch before its withdrawal in 1911 and sale to the Bute Works Supply Company, finishing up as the Weston, Clevedon & Portishead Railway No.4 *Hesperus* until being scrapped in 1937 (see page 131).

West Cornwall Railway

The West Cornwall Railway was a standard gauge railway formed in 1846, but it was 1852 before it linked Penzance with Truro. There it met the South Devon Railway broad gauge and it was not until 1866 that a third rail to provide mixed gauge running was constructed, then under the auspices of the Associated Companies (the GW, South Devon and Bristol & Exeter railways). Most of the passenger services then used the broad gauge and the goods trains, the standard. West Cornwall engines converted to the broad gauge were covered earlier in Chapter 2 (South Devon Railway – see page 17) but there was one West Cornwall four-coupled tank locomotive that stayed standard gauge.

Fox (GW 1391), 0-4-0T, 1872

Fox was a small 0-4-0 saddle tank built by the Avonside Engine Co. in 1872. Its dimensions were:

Coupled wheels:	2ft 7in
Cylinders:	11in x 16in
Heating surface:	326.1sqft
Tank capacity:	450 gallons.

It was given the GW number 1391 in 1876 and was subsequently rebuilt at Swindon in 1897 with revised dimensions:

Coupled wheels:	2ft 10in
Cylinders:	11in x 16in
Boiler pressure:	150lb psi
Heating surface:	367sqft
Grate area:	6.5sqft
Weight:	18 tons
Axleload:	11 tons 8 cwt
Tank capacity:	400 gallons

It was used mainly on engineering department work in Devon and Cornwall for many years and spent some time in the Weymouth area before being withdrawn in 1912 and sold to the Gloucester Carriage & Wagon Company who eventually sold it to Cashmore's of Newport for scrap in 1948. It outlived its other West Cornwall standard gauge engines by sixty-seven years!

West Midland Railway

The West Midland Railway was formed in 1860 of the Oxford, Worcester & Wolverhampton Railway, the Newport, Abergavenny and Hereford Railway and the Worcester & Hereford Railway in 1860 and was absorbed into the Great Western Railway in 1863. The GWR numbered its acquired four-coupled tender engines between 171 and 205, the tender singles 206-220, tank engines 221-236 and tender goods engines 237-301.

68 & 69 (GW 225-226), 2-4-0T, 1861

These two 2-4-0 side tank engines were acquired by the West Midlands Railway in 1861 from Beyer, Peacock & Co. and had the following dimensions:

West Cornwall Railway *Fox* (GW 1391) at Gloucester Carriage & Wagon Works, 1 February 1916. (MLS Collection)

Coupled wheels: 5ft 0in
Leading wheels: 3ft 6in
Cylinders: 15in x 20in
Heating surface: 907.74sqft
Grate area: 14sqft
Weight: 30 tons

The GWR renumbered them 225 and 226 in 1863. They were both based at Hereford and worked between Malvern Wells and Hereford and on the Stratford/Honeybourne line. 226 was withdrawn in 1880 and 225 in 1883.

90-92 (GW 194-195), 0-4-2T, 1854, reb.1872
Former Newport, Abergavenny & Hereford Railway locomotives (see pages 37-38).

107, 109 & 111 (GW 197, 199, 201), 2-4-0T, 1862, reb.1879
Beyer, Peacock built six 2-4-0 tender engines for the West Midlands Railway in 1862, numbered 106-111, and three of these, 107, 109 and 111, were renumbered 197, 199 and 201 in 1863 and rebuilt by the GWR in 1879-1881 as express 2-4-0 side tank engines, 201 only fitted with condensing apparatus. This only lasted until 1884 when they were, with a number of 2-2-2 tender engines, rebuilt again as 2-4-0 tender engines, being then only withdrawn between 1914 and 1919. Their dimensions as 2-4-0Ts were:

Coupled wheels: 6ft 0in
Leading wheels: 4ft 0in
Cylinders: 17in x 24in
Heating surface: 1,297sqft
Tank capacity: 1,000 gallons

121, 130 & 131 (GW 228-230) class 2-4-0T, 1856
Former Shrewsbury & Hereford Railway locomotives (see page 46).

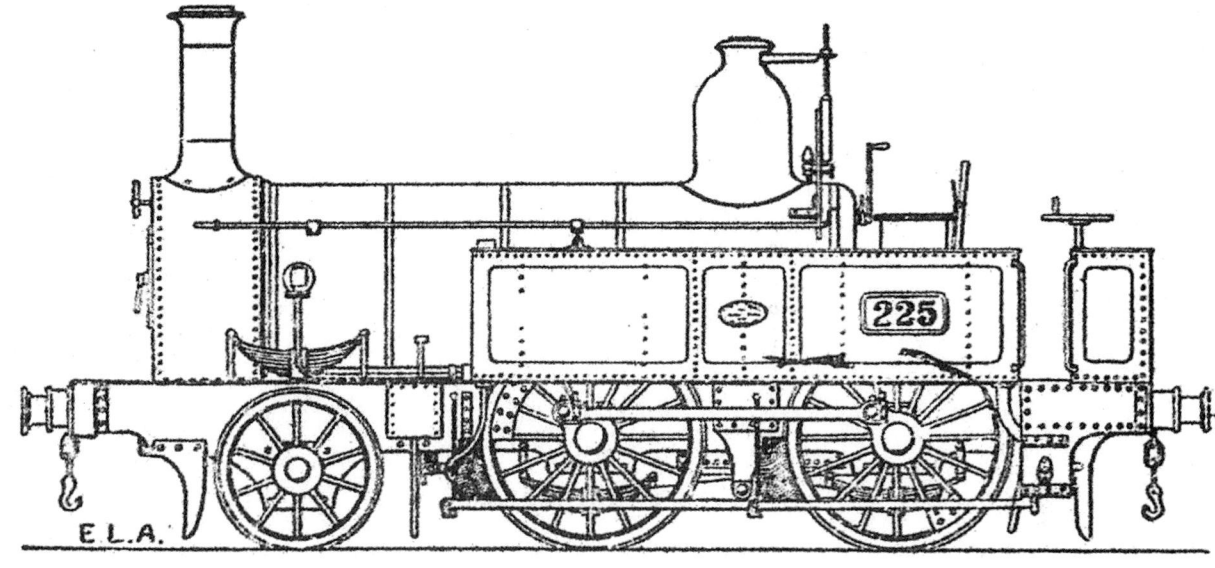

Drawing of the West Midlands 2-4-0T 68 renumbered 225 by the GWR. (RCTS)

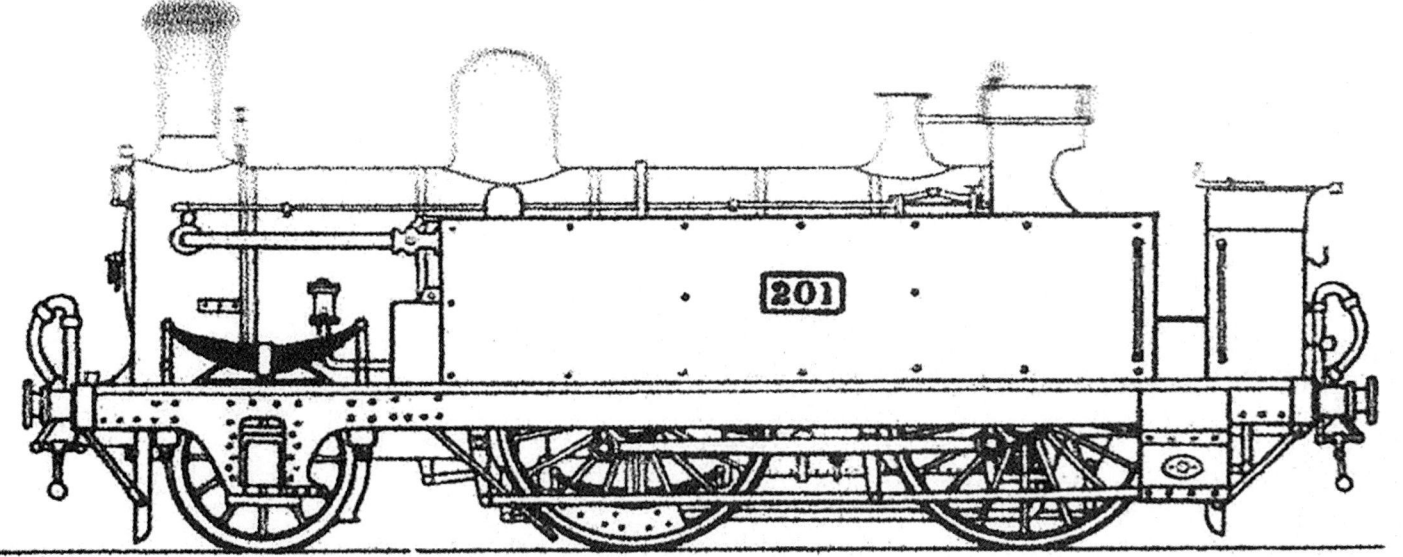

Drawing of the West Midlands 2-4-0 111, rebuilt as a 2-4-0T in 1862, fitted with condensing apparatus and renumbered 201 by the GWR. (RCTS)

Chapter 4
LOCOMOTIVES ABSORBED BY THE GWR 1914–23

Britain's railways were brought under government control during the First World War and the country's largest locomotive works were turned over to munitions production at the expense of much routine repair work with the result that deterioration of the railways' rolling stock and locomotives in particular was serious. At the end of the war, many of the railway companies were in some financial difficulty and did not have the resources for quick recovery and the investment needed to overcome the parlous situation. The most senior Mechanical Engineers of the major railways – Churchward, Maunsell, Fowler, Robinson, Gresley – were brought together in the Association of Railway Locomotive Engineers (ARLE) to design standard engines for the war production effort and afterwards nationalisation of the railways was seriously considered by the government, with Maunsell earmarked as the potential Chief Mechanical Engineer of the proposed state railway. In the event, the Geddes Committee set up by the government was strongly opposed to nationalisation and advocated instead the amalgamation of the numerous private companies into the 'Big Four '– the LMSR, LNER, GWR and SR.

The Companies were formed on 1 January 1923, but in anticipation of this the Great Western Railway took over all the South Wales railways whose primary purpose was the carriage of coal and steel products that had been so vital in the war effort, and was now flagging in the post-war situation. The GWR took command of these railways as a result of the Railways Act 1921 and locomotives of the Alexandra Railway & Dock Company, the Barry Railway, the Cambrian Railways, the Cardiff Railway, the Rhymney Railway and the Taff Vale Railway were absorbed into the GWR fleet on 1 January 1922, a full year before the 'Grouping' of the four main line companies was accomplished. This chapter will describe the numerous four-coupled tanks of those Welsh companies that were 'absorbed' in 1922, some of which had previously been taken over from smaller Welsh railway companies, such as the Brecon & Merthyr or Neath & Brecon. The only non-Welsh railway absorbed at this time was the Midland & South Western Junction Railway which shared resources with the London & South Western Railway – this followed in July 1923 and the relevant locomotive classes from this railway are included in this chapter.

Alexandra Dock Railway

The Alexandra Docks Company was formed in 1865 to construct docks and connect them with the Great Western Railway at Newport. The first dock was opened in 1875 and the Pontypridd, Caerphilly and Newport Railway (PC&N) opened between Pontypridd and Caerphilly in 1884 and from Bassaleg to the docks in 1886, with running powers over the intervening section on the Brecon & Merthyr Railway. Initially, the trains were worked by Taff Vale engines. In 1897, the AD&R absorbed the PC&N and its 9¼ miles to add to the 100 miles it owned of docks lines and sidings. The GWR took over passenger services on the line in 1899 apart from an AD&R supplementary passenger service operated by a steam rail motor. The AD&R took over mineral working from the TVR in April 1906 and provided the motive power, most of which was purchased second hand. The AD&R engine livery was black.

Active, *Trojan* (GW 1340) & *Alexandra* (GW 1341), 0-4-0ST, 1882-97

Three four-coupled saddle tank engines were purchased from the contractors, Dunn & Shute, when their work in the construction of the Town Dock was completed in 1903. *Active* had been built by Hunslet in 1882 and initially used by Isaac Llewellyn and named *Kate*. It was renamed by Dunn & Shute. Little is known of its dimensions, and it was sold to Newport & Abercarn Colliery in 1915. By 1919, it was with Babcock & Wilcox in Renfrew.

Alexandra's origin and date of construction is unknown, but the GWR held records of its dimensions after the Grouping. These were:

Coupled wheels:	3ft 0in (later given as 3ft 2in)
Cylinders (outside):	12in x 19in
Boiler pressure:	120lb psi
Heating surface:	465.7sqft
Grate area:	6.18sqft
Weight:	18 tons 8 cwt (later 19 tons 9 cwt)
Axleload:	10 tons 14 cwt (later 11 tons 8 cwt)
Tractive effort:	7,750lb

The engine had an extensive overhaul at Swindon between 1922 and 1925, returning to the Cardiff Cathays and Radyr areas numbered 1341 unnamed. It was withdrawn in 1946.

Trojan was built by the Avonside Engine Co. in 1897. Its dimensions are given below together with variations made during its sojourn at Swindon in 1922/3.

Coupled wheels:	3ft 0in
Cylinders (outside):	12½in x 19¾in (later 14in x 20in)
Boiler pressure:	120lb psi
Heating surface:	563.16sqft
Grate area:	8sqft
Weight:	22 tons 17 cwt (later 22½ tons)
Axleload:	13 tons 6 cwt (later 13 tons 3 cwt)
Tank capacity:	420 gallons
Tractive effort:	8,740lb (later 11,100lb)

The former Dunn & Shute contractor's 0-4-0ST 1341, formerly *Alexandra*, at Alexandra Dock Junction in the 1930s. Note the unusual shape of the saddle tank. (H.C. Casserley/MLS Collection)

Alexandra Dock Railway 0-4-0ST *Trojan*, GW 1340 after withdrawal and awaiting sale together with ex-Cardiff Railway 0-4-0ST 1339, 1934. (S.J. Rhodes/Bob Miller/MLS Collections)

Former GW 1340 *Trojan* shortly after sale to Alders Ltd of Tamworth in 1947. (H.W. Robinson/Bob Miller/MLS Collections)

GW 1340 *Trojan* at the premises of Alders Ltd of Tamworth, c1959. Note the provision of a stovepipe chimney and the modified side window shutters of the cab. (Bob Miller/MLS Collections)

It was renumbered 1340 in 1922 but retained its name. Although mainly, like 1341, at Cathays and Radyr, it was briefly based at Oswestry and later in 1929 seen around the Greenford/Park Royal area. It was withdrawn in 1932 and sold to the Victoria Colliery Co. at Wellington in 1934. In 1947 it was further sold to Alders of Tamworth and was still operational there in 1965.

1-2 Steam Railmotors 0-4-0T, 1904

Two steam railmotors were built in 1904/5 by the Glasgow Railway & Engineering Co. of Govan. The locomotive part of the carriage was of 0-4-0T wheel arrangement with the rear of the single coach carried on a four wheel bogie. They were numbered 1 and 2. The known dimensions of the two railmotors were:

	Railmotor No.1	Railmotor No.2
Coupled wheels:	3ft 0in	
Cylinders:	9in x 14in	9in x 14in
Boiler pressure:	160lb psi	160lb psi
Heating surface:	347sqft	
Weight:	31½ tons	35 tons
Water capacity:	350 gallons	350 gallons
Coal capacity:	1 ton	1 ton
Seating capacity:	52	54

They operated the local service between Caerphilly and Pontypridd. No.1 was withdrawn in 1911 and its coach converted to a normal carriage whilst No.2 was withdrawn from traffic in 1917 when the Caerphilly-Pontypridd service was withdrawn as a wartime economy. It is not known whether its coach element was retained.

14 (GW 1426) '517' class 0-4-2T, 1877

When the AD&R Railmotor No.1 was withdrawn in 1911 after a dubious seven years of operation it was replaced by a locomotive hauled train with Railmotor No.2 in reserve. The company purchased a GW '517' class 0-4-2T, GW 1426, which it renumbered 14. Originally built

Alexandra Dock Railway Steam Railcar No.1 built in 1904 and withdrawn in 1911. (F.K. Davies/John Hodge Collections)

54 • FOUR-COUPLED TANK LOCOMOTIVE CLASSES ABSORBED BY THE GREAT WESTERN RAILWAY

Alexandra Dock Railway Steam Railcar No.2 built in 1905 and withdrawn in 1917. (F.K. Davies/John Hodge Collections)

in 1877, it was reboilered in 1919 by Hawthorn, Leslie & Co. – a boiler pressured to 150lb psi, heating surface of 1,009sqft and grate area of 13.14sqft. It returned to the GWR in 1922 adopting its former number once more. It was withdrawn in 1934. (Full details of the class '517' dimensions were given in my book *Four-Coupled Tanks Built by the GWR*, P&S 2023.)

Barry Railway

The Barry Railway came into being after colliery owners' frustration at the congestion of shipping at Cardiff Docks and the subsequent Parliamentary Bill sanctioning the Barry Dock and Railway Bill in 1884. The first trains ran in 1888 and Barry Docks opened in 1889. It grew to be the largest coal shipment dock in the country as annual tonnages grew rapidly up to the beginning of the First World War, and whilst most of the Barry Railway's revenue came from coal haulage from the valleys to the docks, it ran passenger services, culminating in the development of Barry Island as a major day trip destination. The South Wales railways were complex and had many joint agreements and mutual running powers (as well as bitter commercial rivalries, especially with the Great Western Railway).

'E' class 0-6-0T, 1889 rebuilt as 0-4-2T (GW 781, 785), 1909

Five small Hudswell Clarke 0-6-0 tanks were acquired by the Barry Railway in 1889 and in 1909 one of them, 33, was converted to an 0-4-2T by removal of the rear coupling rods and fitted with auto working equipment. It was then repainted and lined out in the company's passenger livery for use on the Barry-Llantwit Major service. The auto working ceased by 1910 but the engine continued on the same service and a second 'E' tank, 53, built in 1891, was similarly converted as a spare. Their dimensions were:

Coupled wheels:	3ft 6½in (thickened from 3ft 3½in when converted)
Trailing wheels:	3ft 3½in
Cylinders:	14in x 20in
Boiler pressure:	140lb psi (later 150lb psi)
Heating surface:	562sqft
Grate area:	9sqft
Weight:	27½ tons (later 32 tons 4 cwt after reboilering)
Axleload:	9½ tons (later 12 tons 14 cwt)
Tank capacity:	660 gallons
Coal capacity:	1½ tons
Tractive effort:	11,810lb

The whole class was renumbered 781-785 in 1922, and at some stage their rear coupling rods were restored and became 0-6-0Ts once more. The vacuum brakes were removed from them by the GWR and they were withdrawn and sold in 1932. 785 had run just about half a million miles and 781 rather more, but how much as an 0-4-2T is unknown.

The Barry Railway 'E' 0-6-0T, No.33, converted to run as an 0-4-2T in 1909 and seen here as auto fitted, the control wires visible to the roof of the trailing vehicles. It appears to be at Barry Town station, 1909.
(A.C. Roberts/F.K. Davies/John Hodge Collections)

'C' class 2-4-0T, (GW 1321-1322), 1889
The Barry's first passenger engines were four 2-4-0 side tank engines designed and constructed by the Sharp, Stewart Company in 1889/90. They were numbered 21, 22, 37 and 52. Their dimensions were:

Coupled wheels:	5ft 3in
Leading wheels:	3ft 6in
Boiler pressure:	150lb psi
Heating surface:	1,041sqft
Grate area:	14.25sqft
Weight:	41 tons 2 cwt
Axleload:	16 tons 2 cwt
Tank capacity:	800 gallons
Tractive effort:	14,040lb

They were built for the short branch from Barry to Cogan and worked passenger services between Barry and Cardiff until 1897. As the Barry passenger services were extended to Trehafod, their water tank and coal bunker capacities were insufficient, and they were replaced by the newly introduced 'J' 2-4-2Ts. In 1898 Nos.21 and 22 were rebuilt as 2-4-2Ts to overcome this deficiency, with 3ft 6in trailing wheels, a new bunker holding 2¼ tons of coal and an additional 570 gallons of water giving a total tank capacity of 1,370 gallons. In 1898 the Port Talbot Railway purchased Nos. 37 and 52, the latter converted at their request to the 2-4-2T wheel arrangement. As the class 'J's took over the passenger work No.21 was utilised for special working including the Directors' and Engineers' saloons and the General Manager's special vehicle. No.22 worked colliers' trains or services on the Vale of Glamorgan. When the steam railmotors were discontinued in 1914 both were converted to trailers and 21 and 22 were fitted with steam heating apparatus to haul these vehicles on the Vale of Glamorgan to Bridgend. The GWR numbered these two locomotives 1321 and 1322 and 1322 was rebuilt at Swindon in 1924 with a 165lb psi 'Metro' boiler, high-roofed cab and enlarged bunker. Tractive effort increased to 15,440lb and weight to 47 tons 2 cwt. Both locomotives exceeded 700,000 miles and were withdrawn in 1926 (1323) and 1928 (1322).

The Barry Railway's first passenger tank, No.22, a 2-4-0T built by Sharp, Stewart Co. in 1889. (LGRP/Bob Miller/MLS Collections)

No.22, rebuilt in 1898 as a 2-4-2T with additional tank and bunker capacity, at Barry, c1900. (Real Photographs/Bob Miller/MLS Collections)

'G' class 0-4-4T, (GW 2-4, 9), 1892

The Barry Railway's Locomotive Superintendent, J.H. Hosgood, designed an 0-4-4 side tank passenger engine in the early 1890s and the first two, numbered 66 and 67, were built by the Vulcan Foundry and delivered in August 1892. Two more were constructed by the Sharp, Stewart Company in March 1895. Their dimensions were:

Coupled wheels:	5ft 7½in
Trailing bogie wheels:	3ft 0in
Cylinders:	18in x 26in
Boiler pressure:	150lb psi
Heating surface:	1,126sqft
Grate area:	21sqft
Weight:	56 tons 1 cwt
Axleload:	18 tons 3 cwt
Tank capacity:	1,400 gallons
Bunker capacity:	1½ tons
Tractive effort:	14,930lb

These locomotives proved themselves very capable and were kept in excellent condition. No.67 was experimentally fitted with piston valves between 1902 and 1910. This locomotive received a heavier 3A boiler in 1920 with 160lb psi pressure, 17½in x 26in cylinders and 5ft 8in coupled wheels, with a tractive effort of 15,925lb. It had an increased bunker capacity of 2 tons but slightly reduced tank capacity of 1,280 gallons. They were renumbered 2, 3, 4 and 9 by the GW.

They worked the Barry-Trehafod services and after introduction of the 'J' class were working mainly at the northern end of the Barry system. They were largely replaced after the Grouping by 0-6-2Ts and were withdrawn between 1925 and 1929, the rebuilt 67 (GW 3) being the last survivor. The longest

Barry Railway class 'G' 0-4-4T No.68, built in 1895 by the Sharp, Stewart Co. to J.H. Hosgood's design, as built in works grey livery for the company's official photograph. (Bob Miller/MLS Collections)

'G' 0-4-4T No.68 in Barry Railway livery at Barry, 26 April 1910. (K. Nunn/LCGB/MLS Collections)

Barry Railway 'G' 0-4-4T renumbered 4 by the GWR, at Swindon, c 1923. (Real Photographs/Bob Miller/MLS Collections)

mileage achieved was 902,362 by this locomotive.

'J' class 2-4-2T, (GW 1311-1321), 1897

The Barry Railway's final passenger class, the 'J' 2-4-2 side tank, designed by J.H. Hosgood with the standard parts interchangeable with the class 'G' 0-4-4Ts. 86-88 were built by Hudswell, Clarke in 1897 and eight more built by Sharp, Stewart in 1898/9, numbered 89-91 and 94-98. There were minor differences between the two batches, mainly the boiler pitch and tank capacity, spring gear and sanding arrangements and shape of the cabs. Their dimensions were:

Coupled wheels:	5ft 7½in (later 5ft 8in)
Leading & trailing wheels:	3ft 6in
Cylinders:	18in x 26in (later 17½in x 26in)
Boiler pressure:	150lb psi (later 160lb psi)
Heating surface:	1,126sqft (later 1,138.75sqft)
Grate area:	21sqft (later 20.5sqft)
Weight:	60 tons 18 cwt (later 59 tons 14 cwt)
Axleload:	21 tons (later 19 tons 18 cwt)
Tank capacity:	1,600 gallons (1,550 Sharp, Stewart locos)
Bunker capacity:	3½ tons
Tractive effort:	14,930lb (later 15,925lb)

These engines took over from the 2-4-0Ts and 0-4-4Ts the main passenger services between Barry, Cardiff and Pontypridd and were maintained in excellent condition. They remained allocated to the Barry depot for the whole of their lives.

New boilers of type 2C (1,079sqft heating surface and 20.5sqft grate area) were provided from 1909 for 86, 88, 90, 91 and 94, and type 3A with 160lb psi pressure, and reduced cylinder diameter of 17½in, for 88, 91, 94, 95, 97 and 98 between 1911 and 1922. The engines were renumbered 1311-1321 by the GWR in 1922 and 90 (1315), and 95-97 (1318-1320) were rebuilt at Swindon, most in 1924, with new smokeboxes, GWR chimney, and GWR style bunker. 1312 (the former 87) was also rebuilt later in 1926 with a single-row superheater, 5ft 7in coupled wheels, 165lb psi boiler pressure, tank capacity 1,560 gallons and a revised weight of 56 tons 7 cwt. Its tractive effort was enhanced to 16,670lb. It was the last survivor of the class, being withdrawn in July 1930, the rest going between 1926 and earlier in 1930. Their mileages ranged from 737,882 to 892,166. They were eventually replaced on the Barry-Rhondda Valley services by the Taff Vale 0-6-2 'A' tanks.

Barry Railway 'J' 2-4-2T No.90 as built by Sharp, Stewart in 1898 in grey photographic livery.
(F. Moore/MLS Collection)

No.88 built by Hudswell, Clarke in 1897 in Barry Railway livery at Barry shed, 25 April 1910.
(K. Nunn/LCGB/ MLS Collection)

1313 (former Barry Railway 88) at Barry shed, shortly before withdrawal in 1928.
(Photomatic/MLS Collection)

Hudswell Clarke No.86 at Cardiff Riverside with a Clarence Road-Pontypridd train, 11 August 1913. (K. Nunn/LCGB/MLS Collections)

Sharp, Stewart No.97 at Cardiff Riverside with the 1.4pm Barry Island-Clarence Road train, 11 August 1913. (K. Nunn/LCGB/MLS Collections)

Steam Railmotor No.2 built by the North British Loco Co. in 1905 for the Barry Railway, 1905. (F.K. Davies/John Hodge Collections)

1-2 Steam Railmotors, 0-4-0T, 1905
The Barry Railway had two steam railmotors built in 1905 by the North British Locomotive Company of Glasgow. Numbered 1 and 2, their dimensions were:

Coupled wheels:	3ft 7½in
Cylinders:	12in x 16in
Boiler pressure:	160lb psi
Heating surface:	598sqft
Grate area:	11.5sqft
Weight:	50¾ tons
Tank capacity:	500 gallons
Coal capacity:	¾ ton
Seating capacity:	50

They operated primarily on the Vale of Glamorgan between Barry and Bridgend and in 1914 they were withdrawn, the coach element converted to a standard trailer and were then loco-hauled over the same route.

Steam Railmotor No.2 in service with its crew, c1906. (F.K. Davies/John Hodge Collections)

Brecon & Merthyr Railway
The Brecon & Merthyr Railway started with various schemes to connect Brecon with the ironworks at Dowlais and then to link Merthyr with the Brecon-Talyllyn-Pant section opening in the early 1860s with connections via the Taff Vale

Railway to Merthyr. It then, in conjunction with the Rhymney Railway, opened up the route from Rhymney through New Tredegar, Bargoed, Bedwas and Machen to Bassaleg and eventually Newport Dock Street. The routes of the B&M were established by 1868 with mutual running powers between the B&M and the RR. It was absorbed by the Great Western Railway on 1 July 1922 and its locomotives added to the GW stock in October. Brecon lost its rail connections through passenger service closures in December 1962 and its freight between Brecon and Merthyr in May 1964, and thereafter the freight traffic dwindled as the pits closed, the last being the closure of Bedwas Colliery in 1980. The B&M workshops were at Machen.

'Tiny' 0-4-0ST, 1862

A small 0-4-0 saddle tank was built by Manning, Wardle in 1862 but although owned by the Brecon & Merthyr Railway, was used initially on the Hereford, Hay & Brecon Railway and subsequently for the contractors building parts of the Cambrian at Llynclys. It had 2ft 11½in coupled wheels and 9½in x 14in cylinders and was sold to the Cambrian contractors in 1868 without ever operating on the B & M.

Usk, 2-4-0, 1865, reb. 2-4-0T, 1895.

Usk was one of two 2-4-0 tender engines built by Sharp, Stewart & Co. for the Hereford, Hay & Brecon Railway, but on completion in 1865 they were delivered to the Cambrian and then transferred to the Brecon & Merthyr Railway. After years on Brecon-Hereford services, *Usk* was used on the Newport-Rhymney trains until 1895 when it was rebuilt as a 2-4-0 side tank engine at the B&M Machen works. Its dimensions as a tank engine were:

Coupled wheels:	5ft 6in
Leading wheels:	3ft 6in
Cylinders:	16in x 20in
Boiler pressure:	120lb psi
Heating surface:	914.8sqft
Grate area:	11.6sqft
Tank capacity:	700 gallons

It was renumbered 21 in 1895 and was withdrawn in June 1904 and replaced by a new 'Metro' tank that assumed its number (see page 63).

44 (GW 1391) ex-LSWR 0376, 4-4-2T, 1879

A former L&SWR Adams 4-4-2 side tank engine was available for sale by the Bute Works Supply Company in 1914 and it was purchased as an additional engine for the Newport-Brecon service. It had been built in 1879 as a 4-4-0T but converted to the 4-4-2T arrangement in 1883. The L&SWR had placed it on their duplicate list in 1903 as 0376 and it became B & M 44. Its dimensions were:

Coupled wheels:	5ft 6in
Bogie wheels:	2ft 6in
Trailing wheels:	3ft 0in
Cylinders (outside):	17½in x 24in
Boiler pressure:	140lb psi
Heating surface:	1,047sqft
Grate area:	16sqft
Weight:	58 tons 19 cwt
Axleload:	17 tons 6 cwt
Tank capacity:	1,650 gallons
Tractive effort:	13,260lb

Although a free steaming and good riding engine, it proved unsuitable for the long steep banks on the Newport-Brecon line because of its large diameter coupled wheels and was used on the Newport-Rhymney line. The GW allocated

Former L&SWR 0376 of the Adams 0415 class, bought by the B & M and renumbered 44, after purchase and repainting, c1914. (F.K. Davies/John Hodge Collections)

it the number 1391 but although overhauled at Machen in 1922 and newly painted a dark crimson-lake, it was condemned by the GW in September 1922 as life-expired.

9-12, 21, 25 (GW 1402/12/52/58/60) Met tanks 2-4-0T, 1888

There was a need to replace older passenger tender engines in the 1880s and trials were conducted with Great Western 2-4-0 'Metro' tanks in 1888. These were successful and the B & M therefore ordered four locomotives of the class direct from R. Stephenson & Co. They were numbered 9-12. They were delivered at the end of 1888 and beginning of 1889. A further example, numbered 25, was built at the company's Machen works in 1898 and the final example, 21, was built as a replacement for the 1863 engine *Usk* in 1904. Their dimensions were similar to the GW 'Metro' tanks, this group being:

Coupled wheels:	5ft 0in
Leading wheels:	3ft 6in
Cylinders:	16in x 24in
Boiler pressure:	150lb psi
Heating surface:	1,156sqft
Grate area:	15.25sqft
Weight:	43 tons (21-46 tons 1 cwt)
Axleload:	15 tons 8 cwt
Tank capacity:	800 gallons
Tractive effort:	13,055lb

Their livery was brick red with polished brass work. They were based at Brecon and Bassaleg. No.21 operated the Newport-Rhymney service from 1916 until its withdrawal in 1921. After 1922 they were allotted GW numbers in the 14XX range infiltrating the GW 'Metro' tank series, but apart from 1460 (ex-No.11) they were withdrawn in 1922/3 before renumbering. 1460 was withdrawn in October 1924.

'Metro' tank No.12 on shed, 1910. (MLS Collection)

Two photos of 'Metro' tank No.9, the first built by R. Stephenson & Co. for the B&M in 1888, working trains between Newport and Brecon in the first decade of the twentieth century.
(MLS Collection)

Another shot of 'Met Tank' No.9 at Machen with a Newport-Brecon train, 1922. (A. Lewis/F.K. Davies/John Hodge Collections)

'Metro' tank GW 1460 (former B & M No.11 still stencilled on the bufferbeam) at Merthyr, c1922. (K. Nunn/LCGB/Bob Miller/MLS Collections)

Burry Port & Gwendreath Valley Railway

With a length of only twenty-one miles, the BP&GV Railway was one of the shortest absorbed by the Great Western Railway in 1922. It was formed in 1865 with its main line from Burry Port on the Carmarthenshire Coast to Cwm Mawr at the head of the Gwendraeth Valley. Goods train activity started in 1869 and there were branches to Kidwelly in 1873 and to Llanelly at Sandy Gate Junction. The company also owned the docks at Burry Port. A light railway order was obtained in 1909 for the economical introduction of passenger services. Fifteen engines were taken into GW stock in October 1922. Its engines just carried names until 1899 and were liveried in green lined out in black and yellow.

Lizzie & *Gwendraeth*, 0-4-0ST, 1869

The first locomotives of the company were two 0-4-0 saddle tanks purchased from the contractors in 1869. They were built by Henry Hughes & Co. of Loughborough in 1868. The few dimensions known about them were:

	Lizzie	*Gwendraeth*
Coupled wheels:	2ft 9in	3ft 9in
Cylinders (outside):	12in x 20in	12in x 20in
Weight:	14-15 tons	

The contractors' engine, *Lizzie*, purchased by the BP&GV Railway in 1869, photographed probably in the 1880s.
(LPC/F.K. Davies/John Hodge Collections)

It is not known how long *Lizzie* worked on the system, but *Gwendraeth* was still there in 1893 when it was reboilered. It was shunting Burry Port docks. It was further rebuilt in 1897 and a cab fitted.

Pioneer/Mountaineer Fairlie 0-4-4-0T, 1870

Two Fairlie patented double engines were acquired, one of which was a standard gauge 0-4-4-0T. It was constructed by the Fairlie Engine & Rolling Stock Company in 1870 and named *Pioneer*. It was intended for the overseas market, with both New South Wales, Australia and Sweden suggested as the intended destination, but Fairlie then agreed to sell it to the BP&GV. It was then renamed *Mountaineer* and undertook a number of trials in comparison with *Gwendraeth*. Few details are known of its dimensions, other than its coupled wheel diameter was 3ft 6in and its outside cylinders, 10in x 18in. It was withdrawn around 1891 and scrapped at Burry Port around the end of the century.

Cambrian Railways

The Cambrian Railways started as a group of independent companies – the Llanidloes & Newtown Railway in 1859, the Oswestry & Newtown Railway in 1860, the Shrewsbury & Welshpool Railway in 1862, the Newtown and Machynlleth Railway in 1863, the Aberystwyth & Welsh Coast Railway also in 1863 and the Oswestry, Ellesmere and Whitchurch Railway in 1864. Close cooperation made sense finally with the setting up of a Joint Committee and a Bill was enacted in parliament to form

Above: The BP&GV standard gauge Fairlie 0-4-4-0T *Pioneer* purchased in 1870. (B.Y. Williams/F.K. Davies/John Hodge Collections)

Below: The BP&GV standard gauge Fairlie 0-4-4-0T *Mountaineer* purchased in 1870 and renamed from the original *Pioneer*. It is seen here at Kidwelly Junction, 24 May 1890, a year before its withdrawal. (Bob Miller/MLS Collections)

the Cambrian Railways in July 1864. By the 1870s, the Cambrian Railways owned 180 route miles and operated another 51 miles on behalf of other companies. The Mid-Wales Railway from Llanidloes to Brecon was amalgamated with the Cambrian Railways in 1904. Although strenuously opposed by the Great Western through much of its existence, that company finally 'absorbed' the Cambrian in January 1922, though the actual takeover happened in March. The Cambrian Railways had inherited a few early locomotives from the pre-1864 railways but the majority of passenger and freight engines acquired by the GWR were designed and built for the Cambrian, many by the Sharp, Stewart Company and after 1900 by its own engineers and Oswestry Works.

3 *Milford*, 0-4-2ST, 1859

No.3 *Milford* was a small 0-4-2 saddle tank built by Sharp, Stewart & Co. for the contractors, Davies and Savin, who built the Llanidloes and Newtown Railway. It operated on the day of opening, 31 August 1859 and was sold to the Cambrian Railway in 1864. Its dimensions were:

Coupled wheels:	4ft 9in
Trailing wheels:	3ft 6in
Cylinders:	14in x 20in
Boiler pressure:	120lb psi
Heating surface:	660.5sqft
Weight:	26 tons 8 cwt
Tank capacity:	700 gallons

As the Cambrian lines were extended to and up the coast, *Milford* was used in the construction process, then after 1870, as a shunting engine at Oswestry and trip working to local quarries. Its nameplates had disappeared by 1888 and it was withdrawn after an accident in Oswestry Yard in 1893.

21 *Lilleshall* 0-4-0ST, 1862

Lilleshall was an 0-4-0 saddle tank built by the Lilleshall Iron Company in 1862 and purchased by Davies and Savin in 1864. It was sold in 1868 for £850 to an unknown buyer. The only other facts known about this engine was that it had 3ft diameter coupled wheels and 13in x 20in outside cylinders.

Llanidloes & Newtown Railway No.3 *Milford*, seen after the fitting of a cab, c1891. (Loco Publishing Co./Bob Miller/MLS Collections)

36-38 *Plasfynnon* 0-4-0ST, 1863

Sharp, Stewart built three 0-4-0 saddle tanks for light branch working in 1863. They were named *Plasfynnon*, *Mountaineer* and *Prometheus*. They were numbered by the Cambrian in 1864 as 36-38. Their dimensions were:

Coupled wheels:	4ft 0in
Cylinders:	14in x 20in
Boiler pressure:	120lb psi
Heating surface:	669sqft
Grate area:	9.75sqft
Weight:	22 tons 6 cwt
Axleload:	13 tons 6 cwt
Tank capacity:	480 gallons
Tractive effort:	8,330lb

A small enclosed cab was provided in later years. They operated the Kerry and Porthywaen branches from Oswestry depot where they were based, being also used for shunting there. 36 and 37 were withdrawn in 1905 and 38 *Prometheus* in 1907.

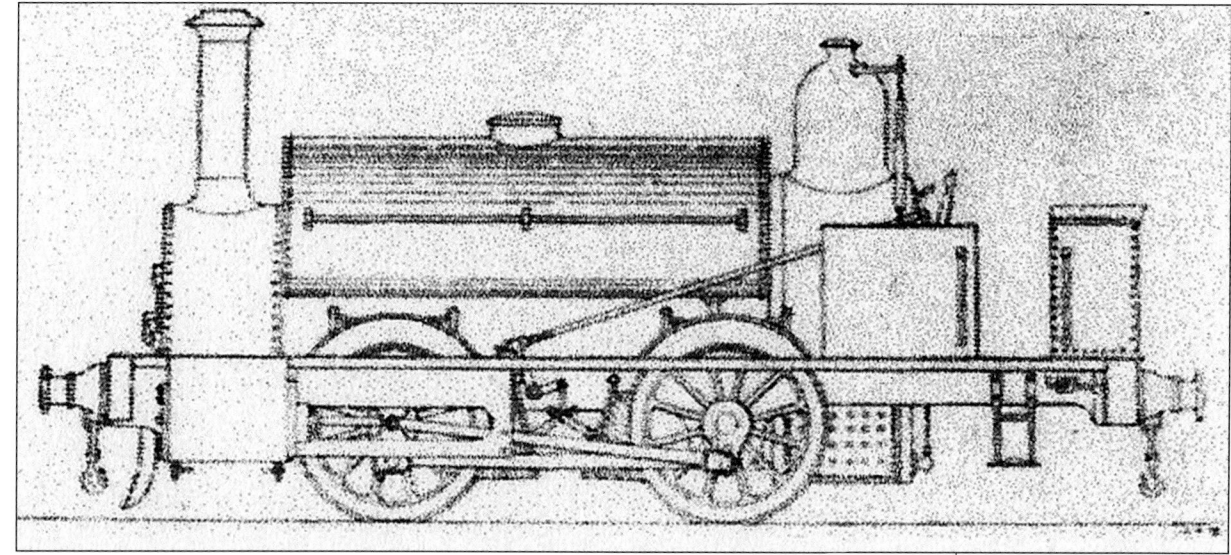

Drawing of Cambrian Railways No.21 *Lilleshall*, an 0-4-0ST built by the Lilleshall Iron Company in 1862 and sold in 1868. (*Locomotive Magazine*/RCTS)

38 *Prometheus* at Oswestry, c1891. (Loco Publishing Co./Bob Miller/MLS Collections)

36 *Plasfynnon* at Kerry on the mixed branch train, July 1904. Note provision of an enclosed cab. (LGRP/Bob Miller/MLS Collections)

36 *Plasfynnon* with the mixed Kerry branch train, c 1903. (Bob Miller/MLS Collections)

2, 12, 33, 37 (GW 1129-1132), 'Metropolitan' 4-4-0T, 1864

In 1905, the Cambrian Railways purchased six Metropolitan Railway 4-4-0 side tank engines which were made redundant by electrification at a bargain price of £500 each, possibly the main reason being that they were found unsuitable for some of the tasks for which they were initially tried. Their condensing gear was removed at Oswestry and their Metropolitan livery was replaced by the standard Cambrian colours and they were numbered 2, 12, 33, 34, 36 and 37. 34 was converted to a tender engine in 1915 and 36 in 1916. They were originally built in 1864 as Met Nos. 10 (Cambrian 2), 11 (12), 12 (33), 13 (34), 15 (36) and an 1885 built 66 (37). Their dimensions were:

Coupled wheels:	5ft 10in
Bogie wheels:	3ft 0in
Cylinders (outside):	17½in x 24in
Boiler pressure:	150lb psi
Heating surface:	942.6sqft
Grate area:	19sqft
Weight:	44 tons 9 cwt
Axleload:	16¾ tons
Tank capacity:	900 gallons
Tractive effort:	13,390lb

Nos. 2 and 34 were allocated to Machynlleth, and the other four to Aberystwyth. They were found suitable for local passenger work only although two (33 and 37) were later transferred to Oswestry for shunting duties. 34 and 36 were rebuilt in 1915/6. By their absorption by the GW, the four remaining tank engines had revised boiler dimensions of 979.7sqft heating surface and 17.3sqft grate area. Although they were renumbered by the GW as 1129-1132, only No.12 received its new number, 1130. Two were withdrawn in 1922, No.66 in January 1923 and 1130 in June 1923.

44, 56 (GW 1190, 1191) 2-4-0T, 1864

Sharp, Stewart built sixteen 2-4-0 passenger tender engines for Davies & Savin's railways in 1863, the Oswestry & Newtown in 1864 and the Cambrian in 1865. Two of these, *Rheidol* built for the O&N,

Former Metropolitan 4-4-0T No. 10 *Cerberus* with its new Cambrian Railways identity as No.2, at Machynlleth, 2 July 1909. (K. Nunn/LCGB/Bob Miller/MLS Collections)

Former Metropolitan 4-4-0T No. 11 *Latona* with its new Cambrian Railways identity as No.12, at Barmouth on a stopping train for Machynlleth, c 1906. (LGRP/MLS Collection)

No.44, formerly *Rheidol,* after rebuilding as a 2-4-0T at Oswestry in 1907. (F. Moore/Bob Miller/ MLS Collections)

numbered 44 by the Cambrian, and *Whittington* built as No.56 in 1865 were rebuilt as 2-4-0 side tanks at Oswestry in 1907. The frames were extended to seat an enclosed cab and bunker but the dimensions otherwise remained that of the 1964/5 tender engines with new boilers in 1890 (56) and 1894 (44).

Coupled wheels:	5ft 6in
Leading wheels:	3ft 6in
Cylinders:	16in x 20in
Boiler pressure:	150lb psi
Heating surface:	964sqft
Grate area:	11.6sqft
Weight:	35 tons 6 cwt
Axleload:	13 tons 14 cwt
Tank capacity:	500 gallons
Bunker capacity:	1½ tons

They were both allocated to the coastal section, 44 at Portmadoc and 56 at Penmaenpool. 56 operated from 1911 on the Wrexham-Ellesmere branch and 44 moved to Llanidloes. From 1916 both were at Machynlleth for working the Mawddwy branch. The GW renumbered them 1190 and 1191, but both were withdrawn in 1922.

57-59 (GW 1192, 1196-1197) 2-4-0T, 1866

Three small 2-4-0 side tanks were built by Sharp, Stewart for the contractor, Savin, in 1866 and were named *Maglona*, *Gladys* and *Seaham*, being numbered 57-59 by the Cambrian Railways. Their dimensions were, before and after rebuilding with new boilers in 1893/4:

Sharp, Stewart 2-4-0T 59 *Seaham* as provided with the initial overall roof in the 1880s, seen at Oswestry c1891. (LGRP/Bob Miller/MLS Collections)

58 after rebuilding in December 1894 at Oswestry in the first decade of the twentieth century. (Loco Publishing Co./Bob Miller/MLS Collections)

Coupled wheels:	4ft 6in
Leading wheels:	3ft 0in
Cylinders:	14in x 20in
Boiler pressure:	120lb psi (later 150lb psi)
Heating surface:	780sqft (later 800sqft)
Grate area:	10.5sqft (later 10.6sqft)
Weight:	28 tons 11 cwt (later 29 tons)
Axleload:	10 tons 13 cwt
Tank capacity:	500 gallons (later 600 gallons)
Tractive effort:	7,404lb (later 9,255lb)

58 after rebuilding in December 1894 at Blodwel Junction with the Tanat Valley branch train to Llangynog, 1904.
(R.E. Fox-Davies/Bob Miller/ MLS Collections)

GW 1196 (formerly Cambrian 58) as rebuilt by the GWR in 1924 at Oswestry, c1938.
(Photomatic/Bob Miller/ MLS Collections)

GW 1197 (ex-59) at Llangynog with the 5.25pm from Oswestry, 10 May 1947. (W.A. Camwell/Bob Miller/MLS Collections)

They received an overall cab in the 1880s. At first, they operated the Dolgelly and Llanfyllin branches although from 1895, 57 was used on the Elan Valley line. The Tanat Valley line opened in 1904 and the three engines were transferred to operate that line for many years. The GW numbered them 1192 (57), 1196 (58) and 1197 (59) and although their condemnation in 1922 was intended, they were reprieved and their boilers modified with a new heating surface of 785sqft. All three were then given the Swindon 'treatment' with GW standard enclosed cab, new fireboxes and smokeboxes, safety valves and larger bunkers increasing their weight to 33 tons 3 cwt and axleload to 12½ tons. 1192 was transferred to Exeter to work the Hemyock branch in 1927 and was withdrawn in 1929 but the other two soldiered on until 1948, working the branch trains to Llangynog, both amassing over a million miles.

3-9, 23 (GW 10-21) 0-4-4T, 1895

Six 0-4-4 side tanks were designed and built by Nasmyth, Wilson & Co., three in 1895 and three in 1899. They were originally shown as 4-4-0Ts but the Cambrian Engineer, Mr Aston, required the changed wheel arrangement. They were numbered 3, 5, 7-9, and 23 and their dimensions were:

Coupled wheels:	5ft 3in
Trailing bogie wheels:	3ft 1½in
Cylinders:	17in x 24in
Boiler pressure:	160lb psi
Heating surface:	1,010.1sqft
Grate area:	13.3sqft
Weight:	45 tons 9 cwt
Axleload:	15 tons
Tank capacity:	1,200 gallons
Tractive effort:	14,970lb

Their initial operation was around the newly opened branch to

Nasmyth, Wilson & Co 0-4-4T No. 5 as built in 1895 in works grey for photographic purposes.
(Real Photographs/Bob Miller/MLS Collections)

No. 7 working the Wrexham – Oswestry auto train, c1900.
(Loco Publishing Co./Bob Miller/MLS Collections)

No. 8 seen bunker first at Aberystwyth c1912.
(W.L. Good/Bob Miller/MLS Collections)

Wrexham and the Llanfyllin branch and later the Barmouth-Dolgelly trains linked with the GW trains from Ruabon. Nos.5 and 7 worked for a time on the Mid-Wales line. They were renumbered by the GWR as 10, 11, 15, 19-21, but only 10 (former 3), 19 (ex-8), and 20 (ex-9) carried their new numbers. These three received GW style smokebox, chimney, safety valve and bunker. The other three were withdrawn in 1922, with 20 being withdrawn in 1928 and the last two, 10 and 19, in 1932. They finished their lives working local services from Machynlleth to Aberystwyth.

GW 20 as rebuilt with GW fittings in 1923.
(Real Photographs/Bob Miller/MLS Collections)

GW 10 (ex-Cambrian 3) as rebuilt by GWR at Swindon in 1925, at Aberystwyth near the end of its life, c1930. (LGRP/Bob Miller/MLS Collections)

The Manning, Wardle 0-4-0ST *Coel* on the Van Railway, c1901. (Bob Miller/MLS Collections)

Now numbered 22 and nameless, the Manning, Wardle 0-4-0ST is seen at Porthywaen, c1905. (Bob Miller/MLS Collections)

22 formerly *Coel*, Van Railway 0-4-0ST, 1901

A small 0-4-0 saddle tank engine was purchased in 1901 from Manning, Wardle & Co., as there was an urgent need for a small branch engine to replace the elderly engines on the Van branch. It was originally named *Coel* and numbered 22 and its dimensions were:

Coupled wheels:	3ft 0in
Cylinders (outside):	12in x 18in
Boiler pressure:	140lb psi
Heating surface:	364sqft
Grate area:	6.36sqft
Weight:	19½ tons
Axleload:	11½ tons
Tank capacity:	450 gallons
Tractive effort:	7,560lb

It was used on Birmingham Corporation traffic at Rhayader and on the Van branch until 1914 when it was sold to the government's contractors for use at Prees Heath Camp and later sold again for work at a colliery in Wigan.

Cardiff Railway

The Cardiff Railway's origins stemmed from the Bute Dock at Cardiff opened in 1839, a second dock, the Bute East Dock, being opened in 1850. The docks, principally owned by the Marquis of Bute, were serviced primarily by the Taff Vale Railway Company, and the first Cardiff Railway locomotives were owned by the dock company and restricted to its operation in the Cardiff Docks area. The dock company decided to try to break the Taff Vale company monopoly in 1885 and the Marquis, who owned collieries in the Rhondda Valley, sought powers to construct a railway over the route of the Glamorganshire and Aberdare Canal. Nothing came of this but in 1897, parliamentary powers were obtained to construct the Cardiff Railway using the Rhymney Railway to Heath Junction and joining the Taff Vale at Treforest. However, opposition from the TVR ensured through working of freight from the Rhondda to Cardiff Docks was curtailed and the Cardiff Railway was limited to the line from Heath to Coryton and Tongwynlais, with the main activity remaining in the Cardiff Docks complex served by both the Taff Vale and Rhymney railways.

Marquis of Bute No.5 0-4-0T, 1862

From about 1860, the Marquis of Bute obtained his own locomotives for shunting the Bute East and West Docks in Cardiff. One of the first engines he obtained for this purpose was a small 0-4-0 saddle tank built by Manning, Wardle & Co. to their standard design and it was delivered in 1862. It was numbered 5 in the Bute stock and its dimensions were:

Coupled wheels:	2ft 9in
Cylinders:	9½in x 14in
Tank capacity:	250 gallons

With no cab, a stovepipe chimney and ability to ride the sharp curves of the dock lines, it remained there on shunting duties until 1898.

Marquis of Bute No.17 0-4-0T, 1874

Another 0-4-0 saddle tank was ordered from Fox, Walker & Co. and delivered in 1874. It had outside cylinders and an open cab. Its known dimensions were:

Coupled wheels:	2ft 10in
Cylinders:	11in x 18in
Boiler pressure:	140lb psi
Heating surface:	330sqft
Tank capacity:	350 gallons

This was a more powerful engine to supplement or replace the 1862 No.5 and it was also able to work on the tight curves in the dock areas. It survived until 1917 when it was sold to the government, presumably for work at a government supply depot.

Marquis of Bute No.24 0-4-2T, reb. 2-4-2T, c1883

This locomotive, numbered 24, seems to have had a strange career. It started life as a 2-4-0 tank built by Beyer, Peacock although its date of origin is unknown. It was moved from the Marquis of Bute's Hirwaun Colliery in 1883 to Cardiff and appears to have been rebuilt as a 2-4-2T, presumably to enlarge the bunker capacity. It was clearly found unsuitable for shunting at the docks and was rebuilt again as an 0-6-0 saddle tank with new frame, cylinders and saddle tank. Although the GW held dimension details of the rebuilt engine, by 1922 numbered 698, no record is extant for its dimensions as a four-coupled tank engine. It was withdrawn in that condition in 1922.

Marquis of Bute No.3, 6, 13 4-4-0T, ex-NLR Metropolitan, 1861, acquired 1882/3

The Marquis of Bute purchased three 4-4-0 side tank locomotives from the North London Railway in 1882/3, which were numbered 3, 6 and 13. There were already old engines built as early as 1861 by Slaughter, Gruning & Co. They had inside cylinders and lacked any cab cover for the crew. Their dimensions as built in 1861 were:

Coupled wheels:	5ft 3in
Bogie wheels:	3ft 0in
Cylinders:	16½in x 22in
Boiler pressure:	120lb psi
Heating surface:	969sqft
Grate area:	14sqft
Weight:	37 tons
Tank capacity:	850 gallons
Tractive effort:	9,697lb

4-4-0Ts with such large coupled wheels seem an unlikely choice for dock shunting. Whether they were obtained with a view to extending a network beyond the docks is not known and it was not until 1897 that efforts were made to get the necessary powers to build its own line to gain access to the mines in the valleys as the Cardiff Railway. However, by this time these engines were deemed life expired and 3 and 13 were withdrawn by 1985 and 6 by 1898.

5, 6 (GW 1338-1339) 0-4-0ST, 1898

When the Marquis of Bute No.5 was withdrawn in 1898, it was replaced by another 0-4-0 saddle tank from Kitson & Co., with the same number. A similar engine followed in 1899 and was No.6. Their dimensions were:

Coupled wheels:	3ft 2½in
Cylinders:	14in x 21in
Boiler pressure:	160lb psi
Heating surface:	434sqft
Grate area:	8.75sqft
Weight:	25½ tons
Axleload:	12¾ tons
Tank capacity:	850 gallons
Tractive effort:	14,540lb

They were rebuilt in 1916 (No.6) and 1918 (No.5) and renumbered by the GWR as 1338 and 1339. 1339 was withdrawn in 1932 and scrapped in 1934 but 1338 after a period in store was loaned to Stewarts & Lloyds at Landore during the war. In 1943 it was transferred to shunt Bridgwater Docks and stayed there until 1960 when it returned to South Wales and operated with other 0-4-0Ts on Swansea Docks. It was withdrawn in 1963, after running 353,985 miles in GW service almost entirely on docks lines. 1338 was preserved – bought by a private owner in 1964 – and was kept at Bleadon & Uphill station near Weston-Super-Mare

Drawing of Marquis of Bute's 4-4-0T, No.3. (RCTS)

1338 in BR days at Swansea East Dock, c1962. (A.F. Smith/MLS Collection)

1338 at work on Swansea South Dock, 26 August 1963, shortly before withdrawal and preservation. (MLS Collection)

that became the Somerset Railway Museum until the station's lease expired in 1985 and the museum closed. 1338 was moved to the Didcot Great Western Railway Centre in 1987.

1-3 Steam Railmotors 0-4-0T, 1905
The Cardiff Railway acquired two steam railmotors for the Cardiff-Rhydyfelin passenger service in 1911, numbered 2 and 3. The railmotors were built by the Gloucester Carriage & Wagon Company. A third to act as spare (No.1) was built by W. Sissons & Co. of Gloucester in the same year. They handled the traffic for the first three years until passenger numbers outgrew the accommodation after which the vehicles from railmotors

Cardiff Railway Steam Railmotor No.3 built in 1911 by the Gloucester Carriage & Wagon Co., as built, 1911. (F.K. Davies/John Hodge Collections)

The L&NWR 2-4-2T purchased in 1914 and numbered 36 and named *The Earl of Dumfries* as repainted in Cardiff Railway livery, March 1914. (Real Photographs/ Bob Miller/MLS Collections)

2 and 3 were converted as trailers for use with independent steam locomotives. Their dimensions were:

Coupled wheels:	4ft 0in
Cylinders:	12in x 16in
Boiler pressure:	160lb psi
Heating surface:	660sqft
Grate area:	11.5sqft
Weight:	43 tons 8 cwt
Coal capacity:	½ ton
Passenger capacity:	64

36 (GW 1327) 2-4-2T LNWR, 1879, reb. 1898, acquired 1914

As a result of the railmotors being found inadequate for traffic levels, the Cardiff Railway needed to obtain suitable motive power for passenger haulage and purchased in 1914 a 2-4-2 side tank locomotive from the L&NWR. 1181 had been built as a 2-4-0T in 1879 but extended to the 2-4-2T arrangement in 1898. The Cardiff Railway numbered it 36 and named it *The Earl of Dumfries*, a hereditary title of the Marquis of Bute. Its dimensions were:

Coupled wheels:	4ft 8½in
Leading & trailing wheels:	3ft 3in
Boiler pressure:	150lb psi
Heating surface:	961sqft
Grate area:	14.2sqft
Weight:	45 tons 18 cwt
Axleload:	13½ tons
Tank capacity:	900 gallons
Tractive effort:	13,045lb

Although allocated GW number 1327, it was withdrawn in May 1922.

Midland & South Western Junction Railway

The Swindon, Marlborough and Andover Railway was opened between Swindon and Marlborough in 1881 and Grafton and Andover in 1883. Another line, the Swindon & Cheltenham Extension Railway, was opened later that year and the two companies were amalgamated in 1884 as the Midland & South Western Junction Railway. The sixty mile through route from Andover to Cheltenham was not completed until 1891. Locomotive repair shops were opened at Cirencester in 1895 and the Locomotive Superintendent was

James Tyrrell, who held the post from 1903 until 1 December 1923 after the railway and locomotive stock was absorbed into the Great Western Railway, which had occurred on 1 July that year. The twenty-nine engines taken over by the GWR were allocated their new numbers in 1922 in anticipation of their absorption.

Swindon, Marlborough & Andover Railway

4, 0-4-4T Fairlie, 1878

The Avonside Engine Company built an 0-4-4 tank locomotive with a steam driven leading bogie designed by the Fairlie Company. It was exhibited at the Paris Exhibition and loaned to the Swindon, Marlborough & Andover Railway in 1881 and purchased by them in 1882. It was given the number 4. Its dimensions were:

Coupled wheels:	5ft 6in
Rear bogie wheels:	4ft 0in
Cylinders:	16in x 22in
Valve gear:	Walschaerts
Heating surface:	1,094sqft
Grate area:	15.5sqft
Weight:	44 tons
Side & bunker tank capacity:	1,200 gallons
Coal capacity:	2 tons

It was intended for passenger service but was unreliable and inefficient. It was withdrawn in 1892 and used as a stationary boiler at Cirencester workshop.

5-8, 2-4-0T, 1882

Three 2-4-0 side tanks, numbered 5-7, were built by Beyer, Peacock in 1882 to one of that company's standard designs. Their dimensions were:

Coupled wheels:	5ft 6in
Leading wheels:	4ft 0in
Cylinders:	16in x 24in
Heating surface:	952.4sqft
Grate area:	14.8sqft
Weight:	35 tons 5 cwt
Axleload:	14½ tons
Tank capacity:	900 gallons

A fourth 2-4-0T was also built by Beyer, Peacock in 1884, similar but slightly larger and heavier. It was numbered 8 and had these dimension variations from 5-7:

Cylinders:	17in x 24in
Heating surface:	1,145sqft
Grate area:	15.65sqft
Weight:	40 tons 4 cwt
Axleweight:	15½ tons

These four passenger engines worked on the Swindon-Andover section. No.6 was withdrawn in 1906 and sold to the Isle of Wight Railway where it lasted until 1926. No.7 was withdrawn in 1910 and 5 in 1912. No.8 was renumbered 29 in 1912 and sold in 1918 to a Darlington company.

The Swindon, Marlborough & Andover Railway No.4 0-4-4T of 1878, retained as a stationary boiler, seen here, c1888, a few years before its withdrawal from active work in 1892. Note the Fairlie patent plate which looks as though it has just been removed from the tank side. (R.E. Bleasdale/F.K. Davies/John Hodge Collections)

Locomotives absorbed by the GWR 1914–23 • 85

The first 2-4-0T built by Beyer, Peacock in 1882 and painted in Works grey as No.10, although it was renumbered 5 in the Swindon & Marlborough Railway stock list. (MLS Collection)

No.7, 2-4-0T built by Beyer, Peacock for the S & MR in 1882, seen here in M&SJWR livery, c1900. (Loco Publishing Co./Bob Miller/MLS Collections)

No.8, the larger of the four 2-4-0Ts, this one built by Beyer, Peacock in 1884. It is seen here on passenger work at Swindon, c 1900.
(Bob Miller/MLS Collections)

The Midland & South Western Junction Railway
15 (GW 23) 0-4-4T, 1895

Beyer, Peacock built a single 0-4-4 side tank for the Midland & South Western Junction Railway in 1895. Its dimensions were:

Coupled wheels:	5ft 2in
Rear bogie wheels:	3ft 0in
Cylinders:	17in x 24in
Boiler pressure:	140lb psi
Heating surface:	1,025.6sqft
Grate area:	17.7sqft
Weight:	47 tons 18 cwt
Axleload:	15¾ tons
Tank capacity:	1,300 gallons
Tractive effort:	13,310lb

It was renumbered GW 23 and rebuilt in 1925 with a GW standard No.11 boiler. This reduced its overall weight slightly. It worked mainly on the Swindon-Marlborough section and after its rebuilding was routinely on the Swindon Town-Swindon Junction shuttle service. It was withdrawn in 1930.

The 0-4-4T No.15 built by Beyer, Peacock in 1895, at Swindon Town with the shuttle to Swindon Junction, 23 January 1921. (K. Nunn/LCGB/MLS Collections)

17, 18 (GW 25, 27) 4-4-4T, 1897

The next passenger engines were much larger – two 4-4-4 side tank engines built by Sharp, Stewart in 1897. This wheel arrangement was unique for GW engines, either of its own build or from the absorbed companies. They were numbered 17 and 18 and had the following dimensions:

Coupled wheels:	5ft 3in
Bogie wheels:	3ft 0in
Cylinders:	17in x 24in
Boiler pressure:	150lb psi
Heating surface:	1,050sqft
Grate area:	17sqft
Weight:	59¼ tons
Axleload:	15 tons 13 cwt
Tank capacity:	1,900 gallons (side & bunker)
Tractive effort:	14,040lb

They were renumbered 25 and 27 by the GWR and 25 was rebuilt in 1925 with an extended smokebox and GW safety valves. No. 27 was much more substantially rebuilt at the same time with a GW No.10 standard taper boiler, pressured at 165lb psi and weighing 61 tons 11 cwt and increased tractive effort to 15,440lb. Both engines were initially stationed at Cheltenham. After rebuilding No.25 worked the Swindon Town-Junction shuttle service until its withdrawal in 1927. No.27 was transferred to Kidderminster and operated in that area until its withdrawal in 1929.

The prototype M&SWJR 4-4-4T, No.17 built by Sharp, Stewart in 1897, in Works grey, as built. (F. Moore/MLS Collection)

4-4-4T, No.17 in lined M&SWJR livery at Swindon Town, April 1921. (A.W. Croughton/MLS Collection)

4-4-4T, No.18 at Cheltenham with a train for Swindon, c1910. (MLS Collection)

4-4-4T, No.18 on the 2.35pm Swindon-Andover train approaching Marlborough station, 17 April 1914. (K. Nunn/LCGB/Bob Miller/MLS Collections)

4-4-4T, No.18 at Cheltenham, c1922. (MLS Collection)

M&SWJR 4-4-4T, No.18 newly rebuilt with taper boiler and GW high cab, and renumbered 27, 1925. (F. Moore/MLS Collection)

M&SWJR 4-4-4T, No. 27 shortly before withdrawal, c1929.
(W. Potter/Bob Miller/MLS Collections)

M&SWJR 4-4-4T, No. 27 at Handsworth Junction with a down Stourbridge train, c1927.
(Bob Miller/MLS Collections)

Neath & Brecon Railway

The Neath & Brecon Railway started in 1862 as the Dulais Valley Mineral Railway from Neath to Onllwyn and opened in 1864. The extension to Brecon was opened in 1867 and a branch to Ynys-y-geinon Junction with the Swansea Vale Railway in 1877. The Midland Railway provided motive power at the north end until 1903, the N&B engines working between Neath and Colbren Junction only. Although absorbed by the GW in 1922, the LMS retained operation from Brecon to Ynys-y-geinon until 1930, after which the GW operated the line through to Brecon, basically mineral traffic to Onllwyn and Colbren Junction and passenger trains to Brecon.

Progress Fairlie 0-4-4-0T, 1865

The first Fairlie double-ended locomotive was built by James Cross of St Helen's, named *Progress*, and leased to the Neath & Brecon Railway in 1865. It was an 0-4-4-0T with two boiler barrels and four cylinders. The brakes operated on the axles rather than the wheels. The steampipes were made of copper and coiled inside the smokebox before connecting with the steam chests which seems to have been the main weakness of the locomotive. Its dimensions were:

Coupled wheels:	4ft 6in
Cylinders (4 outside)	15in x 22in
Boiler pressure:	120lb psi
Heating surface:	1,993sqft
Grate area:	25sqft
Weight:	42 tons
Tank capacity:	2,000 gallons
Coal bunkers:	2¼ tons

It and a subsequent Fairlie were intended for the haulage of mineral traffic between Neath and Colbren Junction. The company terminated the lease in 1868 and it was auctioned later that year going to an ironworks. It moved subsequently on hire to the Brecon & Merthyr Railway in 1870 and then the same year to the Monmouthshire Canal Company after which no more is known of it.

Mountaineer Fairlie 0-4-4-0T, 1866

A second Fairlie locomotive called *Mountaineer* was built by the same company in 1866, smaller than *Progress* and with conventional braking gear. Its dimensions were:

Coupled wheels:	4ft 0in
Cylinders (4 outside):	10in x 16in
Heating surface:	858sqft
Grate area:	12.4sqft
Weight:	34 tons
Tank capacity:	900 gallons

This locomotive seems to have been little more successful than *Progress* though steaming problems seem to have been the main cause of failure. It is reported to have spent excessive time out of traffic under repair and it was finally sold for scrap in 1880.

A primitive photograph of the 0-4-4-0 Fairlie double-ended tank *Progress* during its short sojourn on the Neath & Brecon Railway between 1865 and 1868.
(LPC/F.K. Davies/John Hodge Collections)

The second Fairlie 0-4-4-0T built in 1866, named *Mountaineer* and photographed around 1870. (S.H. Pearce-Higgins/F.K. Davies/John Hodge Collections)

4 (renumbered 5) (GW 1392) 4-4-0T, 1871

The company was having some difficulty with its motive power and in 1871 purchased a 4-4-0 side tank engine from the Yorkshire Engine Company and numbered it 4. It was similar to the Monmouthshire Railway's No.14 (see page 35) and had a copper capped chimney and brass dome and safety valve seating. Its dimensions were:

Coupled wheels:	5ft 0in
Bogie wheels:	2ft 8in
Heating surface:	993sqft
Grate area:	17.5sqft
Weight:	41 tons 12 cwt
Tank capacity:	830 gallons
Bunker capacity:	¾ ton

It was renumbered 5 sometime between 1877 and 1884 and fitted with vacuum brakes in 1891 and a cab in 1893. It was reboilered in 1898 with slightly diminished heating surface and grate area but – with the cab and extra braking gear – weighed 45½ tons with an axleweight of 15¾ tons. It was the Company's principal passenger engine for the rest of the N&B's existence, mainly confined to the line south of Colbren Junction.

After absorption by the GWR it was renumbered 1392 and received a number of GW standard parts – smokebox, safety valves, chimney and cab shape. These and other alterations during overhaul in 1921 resulted in the following revised dimensions:

N & B No.4, the 4-4-0T built by the Yorkshire Engine Co. in 1871, seen here in its original condition. (F. Moore/MLS Collection)

Renumbered 5, the 4-4-0T seen here as rebuilt with cab in 1893. Note the tool boxes above the buffer beam. (MLS Collection)

N & B No.6, the Sharp, Stewart 2-4-0T similar to the Barry class 'C', as built in 1892. (Loco Publishing Co./MLS Collection)

Bogie wheels:	2ft 6in
Boiler pressure:	140lb psi
Heating surface:	966.3sqft
Tank capacity:	800 gallons
Tractive effort:	13,755 lb

It was withdrawn in 1926.

6 (GW 1400) 2-4-0T

With continuing motive power difficulties and to cover No.5 when under repair, the N & B ordered a Sharp, Stewart 2-4-0 side tank of their design, similar to that provided to the Barry Railway (see page 56). It was delivered in 1892, had continuous vacuum brake, and was numbered 6. Its dimensions were:

Coupled wheels:	5ft 3in	Boiler pressure:	150lb	Weight:	41 tons 2 cwt
Leading wheels:	3ft 6in	Heating surface:	1,041sqft	Axleload:	16 tons 2 cwt
Cylinders:	17in x 24in	Grate area:	14.25sqft	Tank capacity:	800 gallons

A new boiler was supplied in 1908 and the engine acquired GW standard fittings – smokebox, chimney. The new boiler had an increased pressure of 160lb psi and increased heating surface to 1,104.2sqft. Tractive effort was then 14,970lb. The GWR numbered it 1400 in 1922 and it was withdrawn along with its N & B passenger sister in 1926.

Port Talbot Railway

The Port Talbot Railway was incorporated in 1894 to develop Port Talbot Docks and its railway network and build rail connections to the mineral rich GWR Llynfi, Garw and Ogmore Valleys. The first section was opened through Maesteg in 1897 and its 33 route miles were completed in 1898. It involved some steep gradients into the valleys, especially beyond Duffryn Yard to Bryn Tunnel (including a 1 in 40 section). Its locomotive shed was at Duffryn Yard and, like the other Welsh railway companies, was absorbed by the Great Western in January 1922, although because of the GWR dominance in the area, its operations were taken over by that company in 1908 and its locomotives taken into GW stock in July of that year. It also owned a steam railmotor for passenger work but as the locomotive element was, unusually, six-coupled, it falls outside the scope of this book.

37 (GW 1189) ex-Barry Rly 'C' 2-4-0T, 1890

The Port Talbot Railway acquired a Barry Railway 'C' class 2-4-0 side tank in 1898, a locomotive that had been built for that railway by the Sharp, Stewart Company in 1890. It was numbered 36 on the Barry Railway and retained that number on the PTR. Its dimensions as recorded by the GWR later differed slightly from the Barry engines and were:

Coupled wheels:	5ft 3in
Leading wheels:	3ft 6in
Cylinders:	17in x 24in
Boiler pressure:	160lb psi
Heating surface:	1,041sqft
Grate area:	14.4sqft
Weight:	41 tons 2 cwt
Axleload:	16 tons 2 cwt
Tank capacity:	800 gallons
Tractive effort:	14,975lb

It was renumbered 1189 by the GWR and replaced by that

The former Barry class 'C' purchased by the Port Talbot Railway in 1898 and numbered 36, at Swindon during the 1920s before its withdrawal in 1926. (W.H. Whitworth/Bob Miller/MLS Collections)

company's 2-6-2Ts in 1908. It was reboilered with a GW 'Metro Tank' boiler in 1915 and thereafter was retained as the Swindon station pilot or Works shunter. It was withdrawn in 1926 after accumulating over half a million miles since the GWR started recording mileage for the PTR engines in its stock from 1908.

36 (GW 1326) ex-Barry Rly 'C' 52 2-4-2T, 1890

A second Barry class 'C' was purchased in 1898 also but a set of rear wheels was added in line with conversions that the Barry Railway was making to some of its own stock. The 2-4-2T had been No.52 of the Barry Railway but the Port Talbot Railway renumbered it 36. It dimensions were as No.37 above apart from the variation caused by the addition of the rear set of wheels and larger bunker tank:

Trailing wheels:	3ft 6in
Weight:	49 tons 8 cwt
Axleload:	14 tons 11 cwt
Tank capacity:	1,370 gallons

It also received a GW 'Metro Tank' boiler in 1925 when it received its GW number, 1326. After its redundancy on the former PTR system in 1908, it was transferred to Llanelly and worked passenger services to Pontardulais and Llandovery. It was withdrawn in 1930.

Rhondda & Swansea Bay Railway

The purpose of the Rhondda & Swansea Bay Railway was to bring Rhondda Valley coal down to docks at Port Talbot and Swansea – proposed in 1882 and opened from Aberavon to Cymmer Afan in 1885 and extended through the two mile long tunnel to Treherbert in 1890. Danygraig and access to Swansea Docks was achieved in 1894.

The final system totalled nearly 29 miles. Like the Port Talbot Railway, it was operated by the GWR as early as 1906 although not formally absorbed until 1922.

17-19 (GW 1307, 1309-1310) 2-4-2T, 1895

The Kitson Company built three 2-4-2 side tanks for the Rhondda & Swansea Bay Railway in 1895, numbered 17-19. They were similar in many ways to that company's 0-6-2Ts, the dimensions being:

Coupled wheels:	5ft 3in
Leading and trailing wheels:	3ft 8½in
Cylinders:	18in x 26in
Boiler pressure:	150lb psi
Heating surface:	1,170.74sqft
Grate area:	19.28sqft
Weight:	51¾ tons
Axleload:	15 tons 8 cwt
Tank capacity:	1,650 gallons
Coal capacity:	2 tons 3 cwt

The former Barry class 'C' purchased by the Port Talbot Railway in 1898, renumbered 36 by the latter company and 1326 by the GWR at Swindon shortly before withdrawal, c 1930. (MLS Collection)

The Kitson 2-4-2T No.17, as built for the R&SB Railway in 1895.
(GW Trust)

R & SB No.19 rebuilt at Swindon in 1922 with 45XX taper boiler and high roof, 1922.
(GW official photo/R.K. Davies/ John Hodge Collections)

GW 1310, the former R&SB No.19, at Barry, 17 November 1923. (A.W. Croughton/F.K. Davies/ John Hodge Collections)

They were rebuilt with Swindon boilers of 165lb psi, but decreasing the engine's weight to 50¾ tons, and No.19 was more drastically rebuilt returning to traffic from Swindon Works in 1922 with a 45XX taper boiler and high cab roof. It now weighed 51 tons 19 cwt. The GW renumbered the three engines 1307, 1309 and 1310 in 1922. They worked the R&SB lines and the GW in the Blaenrhondda area, though the rebuilt 1310 was transferred to Barry for the Barry-Cardiff passenger service. It remained there until withdrawal in 1930, though spent more time on local goods and shunting work than the passenger activity for which it had been sent.

Rhymney Railway

The Rhymney Railway and the Taff Vale were two of the most important railways in South Wales before 1922 along with the Great Western Railway itself. The Rhymney Railway (RR) covered 51 miles of track starting with a section from Rhymney to Hengoed in 1858 and developing lines between Cardiff, Caerphilly and Rhymney, with branches and connections, particularly with the GWR at Aberdare, the L&NWR at Nantybwch and the Taff Vale at Taff's Well. It also had close links and joint running powers with the Brecon & Merthyr Railway. The first workshops were on Cardiff Docks, but it built its main Works at Caerphilly in 1901 and had engine sheds at Cardiff, Rhymney, Dowlais, and Senghenydd and shared the GW shed at Merthyr.

With the announced railway mergers under the 'Grouping', preceded by the absorption of the South Wales valley railways into the Great Western in 1922, most of those railways cut their costs to the bone, reducing maintenance and allowing their locomotive fleet to run up mileages much greater than their maintenance schedules would normally allow, creating a headache for the motive power department of the Great Western when it took over and found most of its inherited locomotives were overdue for major overhaul. The major exception was the Rhymney Railway whose locomotive fleet, maintained at the relatively new Caerphilly Works, was in excellent condition, with many of the engines being of recent construction. For thirty-five years, the motive power strategy had been held closely under the control of the remarkable Cornelius Lundie, the General Manager, although Richard Jenkins was the appointed Locomotive Superintendent. During this period, the Rhymney Railway motive power was dominated by outside framed 0-6-0 and 0-6-2 saddle tanks with major changes in policy only taking place on his retirement (at age 90) and replacement by C.T. Hurry Riches, the son of Tom Hurry Riches of the Taff Vale Railway.

7-9 & 16, 2-4-0T, reb. from 1873

Four 2-4-0 tender engines were built by the Vulcan Foundry, Nos. 7-9 in 1858, and No.16 in 1861. In 1873, the latter, 16, was rebuilt as a 2-4-0 side tank, the frame being lengthened to carry the cab and small bunker. It was reboilered in 1881 and fitted with Ramsbottom safety valves and Westinghouse brakes. The other three engines were rebuilt in 1880 (No.8) and 1881 (Nos. 7 and 9) with saddle tanks, new boilers, cab and bunker. Their known dimensions after rebuilding were:

Coupled wheels:	5ft 4½in
Leading wheels:	3ft 7½in
Cylinders:	16in x 20in
Boiler pressure:	140lb psi
Heating surface:	948sqft
Grate area:	14.5sqft

They were built for purely passenger work unlike the various 0-6-0STs and 0-6-2STs on freight and mixed traffic activity. The three saddletanks were withdrawn in 1895 but were stored and sold in 1902 to the Bute Works Supply Company. No.16 lived on, still as a side tank, and in 1900 was working at Caerphilly during the construction of the Works there. It was nicknamed *Jupiter* although the name was never carried. It was withdrawn in 1904, stored and not broken up until 1906.

The Rhymney Railway's No.7, rebuilt from an 1858 2-4-0 tender engine in 1881 as a saddle tank fitted with Westinghouse air brakes. It was withdrawn in 1895, stored and sold in 1902. It is seen here in the 1880s.
(Real Photographs/Bob Miller/MLS Collections)

Locomotives absorbed by the GWR 1914–23 • 99

The Rhymney Railway's No.9, also rebuilt from a 2-4-0 tender engine in 1881, seen from the other side, c1885. (F.K. Davies/John Hodge Collections)

The Rhymney Railway's No.16, built as a 2-4-0 tender engine in 1861 and rebuilt in 1873 as a side tank, c1880. (LPC/F.K. Davies/John Hodge Collections)

62-66 (GW 1324-1325) 2-4-2ST, 1891

Five 2-4-2STs had been built by the Vulcan Foundry in 1891, with 5ft coupled wheels for passenger operations. They were numbered 62-66. They were unaltered until Hurry Riches was appointed locomotive superintendent. They were then classified as 'L'. Three (64-66) got new 150lb boilers and No.65 new cylinders as well. In 1908, Nos.62 and 63 were rebuilt as 0-6-2STs. No.64 was also converted in 1911. Nos.65 and 66 remained as 2-4-2STs. Their dimensions were:

Coupled wheels:	5ft 0in
Leading and trailing wheels:	3ft 8in
Cylinders:	17in x 24in
Boiler pressure:	140lb psi (150lb psi after reboilering)
Heating surface:	1,152.36sqft (later 1,011.4sqft)
Grate area:	15.77sqft
Weight:	50 tons 8 cwt (later 54 tons 8 cwt)
Axleload:	16 tons 17 cwt (later 17 tons 6 cwt)
Tank capacity:	1,000 gallons
Bunker capacity:	3 tons

The 2-4-2STs took over the passenger working from the 2-4-0STs and the two remaining 2-4-2STs were said to be fitted for auto-train working in 1907, although this is not confirmed. It may have been the intention before the purchase of two steam railmotors. No.66 replaced No.16 as the Caerphilly Works pilot engine in 1909. After the withdrawal of the railmotors, 66 was converted for auto-train working in 1915. 65 was retained on Cardiff Docks engaged in general shunting at the end of the First World War. They were renumbered 1324 and 1325 by the GW in 1922. Both had the Westinghouse brake system replaced by vacuum brakes in 1924/5, 1325 returning as the Caerphilly Works shunter during the day and running a workman's train to Cardiff at the beginning and end of each day. Both were withdrawn in 1928 having run in excess of 600,000 miles.

Rhymney Railway 2-4-2ST No.65 as built in 1891, in Works grey. It was renumbered 1324 in 1922. (LGRP/Bob Miller/MLS Collections)

Rhymney Railway 2-4-2ST No.64 seen in the early 1900s before rebuilding as an 0-6-2ST in 1911. It was withdrawn in 1923 without renumbering. (K. Nunn/LCGB/Bob Miller/MLS Collections)

Rhymney Railway 2-4-2ST No.65 seen shortly after the First World War in the Cardiff Docks area, c1920. (Real Photographs/MLS Collection)

Rhymney Railway
2-4-2ST GW 1324 (formerly RR 65) awaiting works attention when the Westinghouse brake was replaced – note the pump still fitted here, 1924. (Photomatic/MLS Collection)

1-2 Steam Railmotors 0-4-0T, 1907
Hudswell Clarke built two small 0-4-0 tank locomotives for the Rhymney Railway in 1907 to the design of the Company's engineer, C.T. Hurry Riches. They were combined with coach portions built by Cravens Ltd to form steam railmotors. They were fitted with Westinghouse brakes and the coaches with electric lighting. Their dimensions were:

Coupled wheels:	3ft 6in
Cylinders:	12in x 16in
Boiler pressure:	175lb psi
Heating surface:	689.72sqft
Grate area:	14.59sqft
Weight:	45 tons (empty)
Water capacity:	700 gallons
Coal capacity:	1 ton
Seating capacity:	64

The Hudswell Clarke Steam Railmotor No.1 built in 1907 with the stubby little locomotive more traditional in form than other steam railmotors, 1907.
(RR Official /F.K. Davies/John Hodge Collections)

Car No.1 was short-lived, being withdrawn in 1910. No.2 lasted until 1919. Both locomotives were then rebuilt as 0-6-0Ts, numbered 120 and 121 by the RR and 661-662 by the GWR, and both were withdrawn in 1925.

Swansea Harbour Trust Railway

Swansea Docks was served by tramways from the end of the eighteenth century, but it was 1850 before the opening of the South Wales Railway serving the docks with steam hauled traffic. The Swansea Harbour Trust was incorporated in 1854 and the South Wales Railway became part of the GWR in 1863. A number of other railways was bringing coal and other traffic to the docks in the latter half of the nineteenth century and the Swansea Harbour Trust was contracted to perform all dock shunting. The Trust contracted out the provision of the shunting power, first to John Dickson in 1879, then to William Westlake in 1885 and finally to Christopher Rowland in 1891. Rowland's contract ended in 1905 when the Swansea Harbour Trust (SHT) acquired six locomotives of its own. After the death of Rowland in 1910, his plant and locomotives were purchased by the SHT. Some additional power was also provided by Powlesland & Mason, some still operating for that company after the SHT was taken over by the GWR in October 1923.

At the end of my first six month's employment with BR in 1957, I used my first 'free ticket' to visit Swansea. In order to catch the dock tanks on shed before they started their day's labour, I travelled down from London overnight on the 12.45am Paddington newspaper train with 5084 *Reading Abbey* to Cardiff and 6969 *Wraysbury Hall* from Cardiff to Swansea arriving around 5.30am and causing the shed foreman at Swansea East Dock a mild shock when I presented my shed permit to him before the 6am shift commenced. I caught a number of the dock tanks on shed before making my way on foot to Danygraig to observe more of the former SHT and P&M 'pugs' going about their business.

1, 3-7 0-4-0ST Westlake, 1885

Seven 0-4-0 outside cylinder saddle tanks were owned by William Westlake. No.1 was supplied by Hawthorn, Leslie in 1885 and had 3ft 6in diameter wheels and 14in x 20in cylinders. Two more were supplied between 1885 and 1888 and little is known about them. No.4 was another slightly smaller Hawthorn, Leslie engine with 3ft wheels and 12in x 18in cylinders. No.7 was a Manning, Wardle engine

Westlake's No. 1, a Hawthorn Leslie 0-4-0ST of 1885, sold in the 1890s and seen working on Birkenhead Docks as late as April 1960, named *Glanmor*. (F. Jones/F.K. Davies/John Hodge Collections)

The Swansea Harbour Trust No.10, built in 1904 and used that year to haul a royal train (a Swansea & Mumbles Railway coach) for the visit of King Edward VII to cut the first turf of the proposed King's Dock, 20 July 1904. The numberplate shows 'R No.10', the R presumably indicating Rowland's ownership. (Bob Miller/ MLS Collections)

built in 1882 and obtained from the contractors S. Pearson & Son sometime after completion of King's Lynn Harbour in 1884. It is possible that it was acquired as late as 1892 or 1893. It had, like No.4, 3ft wheels and 12in x 18in cylinders. All appear to have been sold in the 1890s.

1-4, 7-10 (GW 886, 926, 930, 933) 0-4-0ST Peckett, 1891

Westlake's successor, Rowland, quickly sought replacements for the Westlake engines and three Peckett 0-4-0 saddle tanks, numbered 1-3, were delivered in 1891. They were successful and were soon multiplied, No.4 being delivered in 1895, two more, Nos. 7 and 8, in 1899, another, 9, in 1902 and the final one, 10, in 1904. Their dimensions were:

Coupled wheels:	3ft 3in
Cylinders:	14in x 20in
Boiler pressure:	140lb psi (No.10 – 150lb psi)
Heating surface:	533sqft
Grate area:	8sqft
Weight:	24½ tons
Tank capacity:	700 gallons
Tractive effort:	11,960lb

Nos. 1-3 were sold by 1910 and No.4 in 1911. The other four were taken over by the Swansea Harbour Trust in 1910 and by the GWR in 1923 and renumbered 886, 926, 930 and 933. 933 (the SHT No.10) was withdrawn in 1927 and sold, working for a while on

the Swansea & Mumbles Railway before being sold on several times lasting eventually until 1959 at a colliery in Northumberland. 926 was sold in 1929 and remained in South Wales, being scrapped in 1938. The other two had been withdrawn by 1929.

1-3 (GW 150) 0-4-0ST, Hudswell Clarke, 1905

The first locomotives ordered by the Swansea Harbour Trust itself rather than by contractors were three Hudswell Clarke 0-4-0 saddle tanks in 1905. They were numbered 1-3, the previous SHT locomotives bearing those numbers having been set aside and subsequently sold. Their key dimensions were:

Coupled wheels:	3ft 3½in
Cylinders:	14in x 20in
Boiler pressure:	150lb psi
Heating Surface:	568.5sqft
Grate area:	9.1sqft
Weight:	27¾ tons
Tank capacity:	700 gallons
Tractive effort:	12,650lb

Nos. 1 and 2 were sold in 1915 as the work on Swansea Docks declined during the First World War, with No.1 going to the Ministry of Munitions and No.2 remaining in South Wales until 1919 before ending up in Rotherham at a chemical works and lasting until 1949. No.3 became GWR 150 and was scrapped in 1929.

4-6 (GW 5/701/1140), 0-4-0ST, 1905

Another three saddle tanks were ordered simultaneously from Andrew Barclay & Co. and were delivered in April 1905. They were numbered 4-6. Their dimensions were:

The **Swansea** Harbour Trust No.9 of 1902, renumbered 930 by the GWR, seen here c1923. Note the recently removed Rowland/SHT numberplate on the tankside. (Real Photographs/MLS Collection)

Hudswell Clarke SHT No.3 of 1905, renumbered 150 by the GWR and seen here on Swansea Docks, c1928. (GW Trust)

Coupled wheels:	3ft 5in	Grate area:	9.5sqft
Cylinders:	14in x 22in	Weight:	28 tons
Boiler pressure:	160lb psi	Tank capacity:	700 gallons
Heating surface:	643sqft	Tractive effort:	14,305lb

SHT No.5, subsequently GW 701, seen here after nationalisation ex-works at Swindon as 1140, 24 June 1951. (MLS Collection)

1140 in more workaday condition at Swansea East Dock shed, 21 April 1958. (MLS Collection)

Weight:	33½ tons
Tank capacity:	1,000 gallons
Tractive effort:	14,945lb

They were renumbered 929 and 968 by the GWR and became GW 1141 and 1143 in 1946 although the numbers were not applied until after nationalisation in 1948. 1141 was withdrawn in 1952 but 1143 lasted until November 1960, the last of the SHT saddle tanks in service. It had however departed from Swansea Docks in its last year to shunt at Clee Hill quarries. It had achieved well over half a million miles in traffic since its absorption by the GWR in 1923.

1140 under repair at Swansea East Dock shed on the occasion of the author's early morning visit, August 1957. (David Maidment)

Nos. 4 and 6 were also sold in 1915, both going to the Blaenavon Co. and are believed to have still been working there at least up to the onset of the Second World War. The remaining Barclay tank, No.5, was renumbered 701 by the GWR and 1140 under the GWR 1946 renumbering scheme. It was withdrawn in 1958.

11, 12, (GW, 929/1141, 968/1143) 0-4-0ST, Peckett, 1906

The SHT acquired two more Peckett 0-4-0 saddle tanks in 1906 and 1908 and numbered them 11 and 12. They were larger than the Rowland Peckett engines and their dimensions were:

Coupled wheels:	3ft 7in
Cylinders:	15in x 21in
Boiler pressure:	160lb psi
Heating surface:	719sqft
Grate area:	10.5sqft

Large Peckett 1143 (former SHT No.12) built in 1908 and seen at Danygraig shed, along with 1151 and 1104, 4 May 1952. (W. Potter/MLS Collection)

13 (GW 974/1144) Hawthorn Leslie, 0-4-0ST, 1909

The Swansea Harbour Trust continued their piece-meal additions as they pensioned off or sold earlier dock tanks. No.13 was a Hawthorn, Leslie 0-4-0 saddle tank built in 1909 and had the following dimensions:

Coupled wheels:	3ft 6in
Cylinders:	14in x 22in
Boiler pressure:	150lb psi
Heating surface:	590sqft
Grate area:	8.87sqft
Weight:	27½ tons
Tank capacity:	650 gallons
Tractive effort:	13,090lb

It was renumbered 974 by the GWR, and 1144 in the 1946 renumbering, acquiring the number's fixing in 1948. It was withdrawn in April 1960.

Above: **The Hawthorn,** Leslie 1144 (former SHT No.13) on Swansea East Dock shed on the occasion of the author's early morning visit, August 1957. (David Maidment)

Below: **The Hawthorn,** Leslie 1144 (former SHT No.13) seen shunting on Swansea Docks, 17 September 1959. (MLS Collection)

14 (GW 943/1142) Hudswell Clarke 0-4-0ST, 1911

Yet another variation! Almost every new saddle tank had a slightly different wheel diameter, cylinder dimension, heating surface and grate area. This one, SHT No.14 built by Hudswell, Clarke in 1911, had the following dimensions:

Coupled wheels:	3ft 4in
Cylinders:	15in x 22in
Boiler pressure:	160lb psi
Heating surface:	731.2sqft
Grate area:	10.13sqft
Weight:	28¾ tons
Tank capacity:	980 gallons
Tractive effort:	16,830lb

It was renumbered 943 by the GWR in 1923, received a GW safety valve bonnet, was renumbered 1142 in 1946 and was withdrawn in November 1959.

The Hudswell, Clarke 943 (former SHT No.14), c1946 before its final renumbering as 1142. (Real Photographs/Bob Miller/MLS Collections)

1142 (former SHT No.14) after renumbering from 943, at Danygraig shed, with a GW 1101 0-4-0T and a 57XX pannier tank No.4666, c1959. (MLS Collection)

The final SHT Peckett 0-4-0ST, 1145 (ex-SHT 18) at Danygraig shed, 13 April 1952. (MLS Collection)

18 (GW 1098/1145) Peckett 0-4-0ST, 1918 The next locomotives acquired by the Swansea Harbour Trust were three Peckett 0-6-0STs and then in 1918 a final Peckett 0-4-0 saddle tank, No.18. Its dimensions were similar to the 1906 built Nos.11 and 12. It was renumbered 1098 in 1923 and 1145 in 1946.

SHT - Powlesland & Mason Engines

The Powlesland Company hauled GWR traffic over the Swansea Docks area from 1865 and was joined by Mason in 1875 to become Powlesland & Mason. They continued with the GWR business on the docks until taken over by the GWR in 1923. The initial locomotives used in the nineteenth century are little known. 1, 3 and 4 were 0-4-0 saddle tanks built by the Brush Electrical Company (also known as the Falcon Engine & Carriage Works) and were sold before 1914. No.2 was an 0-6-0 tank. Another No.2 was acquired in 1909 and was an 0-6-0ST.

5, 6 (GW 795, 921) Brush Electrical 0-4-0ST, 1903 Nos. 5 and 6 were 0-4-0 saddle tanks built by the Brush Electrical Company in 1903 and 1906. Their dimensions were:

Coupled wheels:	3ft 7in	(later 3ft 6in)
Cylinders:	14in x 21in	(later 14in x 20in)
Boiler pressure:	140lb psi	
Heating surface:	561sqft	
Grate area:	9.45sqft	(No.6 – 8.7sqft)
Weight:	26 tons 3 cwt	(No.6 – 24 tons 17 cwt)
Tank capacity:	660 gallons	(No.6 – 680 gallons)
Tractive effort:	11,105lb	

No.5 was renumbered 795 in 1923 and rebuilt as a pannier tank in 1926. It was withdrawn in 1929 and sold to Pontardawe Steel Works and continued to carry its 795 numberplate. When owned by Richard Thomas & Baldwins in 1947 it retained its numberplates and gained the name *Dorothy* on the pannier tank side. It was not condemned until 1963. No.6 remained largely unchanged, was

Brush Electrical P & M No.5 renumbered 795 by the GWR and rebuilt as a pannier tank in 1926. It was sold to the Pontardawe Steel Works in 1929 and named *Dorothy* in 1947. It is seen at the RTB steel works at Pontardawe in the early 1950s. (N. Fields/MLS Collection)

Brush Electrical No.6 for the Powlesland & Mason Company, renumbered 921 by the GW and seen here at Swansea in June 1926. It was subsequently sold and converted to burn oil and is now displayed in the Mountsorrel Railway Museum near Loughborough. (F.M. Gates/F.K. Davies/John Hodge Collection)

Peckett 0-4-0ST GW 696 (ex-P & M No.3) at Swansea East Dock, 2 June 1950. It was renumbered 1150 in 1946 but had still not received its new number when this photo was taken. *(MLS Collection)*

renumbered 921 in 1923 and was sold in 1928 to a Sugar Beet Company and it finished up in Kent at Kingsworth and was converted to burn oil, still operational in 1964. It was then presented to the Leicester Museum of Technology (see page 135).

3, 4, 11, 12 (GW 696, 779, 927, 935/1150-1152), Peckett 0-4-0ST, 1907

A Peckett 0-4-0 saddle tank was acquired in November 1907 and numbered 11 and a similar engine, 12, was added in January 1912. Another, No.3, replacing an earlier engine that had been sold, was built in 1913 and No.4 in 1916. Their dimensions were:

Coupled wheels:	3ft 7in
Cylinders:	15in x 21in
Boiler pressure:	150lb psi
Heating surface:	712sqft
Grate area:	10½sqft
Weight:	33½ tons
Tank capacity:	1,000 gallons
Tractive effort:	14,010lb

They received GW mountings including chimney after 1923 and were renumbered 696, 779, 927 and 935. No.11 (927) was withdrawn in 1928 but the other three were renumbered 1150-1152 in 1946. 1150 was withdrawn in 1952 but the other two lasted until the 1960s with 1151 (ex-P & M 4, GW 779) surviving until 1963 when it was sold to Hayes of Bridgend for scrap although it was used by that firm for shunting its sidings until 1965.

Peckett 0-4-0ST GW 779 (ex-P & M No.4) at Swansea East Dock. It was renumbered 1151 in 1946 but had still not received its new number when this photo was taken, c1947. (MLS Collection)

Peckett 0-4-0ST 1151 (ex-P & M No.4, GW 779) at Danygraig, June 1948. 1153 is behind. (N.Harrop/MLS Collection)

Peckett 0-4-0ST 1152 (ex-P & M No.12, GW 935) at Swansea East Dock, 21 April 1957. (MLS Collection)

Peckett 0-4-0ST 1152 (ex-P & M No.12, GW 935) with a freight on Swansea Docks, 7 September 1949. (W. Beckerlegge/F.K. Davies/ John Hodge Collections)

7 (GW 925) Avonside 0-4-0ST, 1874, acquired 1906-9

Four 0-4-0 saddle tanks were built by the Avonside Engine Co. in 1874 for the South Devon broad gauge railway, named *Rook, Crow, Lark & Jay*. They became GWR 2176-2179 in 1876 and were converted to standard gauge in 1892, as GW 1330-1333. They were purchased by the P&M between 1906 and 1909 and numbered 7-10. 8, 9 and 10 were sold to the Ministry of Munitions in 1914, but No.7 remained at Swansea Docks and was renumbered 924 in 1924. See page 21 for its previous history – its post-1923 dimensions were recorded as:

Coupled wheels:	3ft 0in
Cylinders:	14in x 18in
Boiler pressure:	135lb psi
Heating surface:	915.63sqft
Grate area:	9.9sqft
Weight:	26 tons 11 cwt
Tank capacity:	700 gallons
Tractive effort:	11,245lb

It was withdrawn in 1929.

14 (GW 928) Barclay 0-4-0ST, 1912

Powlesland & Mason's No.14 was purchased from Andrew Barclay & Co. in 1914 and was similar in many ways to the Swansea Harbour Trust No.5 (see pages 105 & 106).

Barclay No.14 of the P & M Company shunting on Swansea Docks c1920. (J.A. Peden/MLS Collection)

The only dimensions recorded by the GWR were 14in x 22in cylinders and boiler pressure of 160lb psi. It was renumbered 928 by the GW in 1923 and was withdrawn in 1927.

***Dorothy* (GW 942/1153) Hawthorn Leslie 0-4-0ST, 1903, acquired 1919**
The last acquisition of the P & M before the takeover by the GWR was a Hawthorn, Leslie 0-4-0 saddle tank of 1903, originally constructed for Spring Vale Furnaces in Bilston. To add confusion, it was named *Dorothy* long before GW 795 acquired that name after being sold by the GW. It was renumbered 942 by the GWR in 1923 and the

Powlesland & Mason's 1903 Hawthorn Leslie 0-4-0ST, formerly named *Dorothy*, renumbered 942 (later 1153) by the GWR at Swansea East Dock, 9 June 1935.
(F.K. Davies/John Hodge Collection)

1153 shunting at the RTB Cwmfelin Works, 11 April 1950. (F. Jones/R.K. Davies/John Hodge Collection)

1153, the Hawthorn, Leslie 0-4-0ST of 1903 acquired in 1919, and previously numbered 942 by the GWR. It is seen at Danygraig shed, 13 April 1952. (MLS Collection)

name was removed. In 1926 it received GW boiler mountings. Its dimensions were:

Coupled wheels:	3ft 6in
Cylinders:	14in x 20in
Boiler pressure:	120lb psi
Heating surface:	533.65sqft
Grate area:	9.27sqft
Weight:	26 tons 13 cwt
Tank capacity:	550 gallons
Tractive effort:	9,520 lb

It was renumbered 1153 in 1946 and was withdrawn in 1955.

Taff Vale Railway

The Taff Vale Railway was the oldest, the largest and the most successful of the Welsh Valley railways. Incorporated in 1836, only a year after the Great Western, its main line ran from Cardiff Bute Docks to Merthyr to connect with the Dowlais area iron industry and then spread rapidly between 1840 and 1860 to eventually own 112 miles of track and move over eight million tons of originating freight and eight million passengers annually before being absorbed by the Great Western in 1922, its fleet of 274 locomotives being taken into GW stock in October of that year. The TVR ran alongside the River Taff from Cardiff to Pontypridd and by 1856 had extended to Treherbert and the vast coal reserves in the Rhondda Valley and subsequently to the 'Little Rhondda' – Maerdy and Ferndale. Because of congestion at Cardiff Docks, it built a dock at Penarth, but problems continued until the Barry Railway was formed and built Barry Docks. Coal traffic was its bedrock, enabling it to pay high dividends to its shareholders right up to the GWR take-over and formed a substantial part of the GWR's revenue for years to come. The most important depot on the TVR was Cardiff Cathays with others at Penarth Dock, Radyr, Merthyr, Abercynon, Treherbert and Aberdare.

In the early years, its locomotives were tender engines – 0-6-0s, mostly double-framed, for freight and 2-4-0s and 0-4-2s for passenger work. No tank engines were built before the 1860s. Between the 1840s and 1873, a number of men acted as locomotive superintendent, but in October of the latter year Tom Hurry Riches was appointed and held the post until he died in office in September 1911. He shifted the TVR's locomotive policy from tender engines to tank engines and double-framed to single-framed locomotives.

4, 5, 59, 66 'J' class 0-4-4T, 1876

The Taff Vale 'J' class of 0-4-4 side tank engines started life as double framed 0-6-0 engines built as early as 1861. No.4 had been named *Dinas* and No.5 *Llancaiach* but both had lost their names by 1866. The rebuilding was authorised in July 1875 for the purpose of providing locomotives for the Ferndale branch passenger working. The frame was extended at the rear to be able to fit a bogie replacing the rear set of driving wheels. The four engines were reboilered and were fitted with side tanks, small bunker and enclosed cab. The livery was lined black with brass dome and copper capped chimney.

In 1881, it was decided to rebuild two more 0-6-0 goods engines to the same design, the 1881 example numbered 59 and the 1883 rebuild 66. Dimensions of the four were:

Coupled wheels:	4ft 8in
Rear bogie wheels:	2ft 9in
Cylinders:	16in x 24in
Boiler pressure:	130lb psi
Heating surface:	902.4sqft
Grate area:	14sqft
Weight:	44 tons 11 cwt
Axleload:	14 tons 12 cwt
Tank capacity:	1,177 gallons
Coal capacity:	2 tons 18 cwt

By the 1890s they were replaced on the Ferndale branch and operated the Llantrisant and Cowbridge branches and 4 and 5 were renumbered 260, 261. These first two were withdrawn in 1893. The other two were not renumbered 277 (ex-59) and 278 (ex-66) until

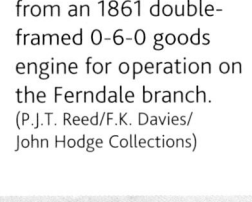

TVR 4 as rebuilt in 1875 from an 1861 double-framed 0-6-0 goods engine for operation on the Ferndale branch.
(P.J.T. Reed/F.K. Davies/ John Hodge Collections)

Locomotives absorbed by the GWR 1914–23 • 119

TVR 59 after rebuilding in 1897 with a new boiler. It is thought to have been converted in 1881 from 0-6-0 goods engine No.17 (of 1859).
(Bob Miller/MLS Collections)

No.59 after rebuilding in 1897 with a new boiler, seen shortly before renumbering as 277 and withdrawal in 1906.
(Moore/MLS Collection)

much later, 277 in 1899 before being reprieved for a year in 1901 and withdrawn in 1902. No. 59 was rebuilt in 1897 with a new boiler and Ramsbottom safety valves and other minor variations which increased its weight to 47 tons 11 cwt. It was renumbered in 1905 and withdrawn in 1906.

67-69 (GW 999, 1133, 1184) 'I' class 4-4-0T, 1884

Tom Hurry Riches designed a 4-4-0 bogie side tank engine in 1884 and Nos. 67-69 were delivered between July 1884 and September 1885. They were intended for branch passenger work and were painted in the TVR livery of black with brass dome and capped chimney. Initially they had half cabs open at the back, which were later enclosed. Their dimensions were:

Coupled wheels:	5ft 3in
Bogie wheels:	2ft 9in
Boiler pressure:	140lb psi
Heating surface:	956.14sqft
Grate area:	16sqft
Weight:	45 tons 8 cwt
Axleload:	15½ tons
Tank capacity:	960 gallons
Coal capacity:	1¼ tons

They were designed as class 'I' in the 1890s and mainly worked the Llantrisant and Cowbridge branches with the class 'J' 0-4-4Ts until replaced by the steam railmotors in 1904/5. They became 285-287 in the surplus stock in 1905, but when the railmotors were found to be inadequate for the traffic offering, the 4-4-0Ts were restored and fitted for auto-working. They were often the power for the Cardiff-Penarth-Cadoxton service.

The type of auto working can be seen in the illustrations of the class 'C' TVR 4-4-2Ts which replaced them – an untidy set of wires, rods and pulleys over the roofs of the engine and auto-coaches. As these auto-trains became more popular the load had to be increased to four coaches (two in front and two behind the engine). All three, still numbered 285-287, were rebuilt with larger boilers in 1914 and 1915 with the following changed dimensions:

Boiler pressure:	150lb psi
Heating surface:	1,010.1sqft
Grate area:	16.06sqft
Weight:	50 tons 12 cwt
Axleload:	17 tons 6 cwt
Tank capacity:	1,100 gallons
Coal capacity:	1½ tons
Tractive effort:	12,400lb

TVR No.67 as built in 1884 seen here, c1900. (Real Photographs/MLS Collection)

TVR No.67 from the other side at Cathays, Cardiff, c1900.
(MLS Collection)

No.68 after rebuilding with an enclosed cab and just before fitting with auto gear, 28 July 1905.
(K. Nunn/LCGB/MLS Collections)

They continued to work on auto trains on the Llantrisant and Penarth branches and they were renumbered by the GWR as 1133 (67), 1184 (68) and 999 (69), the latter initially being allotted 1186 until an engine supposedly withdrawn was found to be still operating and 999 was found to be spare. All were withdrawn at the end of 1925, after a lifetime mileage of around 600,000 miles.

170-174 (GW1301-1306) 'C' class 4-4-2T, 1888

Three 4-4-2 side tank engines were built in 1888 to Tom Hurry Riches' design by Vulcan Foundry and were numbered 170-172. Three more were built by the same manufacturer in 1891, 173-175. Unlike the 4-4-0Ts they replaced, they had inside cylinders and balanced slide valves. They were classified as TVR class 'C' and had left hand drive unlike earlier Taff Vale classes. Their dimensions were:

Coupled wheels:	5ft 3in
Bogie wheels:	2ft 9in
Trailing wheels:	3ft 8in
Cylinders:	17½in x 26in
Boiler pressure:	160lb psi
Heating surface:	1,209.5sqft
Grate area:	19sqft
Weight:	57 tons 12 cwt
Axleload:	16 tons 2 cwt
Tank capacity:	1,500 gallons
Coal capacity:	1½ tons

They were reboilered between 1912 and 1918 and other changes made at the same time giving new dimensions of:

Boiler pressure:	173/4 only – 150lb psi
Heating surface:	1,187.1sqft
Grate area:	19.27sqft
Weight:	54 tons 6 cwt
Axleload:	15 tons 6 cwt
Tank capacity:	1,600 gallons
Coal capacity:	2 tons
Tractive effort:	17,200lb (173/4 – 16,100 lb)

The engines retaining the higher boiler pressure were renumbered 1301-1304 by the GWR and the two 150lb psi engines were renumbered 1305 and 1306.

They were replaced on the principal passenger services by 0-6-2Ts in 1895/6 but continued on relief and branch work. 173 was involved with royal train working in 1912. From 1914, the advent of the TVR 'A' 0-6-2Ts caused a cascade of the earlier 0-6-2Ts and they seemed redundant until they were fitted with auto-train working equipment similar to

The first Vulcan Foundry 4-4-2T built for the Taff Vale Railway in 1888, No.170, seen at Bute Dock, c1890.
(MLS Collection)

The second TVR 4-4-2T, 171, c1900. (F. Moore/Bob Miller/MLS Collections)

171 at Cardiff, 28 July 1905. (K. Nunn/LCGB/MLS Collections)

1305, ex-173 with the lower boiler pressure, fitted with the overhead wire TVR push & pull system, c1925. (Real Photographs/MLS Collection)

1304 (ex-175), one of the 4-4-2Ts with 160lb boiler pressure and converted for auto-train working, at Barry, c1926. (H.C. Casserley/MLS Collection)

the 4-4-0Ts around 1917. They were used mainly on the Penarth branch and branches radiating from Pontypridd. The GWR auto train system was adopted in 1925 and the six 4-4-2Ts were withdrawn between 1925 and 1927, the last survivor being 1304 (ex-175).

106, 107 (GW 1342-1343), 0-4-0ST, 1876

Two 0-4-0 saddle tanks were ordered in 1876 from Hudswell, Clarke & Co. specifically for shunting at the top of the Pwllyrhebog Incline. They had outside cylinders, the second being slightly more powerful and were initially numbered 106 and 107. Their dimensions were:

	106	107
Coupled wheels:	2ft 6in	2ft 9in
Cylinders:	8in x 15in	10in x 16in
Heating surface:	194.32sqft	264sqft
Grate area:	3.31sqft	4.67sqft
Weight:	11 tons 8 cwt	15 tons
Tank capacity:	210 gallons	360 gallons

106 was reboilered in 1891 and both were renumbered 266 and 267. 267 was reboilered in 1895. After rebuilding their changed dimensions were:

	266	267
Coupled wheels:	2ft 11in	
Boiler pressure:	120lb psi	130lb psi
Heating surface:	156.6sqft	230.3sqft
Grate area:	3.4sqft	4.6sqft
Weight:	16 tons 7 cwt	
Tank capacity:	285 gallons	345 gallons
Coal capacity:	9 cwt	11 cwt
Tractive effort:	3,415lb	5,050lb

The former TVR 106/266, renumbered 1343 by the GWR, seen at Cathays depot, 15 August 1924 just a year before its withdrawal. (K. Nunn/LCGB/MLS Collections)

The former TVR 107, renumbered 267 in 1895 outside Cathays shed, c1900. (LPC/F.K. Davies/John Hodge Collections)

The former TVR 107/267, renumbered 1342 by the GWR, inside Cathays shed, c 1925. (Real Photographs/MLS Collection)

New 0-6-0Ts (class 'H') were built for the Pwllyrhebog Incline and the 0-4-0STs were made redundant and moved to Cathays Cardiff depot (266) and Radyr (267). They were transferred to the Departmental stock in 1920 and were renumbered 1342 (267) and 1343 (266) by the GWR. 1342 was replaced at Cathays in 1925 and was stored at Swindon, being withdrawn in August 1926. 1343 was replaced in its routine work in 1924 but became spare at Cathays for both Cathays and Radyr shunting work. It was withdrawn in December 1925. 266 (1343) had run up just under 300,000 miles before its withdrawal but 267 (1342), the more powerful engine, had more than doubled that to roughly 675,000.

1-18 Steam Railmotors, 0-4-0T, 1903

The Taff Vale Railway built more steam railmotors than any of the other constituent companies of the Great Western. The first was designed by Tom Hurry Riches and built at the company's own Works at Cardiff in 1903. Nos. 2-7 were built by the Avonside Engine Co. in 1904, 8-13 by Kerr, Stuart & Co. in 1905 and 14-18 by Manning, Wardle & Co. in 1906. Their dimensions were:

	No.1	2-7	8-13	14-18
Coupled wheels:	2ft 10in	2ft 10in	2ft 10in	3ft 6in
Trailer (coach) wheels:	2ft 10in	2ft 10in	2ft 10in	2ft 10in
Cylinders:	9in x 14in	9in x 14in	9in x 14in	10½in x 14in
Boiler pressure:	160lb psi	160lb psi	160lb psi	180lb psi
Heating surface:	299.5sqft	300sqft	300sqft	413sqft
Grate area:	8sqft	8.4sqft	8.4sqft	10sqft
Weight:	33 tons 2 cwt	32 tons	44 tons 11 cwt	
Tank capacity:	530 gallons	550 gallons	550 gallons	560 gallons
Coal capacity:	10 cwt	12 cwt	9 cwt	12 cwt
Seating capacity:	52	56	44	73

Taff Vale Steam Railmotor No.6 built by the Avonside Engine Co. in 1904 at Cardiff Bute Docks station, c1910.
(Lens of Sutton/F.K. Davies/John Hodge Collections)

128 • FOUR-COUPLED TANK LOCOMOTIVE CLASSES ABSORBED BY THE GREAT WESTERN RAILWAY

Steam Railmotor No.11 built by Kerr, Stuart & Co. in 1905, pauses for a crew photograph, c1910.
(R.C. Riley/F.K. Davies/John Hodge Collections)

The Avonside railmotors, Nos. 2-7, had 3rd class passengers only, the others had accommodation for both first and third class passengers. They worked on the company's main line between Cardiff Bute Road, Queen St., Cathays and Maindy and on the following branch lines – Aberdare and Abercynon, Cardiff and Penarth, Pontypridd and Nelson, Pontypridd and Ynysybwl, Pontypridd, Llantrisant and Cowbridge and Porth and Maerdy. Most were withdrawn in 1919 with the trailer vehicles being converted for use as auto trailers with the 4-4-0Ts and 4-4-2Ts.

Vale of Rheidol Railway
3 (GW 1198) 2-4-0T NG, 1896

No.3 *Rheidol* was a small 2-4-0T purchased second-hand in 1903 from Pethick Bros. (contractors) from the Talybont quarries. It had been built in 1896 by Bagnall's to the 2ft 3in gauge for a Brazilian railway but was taken up instead by the British contractor and converted to 1ft 11½in gauge. The main passenger service on the line was operated by two 1902 built 2-6-2 narrow gauge tank engines, with the 2-4-0T carrying out local shunting and engineering train work. Its dimensions were:

Coupled wheels:	2ft 3in
Leading wheels:	1ft 3in
Cylinders:	8in x 12in
Boiler pressure:	140lb psi
Heating surface:	191sqft
Grate area:	5.2sqft
Weight:	13 tons
Axleload:	4 tons 7 cwt
Water capacity:	225 gallons
Tractive effort:	3,245lb

It was renumbered 1198 by the GWR and withdrawn in July 1924 after the construction of two further 2-6-2Ts in 1923.

The 2-4-0T named *Rheidol*, that became No.3 of the Vale of Rheidol Railway at Aberystwyth after purchase from Talybont Quarries in 1903 and as running until 1904. (LPC/F.K. Davies/John Hodge Collections)

The narrow gauge 2-4-0T of the Cambrian Railways Vale of Rheidol system, No. 3 *Rheidol*, at Aberystwyth, 1921. (W.L. Good/F.K. Davies/John Hodge Collection)

Chapter 5
LOCOMOTIVES ACQUIRED BY THE GWR AFTER 1923

Weston, Cleveland & Portishead Railway

The Weston, Cleveland and Portishead Railway was independent of the GWR and remained so until its winding up in 1940 and its assets including locomotives were acquired by the Great Western which was its principal creditor. Among these engines were two six-coupled tank engines. The WC&P had owned four-coupled tank engines but they were withdrawn before the takeover by the GWR and are included for interest although strictly outside the subjects of this book.

A photo of this 1876 2-4-0T No.1 *Cleveland* taken before the demise of the Weston, Cleveland & Portishead Railway in 1940. (Real Photographs/MLS Collection)

1 *Cleveland* Dübs 2-4-0T, 1879
This locomotive was a 2-4-0 side tank built by Dübs in 1879 for the Jersey Railway. It was sold to contractors in 1884 on the North Cornwall Railway and was purchased by the WC&P Railway in 1901, its name *General Don* changed in 1906 to *Cleveland*. No further detail of this locomotive is available.

4 *Hesperus* Sharp, Stewart 2-4-0T, 1876
This locomotive was built by Sharp, Stewart in 1876 for the Watlington & Princes Risborough Railway and became GW 1384 in 1883. It was purchased on behalf of the WC&P in 1911 by the Bute Works Supply Co., and given the number 4, and name *Hesperus*. It was withdrawn in 1937. For dimensions of the locomotive, see the description under 'The Watlington & Princes Risborough Railway', pages 46-48.

Ystalavera Tin Mine
BR 1 *Hercules* 0-4-0ST, 1900
The Ystalavera Tinplate Works was liquidated in 1948 and a Peckett 0-4-0ST of 1900 owned by the company was acquired by the Western Region of BR that year and numbered 1 retaining its name *Hercules*, with a single nameplate on the left cabside. Its dimensions were:

Coupled wheels:	3ft 2½in
Cylinders:	14in x 20in
Boiler pressure:	140lb psi
Heating surface:	532sqft
Grate area:	7.5sqft
Weight:	21 tons
Tank capacity	850 gallons
Tractive effort:	12,120lb

It was overhauled at Danygraig in 1948 and remained in the area being withdrawn from Gurnos in January 1954.

The former Watlington & Princes Risborough engine of 1876, that became GW 1384 and was purchased in 1911 for the WC&P. It is seen here before its withdrawal in 1937. (MLS Collection)

British Railways (Western Region) No.1 *Hercules* at Danygraig after overhaul following acquisition from the Ystalavera Tinplate Company, 27 August 1948. (H.C. Casserley/ MLS Collection)

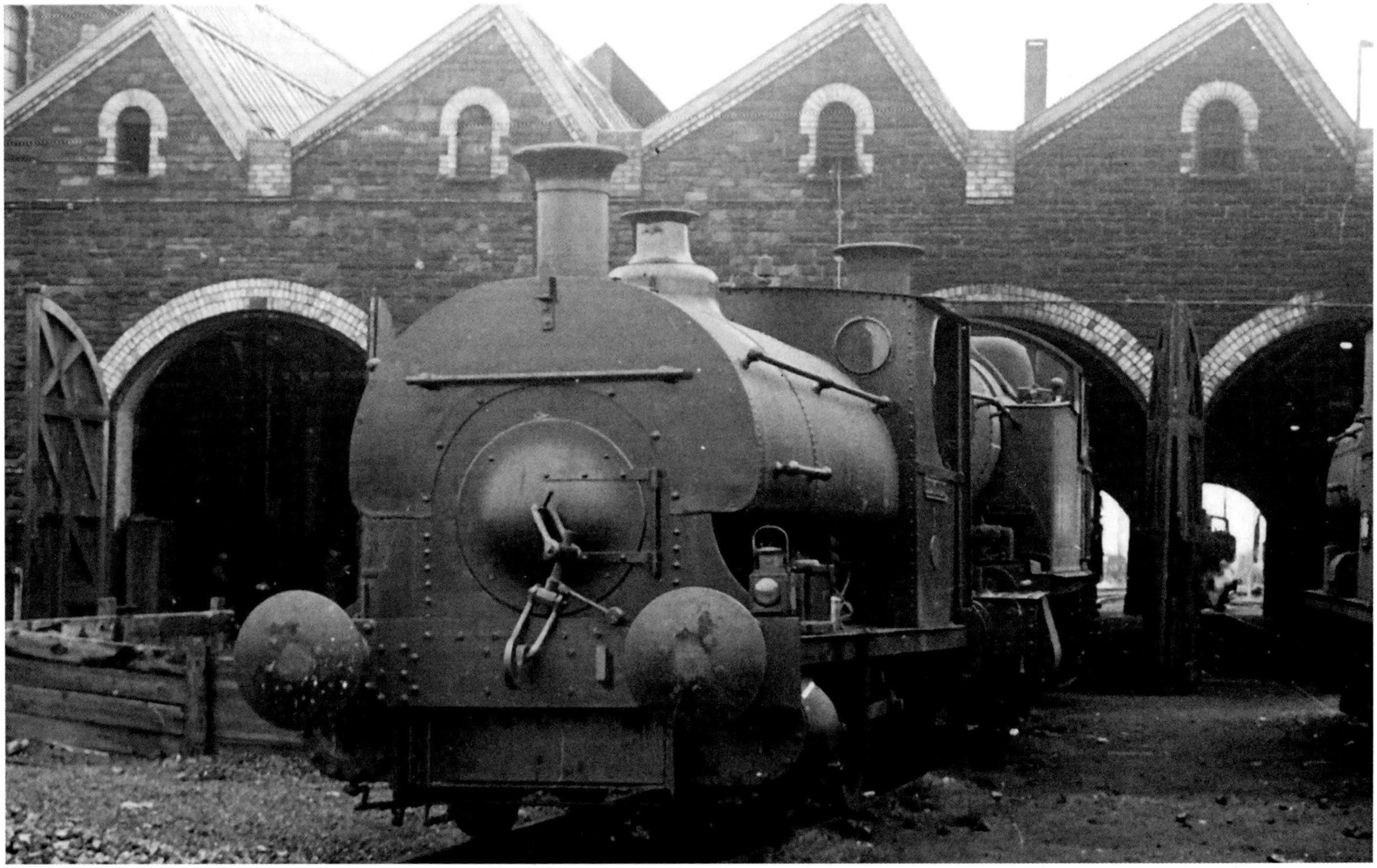

Corris Railway

This narrow gauge tramway of 1858, that became steam locomotive operated in 1879 on 2ft 3in gauge, was taken over by the GWR in August 1930. Passenger services were withdrawn in 1931. Floods of the River Dovey in 1948 eroded the bridge at Machynlleth and the line was closed.

3 (GW 3) Falcon & Co., 0-4-2ST, 1878

Three narrow gauge 0-4-0 saddle tanks were built for the line in 1878 by the Falcon Engine & Car Co. of Loughborough (later the Brush Electrical Engineering Co.). They were numbered 1-3 but the first two

Corris Railway No.3 when it and its two sisters were 0-4-0STs. It is seen at Corris, c1890. (LGRP/F.K. Davies/John Hodge Collections)

Corris Railway No.3 after rebuilding in 1900 and 1926 as an 0-4-2ST at Corris, c1927. It is still extant in this form on the preserved Talyllyn Railway. (LPC/F.K. Davies/John Hodge Collections)

Corris Railway No.4 at Maespoeth, 20 August 1937. (K.D. Rhodes/F.K. Davies/John Hodge Collections)

were withdrawn in 1923 and 1928 respectively before becoming GW property. No.3 was rebuilt as an 0-4-2ST in 1900 and again in 1926, and duly became GW stock until the line's closure when it was sold in 1951 to the Talyllyn Railway, becoming their No.3 *Sir Haydn*. Its dimensions were (and still are):

Coupled wheels:	2ft 6in
Trailing wheels:	10in
Cylinders:	7in x 12in
Boiler pressure:	160lb psi
Heating surface:	166sqft
Grate area:	3.5sqft
Weight:	9 tons
Tank capacity:	200 gallons
Tractive effort:	2,665lb

4 (GW 4) Kerr, Stewart, 0-4-2ST, 1921

The withdrawal of Corris Railway Nos. 1 and 2, followed the purchase of a new 0-4-2ST from Kerr, Stuart & Co. in 1921. The engine had Hackworth valve gear and was initially named *Tattoo*, but this was removed after a short while and the new engine just bore the number 4. It was also sold in 1951 to the Talyllyn Railway where it is still active as their No.4 *Edward Thomas*. Its dimensions are:

Coupled wheels:	2ft 0in
Trailing wheels:	1ft 4½in
Cylinders:	7in x 12in
Boiler pressure:	160lb psi

Heating surface: 115.5sqft
Grate area: 4sqft
Weight: 8 tons
Tank capacity: 140 gallons
Tractive effort: 3,330lb

Wantage Tramway

The Wantage Tramway was a two-mile tramway between Wantage and the GWR station at Wantage Road. Opened in 1873, it was initially served by horse drawn trams with steam power introduced in 1876. The line was closed to passenger traffic in 1925 and freight in 1945. It borrowed a number of locomotives from the GWR in the early days including GW 1329 *Raven* and 1359 *Wye* (see pages 21 and 39) and a Manning Wardle 0-4-0ST engine from the Royal Arsenal Railway. It later used two locomotives. No.7 was a Manning Wardle 0-4-0ST obtained on contract from the Manchester Ship Canal and the other, No.5, was bought by the GWR after the line closed in 1945 and was preserved, first at Wantage Road station and later at Didcot (see Chapter 6 page 138).

Shannon, 0-4-0WT

An 0-4-0 well tank was built by George England & Co. in 1857 for the Sandy & Potton Railway. It was sold in 1862 to the L&NWR as the Crewe Works shunter and in 1872 was named *Shannon*. After an unsuccessful trial on the Cromford and High Peak Railway it was sold to the Wantage Tramway in 1878 for £365. There it was numbered 5 and named *Jane*. In 1946, the GWR bought it for £100 and installed it on display at Wantage Road station, prior to preservation at Didcot. It had heavy repairs at Swindon in 1896 and 1921 and at the Avonside Engine Co. in Bristol in 1929. It had a further heavy repair at Swindon in 1939. Its dimensions are:

Coupled wheels: 2ft 11in
Cylinders: 9in x 12in
Boiler Pressure: 120lb psi
Weight: 15 tons
Tractive effort: 2,500lb

For photo, see page 139.

Chapter 6
PRESERVATION

921 (ex-Powlesland & Mason No.6)

Great Western 921 was built by Brush Electrical Engineering Company in 1906 and was owned by Powlesland & Mason shunting on Swansea Docks until 1924 when that activity was taken over by the GWR. It was sold in 1928 to Berry Wiggins & Co.Ltd. of Kingsnorth in Kent and was finally withdrawn in 1964. It was presented to the Leicester Museum of Technology in 1968. In 1992 it was exhibited at the Snibson Discovery Museum at Coalville until that museum's closure in 2015. Plans to develop that site in 2018 threatened access to the locomotive and in 2019 it was moved to the Mountsorrel Railway Museum near Loughborough where it is currently on display. For full details of the locomotive, see page 111.

Brush Electrical P & M No.6 renumbered 921 by the GWR and sold to Berry, Wiggins & Co. in 1931 and converted by them to oil burning in 1932. The locomotive is now displayed in the Mountsorrel Railway Museum. (MLS Collection)

Cardiff Railway Kitson 0-4-0ST No.5, built in 1898, seen c1922. Note the modified Walschaerts valve gear link above the running plate.
(Real Photographs/Bob Miller/MLS Collections)

1338 (ex-Cardiff Railway No.5)
1338 was built by Kitson for the Marquis of Bute's Railway at Cardiff Docks in 1898 and numbered 5, then the Cardiff Railway and absorbed into the Great Western system in 1922. It ran 354,000 miles in GWR/BR service. It was withdrawn in September 1963 and externally restored and put on display behind the Up platform at Bleadon & Uphill station in Somerset, later the Somerset Railway Museum which closed in 1985. 1338 was brought to Didcot in 1987 and restored to working order. Its boiler certificate has now expired, and it is currently on display in non-working condition. For further details see page 80.

Trojan 1340 (1897, Alexandra Dock & Railway Company)
Trojan was built by the Avonside Engine Co. for Dunn & Shute of Newport Town Dock in 1897 and sold to the Alexandra Dock & Railway Company in 1903. It was numbered 1340 in 1922 but retained its name. Although mainly, like 1341, at Cathays and Radyr, it was briefly based at Oswestry and later in 1929 seen around the Greenford/Park Royal area. It was withdrawn in 1932 and sold to the Victoria Colliery Co. at Wellington in 1934. In 1947 it was further sold to Alders of Tamworth and was still operational there in 1965.

It is now preserved at the Great Western Centre at Didcot, having been restored to working order in 2002. It was withdrawn for its ten-year overhaul in 2011 and work commenced in 2016, with completion in 2021.

Cardiff Railway
Kitson 0-4-0ST No.5, renumbered 1338 in 1922, restored and on display at the Great Western Centre at Didcot, 2019.
(David Maidment)

Comparison of size! 1338 beside 5029 *Nunney Castle* at Didcot, 2017. 1340 can be seen in the background.
(David Maidment)

138 • FOUR-COUPLED TANK LOCOMOTIVE CLASSES ABSORBED BY THE GREAT WESTERN RAILWAY

Above: **1340 *Trojan*** at Alders of Tamworth, 6 July 1959.
(MLS Collection)

Right: **1340 *Trojan*** restored to GWR livery at the Great Western Centre, Didcot, 2019.
(David Maidment)

***Tiny*, 2180, (South Devon Railway, 1868)**
Tiny was a vertical engined broad gauge locomotive built in 1868 for working on Falmouth Docks in Cornwall and numbered 2180 when taken over by the GWR in 1883 and withdrawn immediately for use as a stationary engine to power machinery at Newton Abbot Works until 1927. It was then transferred to the Up platform at Newton Abbot station on display until recently moved to Buckfastleigh for exhibition in the South Devon Railway Museum.

***Shannon* 5, 1857**
This locomotive was built in 1857 by George England & Co. for the Sandy & Potton Railway

and sold in 1862 to the L&NWR for shunting at Crewe Works and numbered 1104. It was given the name *Shannon* in 1872. In 1878 it was sold to the Wantage Tramway, numbered 5 and named *Jane*. The tramway closed in 1945 and the GWR bought the engine in 1946, restored the name *Shannon* and displayed it at Wantage Road railway station until that closed in 1964. It was stored initially on the premises of the Atomic Energy Authority but moved to Didcot in 1969 where it was steamed and operated again. It is now part of the National Collection and in 1975 took part in the 150th anniversary of the opening of the Stockton & Darlington Railway. In 2017 it was repainted in its original Wantage Tramway red livery.

Tiny on display on Newton Abbot station platform, c1956. (GW Trust)

Nos. 3 & 4, Corris Railway 0-4-2ST Both engines were sold to the Talyllyn Railway in 1951 where No.3 was named *Sir Haydn* and No.4 *Edward Thomas*. Both are operational members of the Talyllyn Railway fleet. For details and photographs, see pages 133-134.

Shannon, the former Wantage Tramway engine bought by the GWR in 1946, now exhibited at the Great Western Railway Centre at Didcot, 2017 shortly before being repainted in its original red livery. (David Maidment)

APPENDIX

Included here are a selection of weight diagrams of the most important classes and statistics of building, rebuilding and withdrawal dates of all the classes described in the book. The locomotive dimensions are not repeated here but are included earlier in the appropriate chapter as indicated in the index.

Bristol & Exeter Railway Locomotives Broad Gauge
4-4-0 Saddle Tanks
Statistics

Number	Built	Maker	GWR number	Withdrawn
47	10/1855	Rothwell & Co	2028	12/1879
48	12/1855	Rothwell & Co	2029	3/1879
49	12/1855	Rothwell & Co	2030	6/1884
50	12/1855	Rothwell & Co	2031	6/1884
51	12/1855	Rothwell & Co	2032	12/1882
52	1/1856	Rothwell & Co	2033	7/1880
61	7/1862	Beyer, Peacock & Co	2034	6/1884
62	7/1862	Beyer, Peacock & Co	2035	12/1886
63	7/1862	Beyer, Peacock & Co	2036	7/1880
64	7/1862	Beyer, Peacock & Co	2037	6/1886
65	5/1867	Vulcan Foundry	2038	7/1880
66	5/1867	Vulcan Foundry	2039	5/1892
67	5/1867	Vulcan Foundry	2040	6/1888
68	5/1867	Vulcan Foundry	2041	3/1880
69	6/1867	Vulcan Foundry	2042	5/1892
70	6/1867	Vulcan Foundry	2043	12/1888
71	7/1867	Vulcan Foundry	2044	12/1882
72	7/1867	Vulcan Foundry	2045	5/1892
73	8/1867	Vulcan Foundry	2046	6/1889
74	8/1867	Vulcan Foundry	2047	5/1892

Number	Built	Maker		GWR number	Withdrawn
85	11/1872	Avonside Engine Co		2048	5/1892
86	12/1872	Avonside Engine Co		2049	5/1892
87	3/1873	Avonside Engine Co		2050	5/1892
88	5/1873	Avonside Engine Co		2051	11/1890
89	7/1873	Avonside Engine Co		2052	5/1892

0-4-2ST, No.110
Statistics

Number	Built	Maker	Purchased	GWR No.	Withdrawn
110	5/1864	Manning & Wardle	3/1874	2058	1/1881

0-4-0WT, Nos.91-92
Statistics

Number	Built			GWR number	Withdrawn
91	8/1872			2094	5/1880
92	10/1874			2095	6/1881

Carmarthen & Cardigan Railway
Heron & *Magpie* 4-4-0T, 1861
Statistics

Name	Built	Maker	Sold	GW No.	Withdrawn
Heron	1861	Sharp, Stewart & Co	9/1872	2134	5/1892
Magpie	1861	Sharp, Stewart & Co	9/1872	2135	6/1889

Etna & *Hecla*, 4-4-0ST, 1864
Statistics

Name	Built	Maker	Sold	GW No.	Withdrawn
Etna	1864	Rothwell & Co	12/1868	2132	5/1892
Hecla	6/1864	Rothwell & Co	12/1872	2133	5/1892

Llynvi & Ogmore Railway
Rosa 4-4-0ST, 1863
Statistics

Name	Built	Maker	Sold	GW No.	Withdrawn
Rosa	1863	Slaughter, Gruning & Co	1/1868	2145	10/1885

South Devon Railway
2096-2105 4-4-0ST, 1851
Statistics

Name	Built	Maker	GW number	Withdrawn
Comet	10/1851	Longridge & Co	2096	6/1884
Lance	10/1851	Longridge & Co		12/1873
Rocket	10/1851	Longridge & Co	2097	10/1877
Meteor	11/1851	Longridge & Co	2098	7/1881
Aurora	1/1852	Longridge & Co	2099	11/1878
Priam	11/1851	Haigh Foundry	2100	11/1876
Damon	2/1852	Haigh Foundry	2101	12/1876
Falcon	9/1852	Haigh Foundry	2102	11/1878
Orion	2/1853	Haigh Foundry	2103	4/1878
Ostrich	8/1852	William Fairbairn	2104	12/1877
Ixion	4/1853	Stothert & Slaughter	2105	3/1878
Osiris.	4/1853	Stothert & Slaughter		8/1873

2106-2121 4-4-0ST, 1859
Statistics

Name	Built	Maker	GW number	Withdrawn
Eagle	4/1859	Slaughter, Gruning & Co	2106	12/1876
Elk	4/1859	Slaughter, Gruning & Co	2107	3/1877
Hawk	4/1859	Slaughter, Gruning & Co	2108	12/1885
Lynx	4/1859	Slaughter, Gruning & Co	2109	12/1876
Gazelle	5/1859	Slaughter, Gruning & Co	2110	6/1885
Mazeppa	5/1859	Slaughter, Gruning & Co	2111	6/1885
Giraffe	6/1859	Slaughter, Gruning & Co	2112	10/1877
Lion	6/1859	Slaughter, Gruning & Co	2113	12/1883
Antelope	7/1859	Slaughter, Gruning & Co	2114	12/1884
Wolf	8/1859	Slaughter, Gruning & Co	2115	6/1878
Tiger	5/1860	Slaughter, Gruning & Co	2116	12/1884
Hector	8/1860	Slaughter, Gruning & Co	2117	1/1892
Cato	9/1863	Slaughter, Gruning & Co	2118	10/1877
Dart	12/1864	Slaughter, Gruning & Co	2119	6/1885
Pollux	5/1865	Slaughter, Gruning & Co	2120	12/1882
Castor	6/1865	Slaughter, Gruning & Co	2121	9/1882

2122-2127 4-4-0ST, 1866
Statistics

Name	Built	Maker	GW number	Withdrawn
Gorgon	9/1866	Avonside Engine Co	2122	5/1892
Pluto	10/1866	Avonside Engine Co	2123	5/1892
Sedley	10/1866	Avonside Engine Co	2124	12/1885
Sol	11/1866	Avonside Engine Co	2125	5/1892
Titan	10/1866	Avonside Engine Co	2126	12/1886
Zebra	10/1866	Avonside Engine Co	2127	5/1892

2128-2131 4-4-0ST, 1872
Statistics

Name	Built	Maker	GW number	Withdrawn
Leopard	12/1872	Avonside Engine Co	2128	6/1893
Stag	12/1872	Avonside Engine Co	2129	6/1893
Lance	2/1875	Avonside Engine Co	2130	5/1892
Osiris	3/1875	Avonside Engine Co	2131	5/1892

2132-2135, 4-4-0ST, Secondhand Locomotives
Statistics

Name	Built	Maker	Purchased	GW number	Withdrawn
Etna	1864	Rothwell & Co	12/1868	2132	5/1892
Hecla	6/1864	Rothwell & Co	12/1872	2133	5/1892
Heron	1861	Sharp, Stewart & Co	9/1872	2134	5/1892
Magpie	1861	Sharp, Stewart & Co	9/1872	2135	6/1889

2136, 2-4-0, reb. 2-4-0ST, ex-West Cornwall Railway
Statistics

Name	Built	Maker	Rebuilt	GW number	Withdrawn
Penwith	1853	Stothert & Slaughter	1/1872	2136	12/1888

2137, 2-4-0ST, 1871
Statistics

Name	Built	Maker	GW numbers	Rebuilt Std gauge	Withdrawn
Prince	1871	Ince Forge Company	2137, 1316	1893	1899

2145, 4-4-0ST ex-Llynvi & Ogmore Railway
Dimensions
See Llynvi & Ogmore Railway above

Statistics

Name	Built	Maker	Acquired	Rebuilt 0-6-0ST	GW number	Withdrawn
Rosa	1863	Slaughter, Gruning & Co	1/1868	1874	2145	10/1885

2171, 2-4-0T, 1871
Statistics

Name	Built	Maker	GW numbers	Rebuilt to Std gauge	Withdrawn
King	1/1871	Avonside Engine Co	2171, 2	3/1878	3/1907 (Sold)

2172-2174 class 0-4-0WT, 1873
Statistics

Name	Built	Maker	GW numbers	Converted Std	Withdrawn
Owl	1/1873	Bristol Works	2172, 1327	8/1893	6/1899 (Sold)
Goat	2/1873	Bristol Works	2174, 1328	8/1893	12/1885 (Sold)
Weasel	3/1873	Bristol Works	2173		12/1882 (To Eng Dept)

2175-2179 class 0-4-0ST, 1874, reb. to standard gauge, 1892
Statistics

Name	Built	Maker	GW number	Converted Std	Sold	Withdrawn
Raven	11/1874	Bristol Works	2175, 1329	8/1892	c1906	1919
Rook	11/1874	Bristol Works	2176, 1330, 925	4/1892	3/1906	5/1929
Crow	12/1874	Bristol Works	2177, 1331	8/1892	3/1907	unknown
Lark	12/1874	Bristol Works	2178, 1332	7/1892	3/1906	c1933
Jay	2/1875	Bristol Works	2179, 1333	5/1892	12/1909 unknown	

2180 *Tiny*, 0-4-0WT, 1868
Statistics

Name	Built	Maker	GW number	Withdrawn
Tiny	1/1868	Sara & Co Plymouth	2180	6/1883 (Stationary boiler to 1927)

South Wales Mineral Railway
Princess & *Glyncorrwg* 0-4-0ST & 0-4-2ST, 1863
Statistics

Name	Built	Maker	B&E number	Reb. to Std gauge	Withdrawn
Princess	5/1863	Manning, Wardle		1872	1901 (Sold)
Glyncorrwg	5/1864	Manning, Wardle	110	1872 as 0-6-0ST	1872 (Sold to B&E)

Torbay & Brixham Railway
Queen 0-4-0WT, 1852 Dimensions
Statistics

Name	Built	Maker	Acquired	Withdrawn
Queen	1852	E.B. Wilson	1868	1/1883

Raven (GW 2175) class 0-4-0ST, 1874
Statistics

Name	Built	Maker	GW number	Withdrawn
Raven	11/1874	Bristol Works (S&D)	2175	See S&D 2175-2179 class details

Vale of Neath Railway
1-6 4-4-0ST, 1851
Statistics

Number	Built	Maker	To GWR	Withdrawn
1	10/1851	R. Stephenson & Co	1866	12/1872 (Sold)
2	11/1851	R. Stephenson & Co	1866	6/1872
3	11/1851	R. Stephenson & Co	1866	6/1872 (Sold)
4	11/1851	R. Stephenson & Co	1866	2/1872
5	12/1851	R. Stephenson & Co	1866	12/1872 (Sold)
6	12/1851	R. Stephenson & Co	1866	3/1872

7-9 4-4-0ST, 1854
Statistics

Number	Built	Maker	Reb. 0-6-0T	Withdrawn
7	6/1854	R. Stephenson & Co	1858	6/1874
8	8/1854	R. Stephenson & Co	1858	3/1880
9	10/1854	R. Stephenson & Co	1858	6/1878

Standard Gauge Locomotives absorbed by the GWR before 1914
Birkenhead Railway
32 & 33 (GW 97-98) 2-4-0T, 1856
Statistics

No.	Name	Built	Maker	GWR No.	Withdrawn
32	*Volante*	1/1856	R. Stephenson & Co	97	10/1878
33	*Voltigeur*	2/1856	R. Stephenson & Co	98	2/1880

39 & 6 (GW 95-96), 0-4-0ST, 1856
Statistics

No.	Name	Built	Maker	GWR No.	Rebuilt	Withdrawn
39	*Cricket*	9/1856	Sharp, Stewart & Co	95	8/1890	11/1924
6	*Grasshopper*	11/1957	Sharp, Stewart & Co	96	12/1888	11/1935

Bristol & Exeter Railway
83-84, (GW 1353-1354) 2-4-2T, 1868
Statistics

No.	Built	Maker	GW No.	Withdrawn
83	8/1868	Worcester Engine Co	1353	11/1877
84	9/1868	Worcester Engine Co	1354	11/1877

No. 30 & 33 (GW 1358-1359) 2-4-0T, 1876
Statistics

No.	Built	Maker	GW No.	Withdrawn
30	1876	B&E Bristol	1358	7/1888
33	1876	B&E Bristol	1359	3/1890

No. 93-95 (GW 1378-1380), 0-4-0T, 1875
Statistics

No.	Built	Maker	GW No.	Withdrawn
93	7/1875	B&E Bristol	1378	6/1880
94	12/1875	B&E Bristol	1379	6/1880
95	12/1875	B&E Bristol	1380	5/1880

No. 112 & 113 (GW 1381-1382), 0-4-0WT, 1874 (3ft gauge)
Statistics

No.	Built	Maker	GW No.	Withdrawn
112	1/1874	B&E Bristol	1381	3/1899 (Sold)
113	8/1875	B&E Bristol	1382	3/1899 (Sold)

Bristol Port Railway
Nos. 1 & 2, 0-4-2T, 1854
Statistics

No.	Built	Maker	Rebuilt	Withdrawn
1	1856	St Helens Railway	1865	1890 (Sold)
2	1854	St Helens Railway	1865	1890 (Sold to S&MR withdrawn c1932)

Festiniog & Blaenau Railway (1ft 11½ in gauge)
Nos. 1 & 2, 0-4-2ST NG, 1868
Statistics

No.	Built	Maker	Withdrawn
1	1868	Manning, Wardle & Co	1883 (Sold)
2	1868	Manning, Wardle & Co	1883 (Sold)

Liskeard & Looe Railway
Lady Margaret 2-4-0T, (GW 1308) 1902
Statistics

Name	Built	Maker	GW No.	Rebuilt	Withdrawn
Lady Margaret	1902	Andrew Barclay & Co	1308	1929	5/1948

Llanelli Railway & Dock Company
Loughor 2-4-0T class, 1865
Statistics

Name	Built	Maker	GW No.	Rebuilt	Withdrawn
Lougher	8/1865	Hopkins, Gilkes & Co	901		12/1886
Amman	9/1865	Hopkins, Gilkes & Co	900	1871	6/1884

Llynvi & Ogmore Railway
Nos. 7-9 class 2-4-0ST, 1855, reb. 1868
Statistics

Name	Built	Maker	Rebuilt	GW No.	Withdrawn
7	5/1860	R. Stephenson & Co	c1868	916	9/1875
8	5/1860	R. Stephenson & Co	c1868	917	5/1875
9	8/1855	R. Stephenson & Co	c1868	918	8/1875

Manchester & Milford Railway
Nos. 2, 6 (GW 1304, 1306) 2-4-2T, 1891
Weight Diagram
Although no diagram or drawing of either of these engines has been found, a Sharp, Stewart 2-4-2T Barry class J diagram is shown on page 58.

Statistics

No.	Name	Built	Maker	GW No.	Withdrawn
2	*Plynlimmon*	1891	Sharp, Stewart & Co	1304	7/1916
6	*Cader Idris*	1896	Sharp, Stewart & Co	1306	4/1919

Monmouthshire Canal Co.
Nos. 9-10 (GW 1301-1302), 2-4-0WT, 1849
Statistics

No.	Built	Maker	Rebuilt	GW No.	Withdrawn
9	1849	Sharp Brothers	1875	1302	9/1884
10	1849	Sharp Brothers		1301	11/1877

No. 16 (GW 1303) 4-4-0, 1850, reb. 4-4-0ST 1854
Statistics

No.	Built	Maker	Rebuilt	GW No.	Withdrawn
16	1850	Stothert, Slaughter & Co	1854	1303	9/1882

Nos. 10A, 14, 15 & 41 (GW 1304-1307), 4-4-0T, 1870
Statistics

No.	Built	Maker	Rebuilt	GW No.	Withdrawn
14	1870	Newport Dock St	9/1893	1304	11/1905
41	1871	Newport Dock St	7/1895	1305	1/1905

No.	Built	Maker	Rebuilt	GW No.	Withdrawn
15	1872	Newport Dock St	6/1896	1306	10/1904
10A	1875	Newport Dock St	5/1898	1307	11/1905

No. 42-50 (GW 1345 - 52) 0-6-0ST 1871, reb.0-4-4T, reb.1891/2
Statistics

No.	Built	Maker	GW No.	Rebuilt	Withdrawn
42	1871	Avonside	1345	10/1891	12/06
43	2/1872	Avonside	1346	1/1892	9/1910 (Sold)
44	1872	Avonside	1347	4/1892	10/1907
45	1873	Avonside	1348	10/1891	8/1906
46	1873	Avonside	1349	3/1892	9/1906
48	1875	Dübs	1350	8/1891	8/1913
49	1875	Dübs	1351	5/1892	8/1913
50	1875	Dübs	1352	9/1892	10/1908

No. 47, 5 & 51 (GW 1308-1310) 0-4-4T, 1873
Statistics

No.	Built	Maker	GW No.	Rebuilt	Withdrawn
47	1873	Avonside Engine Co	1308	10/1898	6/1904
5	1874	Avonside Engine Co	1309	3/1897	9/1903
51	1875	Avonside Engine Co	1310	2/1899	4/1908

Newport, Abergavenny & Hereford Railway
Nos. 20-22 (WMR 90-92, GW 194, 195 & 227) 0-4-2 1854, reb. 0-4-2T, 0-4-0T, 1872
Statistics

NA & H No.	Built	WMR No.	Maker	GW No.	Rebuilt	Withdrawn
20	1854	90	Dodds & Co	194	1872	5/1881
21	1854	91	Dodds & Co	195	11/1865	11/1879
22	1854	92	Dodds & Co	227	c1862	3/1870 (Sold)

Oxford, Worcester & Wolverhampton Railway
No. 35 & 36 (GW 221-222), 0-4-2ST, 1853
Statistics

O.W.& W. No.	Built	WMR No.	Maker	GW No.	Withdrawn
35	11/1853	35	E.B. Wilson	221	6/1872 (Sold)
36	1855	36	E.B. Wilson	222	10/1873 (Sold)

Severn & Wye and Severn Bridge Railway
Wye (GW 1359) 0-4-0T, 1876
Statistics

Name	Built	Maker	Rebuilt	GW No.	Withdrawn
Wye	1876	Fletcher, Jennings	1892	1359	12/1910

South Devon Railway
Saturn (GW 1298-1300) 2-4-0T, 1878
Statistics

Name	Built	Maker	GW No.	Rebuilt	Withdrawn
Saturn	12/1878	Swindon	1298		10/1926
Jupiter	12/1878	Swindon	1299	10/1925	9/1936 (Crane engine)
Mercury	12/1878	Swindon	1300	2/1905	5/1934

Shrewsbury & Chester Railway
No.2 (GW 2) 2-4-0T, 1846, reb.1868
No.15 (GW 15) 0-4-0ST, 1847
No.16 (GW 16) 0-4-0WT, 1849
Statistics

S&C	Built	Maker	GW No.	Rebuilt	Withdrawn
2	11/1846	R.B. Longridge	2	1868	12/1873
15	11/1847	Bury, Curtis & Kennedy	15	1866, 1881, 1887, 1890	8/1904
16	5/1849	Sharp Bros.	16	1872	9/1879

Shrewsbury & Birmingham Railway
No. 6 (GW 40) 0-4-2T, 1849, reb.1862
No.11 (GW 45) 0-4-0WT, 1853, reb.0-4-2ST 1862
Statistics

S&H	Built	Maker	GW No.	Rebuilt	Withdrawn
6	10/1849	Longridge	40	1862, 1873, 1897	1/1904
11	12/1853	Sharp, Stewart	45	1860	10/1877

Shrewsbury & Hereford and Tenbury Railways
121, 130 & 131, 2-4-0WT, 1856
Statistics

WMR	Built	Maker	GW No.	Withdrawn
121	1856	Jones & Co Liverpool	228	5/1872
130	1857	Jones & Co Liverpool	229	1/1878
131	1857	Jones & Co Liverpool	230	1/1878

Watlington & Princes Risborough Railway
No.2 (GW 1384) 2-4-0T, 1876
Weight Diagram

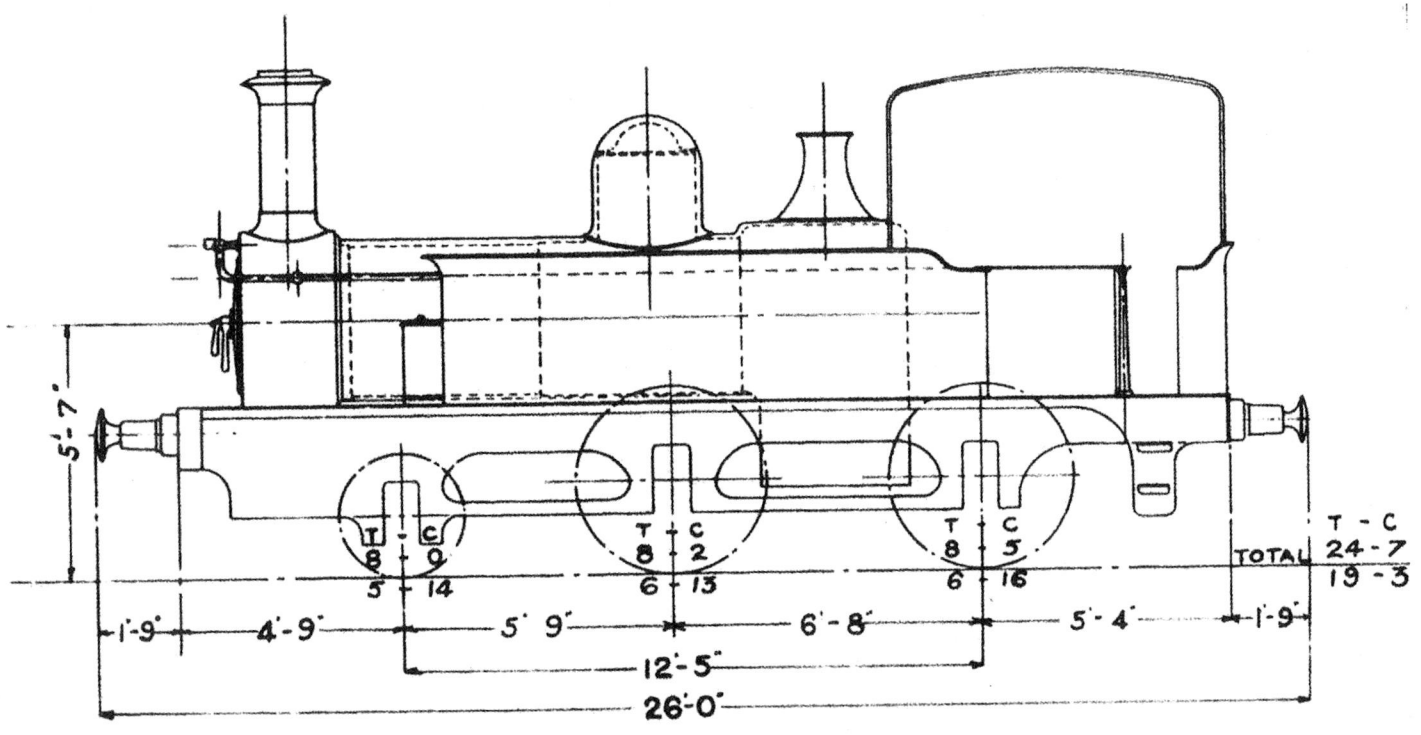

Statistics

W&PR	Built	Maker	GW No.	Rebuilt	Withdrawn
2	2/1876	Sharp, Stewart	1384	11/1899	4/1911 (sold)

West Cornwall Railway
Fox (GW 1391), 0-4-0T, 1872
Statistics

W C Rly	Built	Maker	GW No.	Rebuilt	Withdrawn
Fox	1872	Avonside	1391	1897	7/1912 (sold)

West Midland Railway
68 & 69 (GW 225-226), 2-4-0T, 1861
107, 109 & 111 (GW 197, 199, 201), 2-4-0T, 1862, reb.1879-1884
Statistics

WMR	Built	Maker	GW No.	Rebuilt	Withdrawn
68	1861	Beyer, Peacock	225		9/1883
69	1861	Beyer, Peacock	226		1/1880
107	1862	Beyer, Peacock	197	4/1880	12/1885 (rebuilt as 2-4-0 tender)
109	1862	Beyer, Peacock	199	9/1881	11/1884 (rebuilt as 2-4-0 tender)
111	1862	Beyer, Peacock	201	2/1879	3/1884 (rebuilt as 2-4-0 tender)

90-92 (GW 194-195), 0-4-2T, 1854, reb.1872
Former Newport, Abergavenny & Hereford Railway locomotives (see pages 37, 38 & 49).

Standard Gauge Locomotives absorbed by the GWR between 1914 & 1923
Alexandra Dock Railway
Active, Trojan (GW 1340) & *Alexandra* (GW 1341), 0-4-0ST, 1882-1897
Weight Diagrams

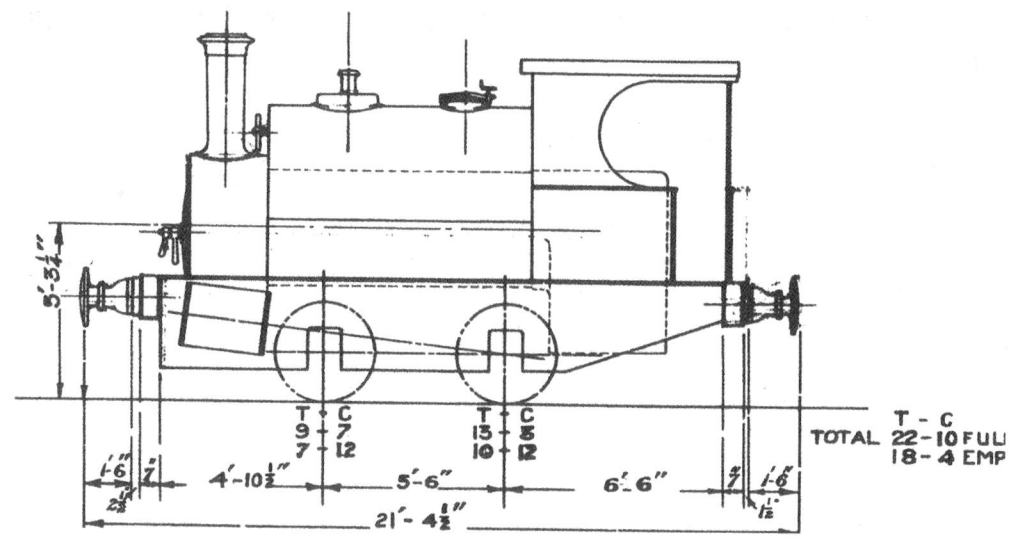

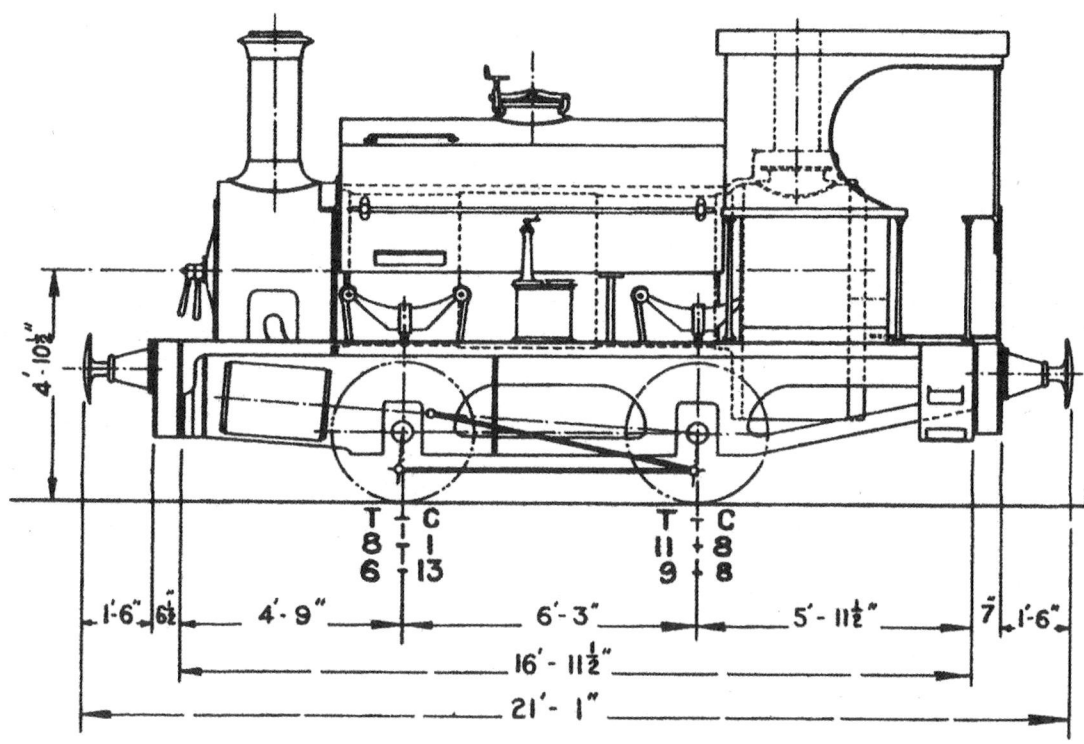

Nos. 1 & 2 Steam Railmotors 0-4-0T, 1904
14 (GW 1426) GW '517' class 0-4-2T, 1877
Statistics

AD&R	Built	Maker	Purchased	GW No.	Rebuilt	Withdrawn
Active	1882	Hunslet	4/1903			1915 (Sold)
Alexandra	Unknown	Unknown	4/1903	1341	4/1925	7/1946
Trojan	1897	Avonside	4/1903	1340	4/1923	7/1932 (Sold)
RM No.1	1904	Glasgow Rly & Eng Co				1911
RM No.2	1905	Glasgow Rly & Eng Co				1917
14	6/1877	Wolverhampton	2/1911	1426	12/1919	11/1934

Barry Railway
'E' class 0-6-0T, 1889 rebuilt as 0-4-2T (GW 781, 785), 1909
Statistics

Barry Rly	Built	Maker	To 0-4-2T	GW No.	To 0-6-0T	Withdrawn
33	1889	Hudswell Clarke	1909	781	By 1923	7/1932 (Sold)
53	1891	Hudswell Clarke	1910	785	By 1923	5/1932 (Sold)

'C' class 2-4-0T (GW 1321-1322), 1889
Statistics

Barry Rly	Built	Maker	GW No.	Rebuilt	Withdrawn
21	9/1889	Sharp, Stewart	1322	8/1898 & 5/1924	5/1928
22	9/1889	Sharp, Stewart	1323	8/1898	8/1926
37	9/1890	Sharp, Stewart			8/1898 (Sold to PTR)
52	9/1890	Sharp, Stewart		11/1898	11/1898 (Sold to PTR)

'G' class 0-4-4T (GW 2-4, 9), 1892
Weight Diagram

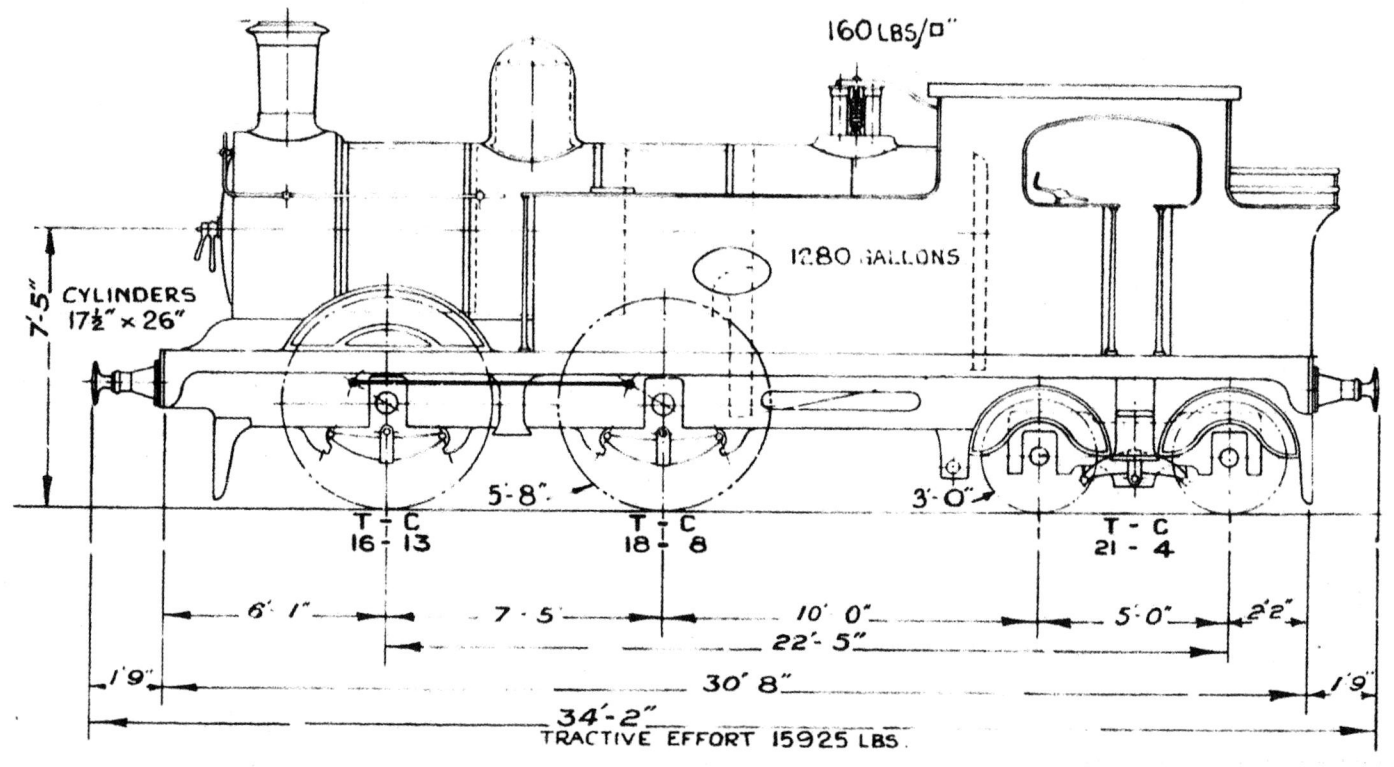

Statistics

Barry Rly	Built	Maker	GW No.	Rebuilt	Withdrawn
66	8/1892	Vulcan Foundry	2		5/1925
67	8/1892	Vulcan Foundry	3	2/1920	4/1929
68	3/1895	Sharp, Stewart	4		10/1926
69	3/1895	Sharp, Stewart	9		12/1927

'J' class 2-4-2T (GW 1311-1321), 1897
Weight Diagrams

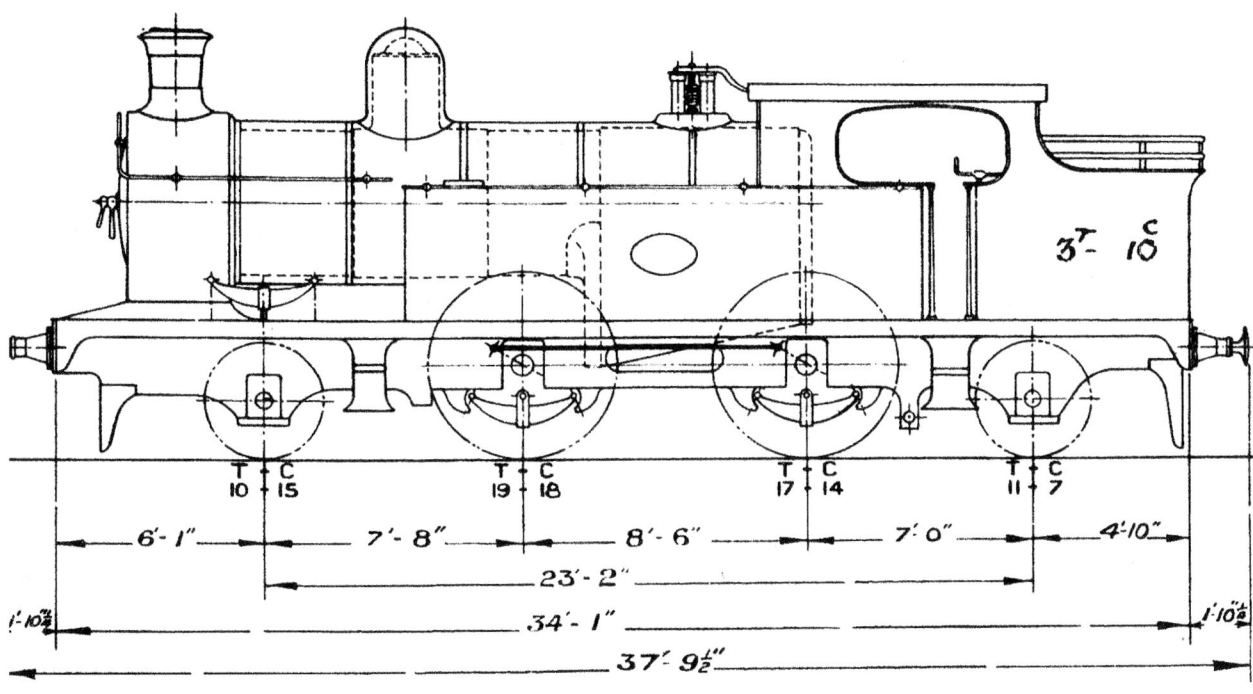

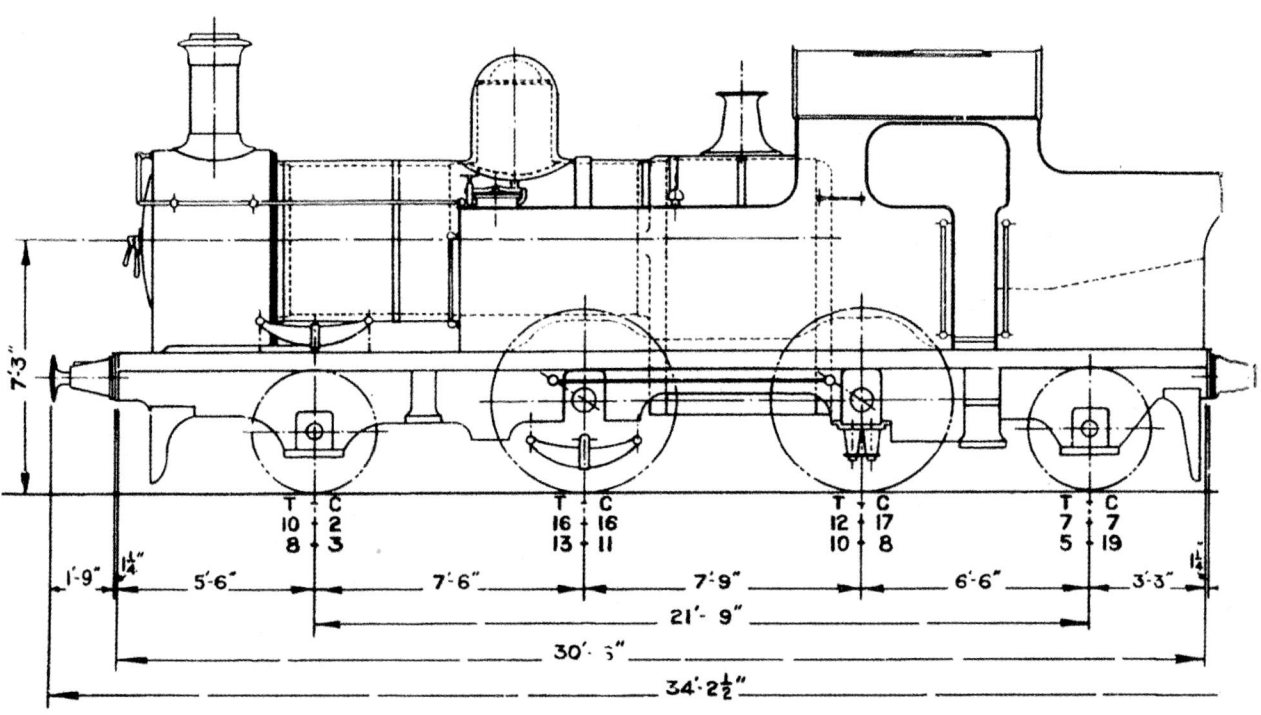

Statistics

Barry Rly	Built	Maker	2C/3A boiler	GW No.	Rebuilt	Withdrawn
86	3/1897	Hudswell, Clarke	7/09 & 4/24	1311		12/1926
87	4/1897	Hudswell, Clarke		1312	9/1926	7/1930
88	5/1897	Hudswell, Clarke	11/09 & 5/21	1313		5/1928
89	5/1898	Sharp, Stewart	11/1919	1314		10/1926
90	5/1898	Sharp, Stewart	3/1909	1315	3/1924	10/1928
91	5/1898	Sharp, Stewart	2/09 & 6/15	1316		10/1928
94	6/1899	Sharp, Stewart	12/09 & 7/21	1317		3/1928
95	6/1899	Sharp, Stewart	2/1911	1318	10/1924	11/1926
96	6/1899	Sharp, Stewart		1319	7/1924	3/1930
97	6/1899	Sharp, Stewart	5/1911	1320	4/1924	6/1930
98	6/1899	Sharp, Stewart	1/1922	1321		2/1926

1-2 Steam Railmotors, 0-4-0T, 1905
Statistics

Barry Rly	Built	Maker	Withdrawn
RM 1	1905	North British, Glasgow	1914
RM 2	1905	North British, Glasgow	1914

Brecon & Merthyr Railway
Tiny 0-4-0ST, 1862
Statistics

B & M	Built	Maker	Withdrawn
Tiny	12/1862	Manning, Wardle	11/1868 (Sold)

'Usk', 2-4-0, 1865, reb. 2-4-0T, 1895.
Statistics

B & M	Built	Maker	Rebuilt	Renumbered	Withdrawn
Usk	1865	Sharp, Stewart	5/1895	21	6/1904

44 (GW 1391) ex-LSWR 0376, 4-4-2T, 1879
Weight Diagram

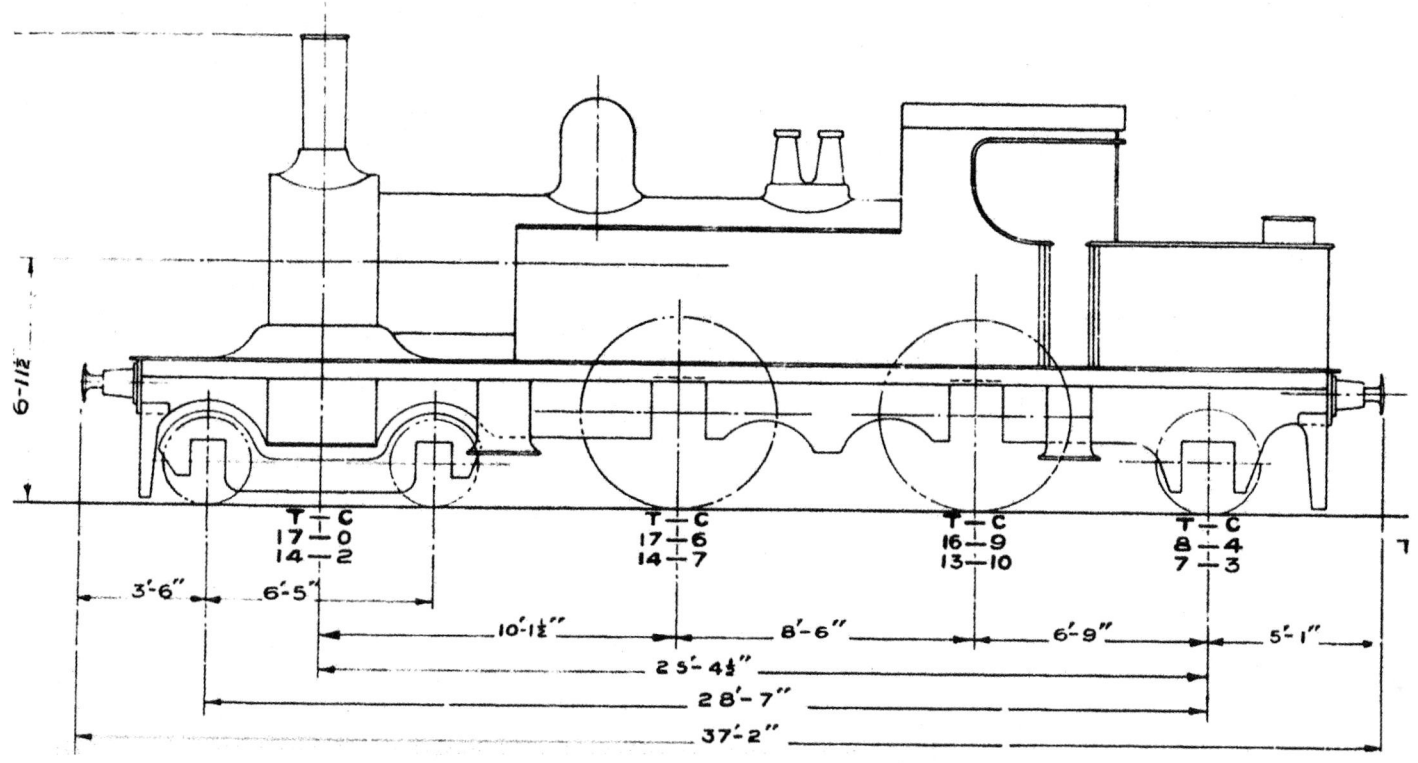

Statistics

B & M	Built	Maker	LSWR No.	Acquired	GW No.	Withdrawn
44	1879	Beyer, Peacock	0376	2/1914	1391	11/1922

9-12, 21, 25 (GW 1402/12/52/58/60) Met tanks 2-4-0T, 1888

Statistics

B & M	Built	Maker	GW No.	Withdrawn
9	12/1888	R. Stephenson	1402	6/1923
10	12/1888	R. Stephenson	1412	4/1923
11	1/1889	R. Stephenson	1460	10/1924
12	2/1889	R. Stephenson	1452	2/1923
25	3/1898	B & M Machen	1458	10/1922
21	4/1904	B & M Machen		12/1921

Burry Port & Gwendreath Valley Railway
Lizzie & Gwendraeth, 0-4-0ST, 1868
Statistics

BP&GV	Built	Maker	Acquired	Rebuilt	Withdrawn
Lizzie	1868	Henry Hughes & Co	1869		Unknown
Gwendraeth	1868	Henry Hughes & Co	1869	1897	c1909

'Pioneer/Mountaineer' Fairlie 0-4-4-0T, 1870
Statistics

BP&GV	Built	Maker	Withdrawn
Mountaineer	1870	Fairlie Engine & Rolling Stock Co	1891

Cambrian Railways
3 Milford, 0-4-2ST, 1859
21 Lilleshall, 0-4-0ST, 1862
Statistics

Cambrian	Built	Maker	Acquired	Withdrawn
3 Milford	1859	Sharp, Stewart & Co	1864	1893
21 Lilleshall	1862	Lilleshall Iron Co	1864	1868 (Sold)

36-38 Plasfynnon 0-4-0ST, 1863
Statistics

Cambrian	Built	Maker	Acquired	Withdrawn
36 Plasfynnon	6/1863	Sharp, Stewart & Co	1864	12/1905
37 Mountaineer	6/1863	Sharp, Stewart & Co	1864	12/1905
38 Prometheus	6/1863	Sharp, Stewart & Co	1864	1/1907

2, 12, 33, 37 (GW 1129-1132), 'Metropolitan' 4-4-0T, 1864
Weight Diagram

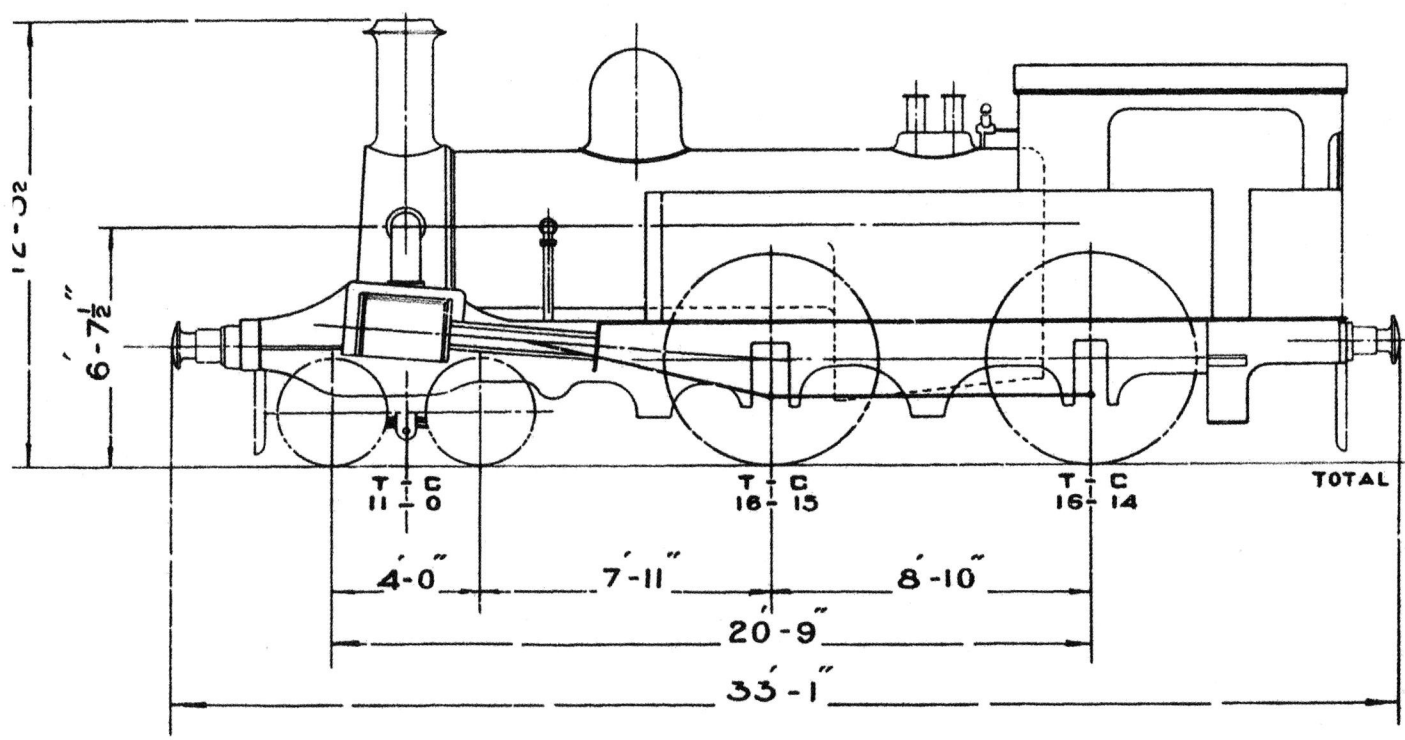

Statistics

Cambrian	Built	Maker	Met	No. Acquired	GW No.	Withdrawn
2	1864	Beyer, Peacock	10	11/1905	1129	9/1922
12	1864	Beyer, Peacock	11	11/1905	1130	6/1923
33	1864	Beyer, Peacock	12	11/1905	1131	7/1922
34	1864	Beyer, Peacock	13	11/1905		3/1915 (rebuilt tender loco)
36	1864	Beyer, Peacock	15	11/1905		2/1916 (rebuilt tender loco)
37	1885	Beyer, Peacock	66	11/1905	1132	1/1923

44, 56 (GW 1190, 1191) 2-4-0T, 1864
Weight Diagram

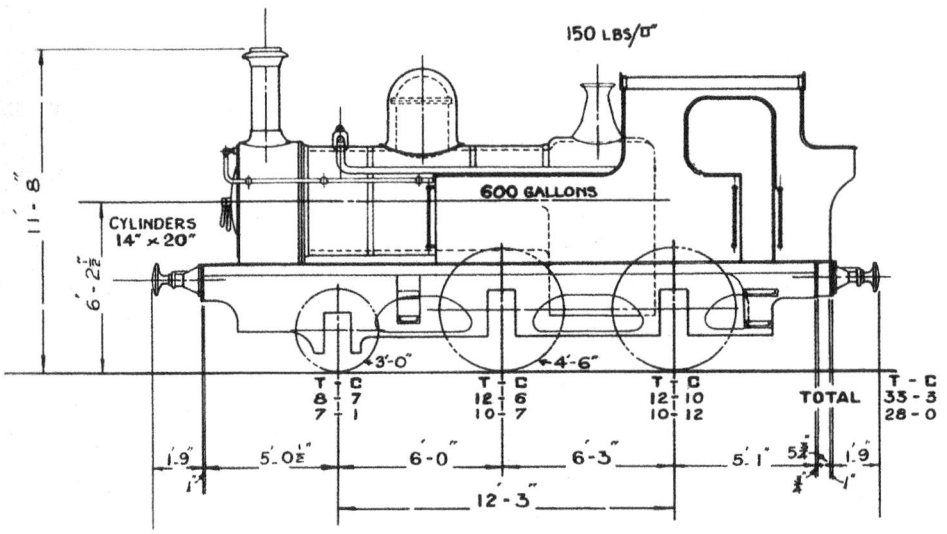

Statistics

Cambrian	Built	Maker	Rebuilt	GW No.	Withdrawn
44 *Rheidol*	3/1864	Sharp, Stewart	1/1907	1190	7/1922
56 *Whittington*	12/1865	Sharp, Stewart	5/1907	1191	10/1922

57-59 (GW 1192, 1196-1197) 2-4-0T, 1866
Weight Diagram

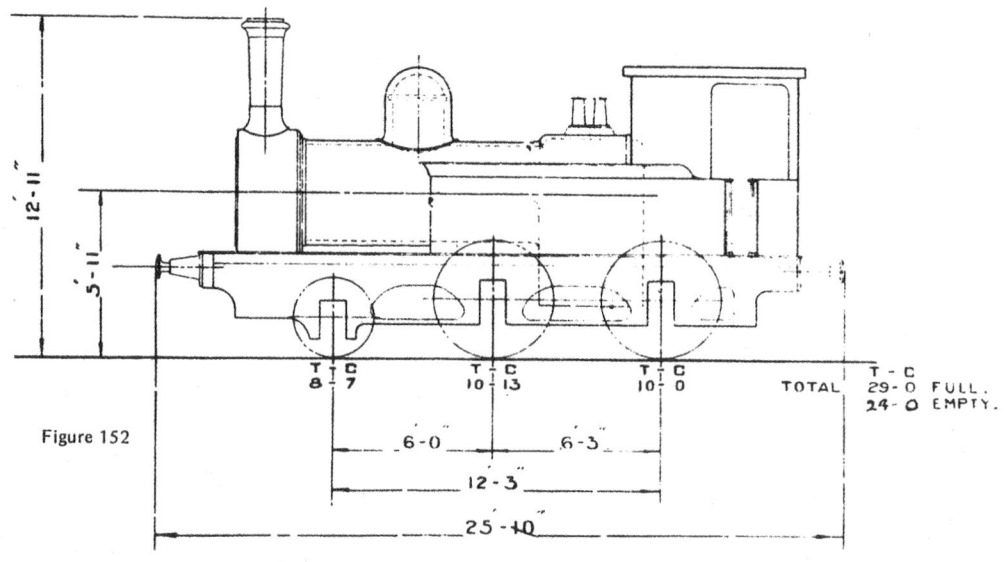

Figure 152

Statistics

Cambrian	Built	Maker	Rebuilt	GW No.	Withdrawn
57 *Maglona*	5/1866	Sharp, Stewart & Co	9/1893 & 7/1923	1192	8/1929
58 *Gladys*	5/1866	Sharp, Stewart & Co	12/1894 & 4/1924	1196	4/1948
59 *Seaham*	5/1866	Sharp, Stewart & Co	2/1894 & 9/1924	1197	4/1948

3-9, 23 (GW 10-21) 0-4-4T, 1895
Weight Diagram

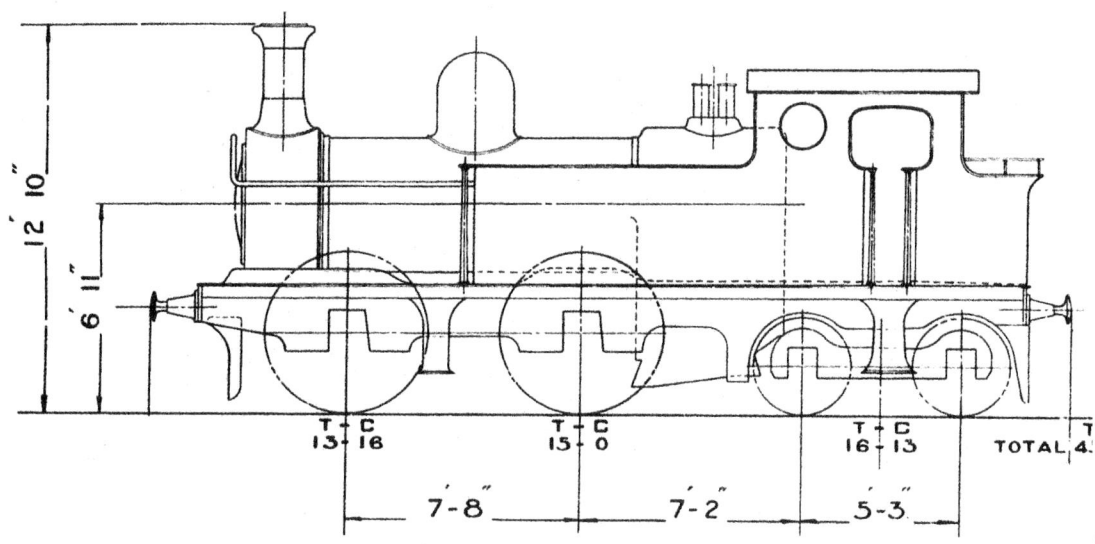

Statistics

Cambrian	Built	Maker	GW No.	Rebuilt	Withdrawn
3	6/1895	Nasmyth, Wilson	10	5/1925	10/1932
5	7/1895	Nasmyth, Wilson	11		5/1922
7	8/1895	Nasmyth, Wilson	15		10/1922
8	6/1899	Nasmyth, Wilson	19	7/1925	10/1932
9	6/1899	Nasmyth, Wilson	20		6/1928
23	7/1899	Nasmyth, Wilson	21		5/1922

22 formerly *Coel*, Van Railway 0-4-0ST, 1901
Statistics

Cambrian	Built	Maker	Withdrawn
22 *Coel*	7/1901	Manning, Wardle & Co	9/1914 (Sold)

Cardiff Railway
Marquis of Bute No.5 0-4-0T, 1862
Marquis of Bute No.17 0-4-0T, 1874
Marquis of Bute No.24 0-4-2T, reb. 2-4-2T, c1883
Marquis of Bute No.3, 6, 13 4-4-0T, ex-NLR Metropolitan, 1861, acquired 1882/3

Statistics

M of Bute	Built	Maker	Acquired	Rebuilt	Withdrawn
3	1861	Slaughter, Gruning & Co	1882		1895
5	2/1862	Manning, Wardle & Co			1898
6	1861	Slaughter, Gruning & Co	1882		1898
13	1861	Slaughter, Gruning & Co	1883		1895
17	6/1874	Fox, Walker & Co			1917 (Sold)
24	Unknown	Beyer, Peacock & Co		1883	1885 (rebuilt as 0-6-0ST)

5, 6 (GW 1338-1339) 0-4-0ST, 1898
Weight diagram

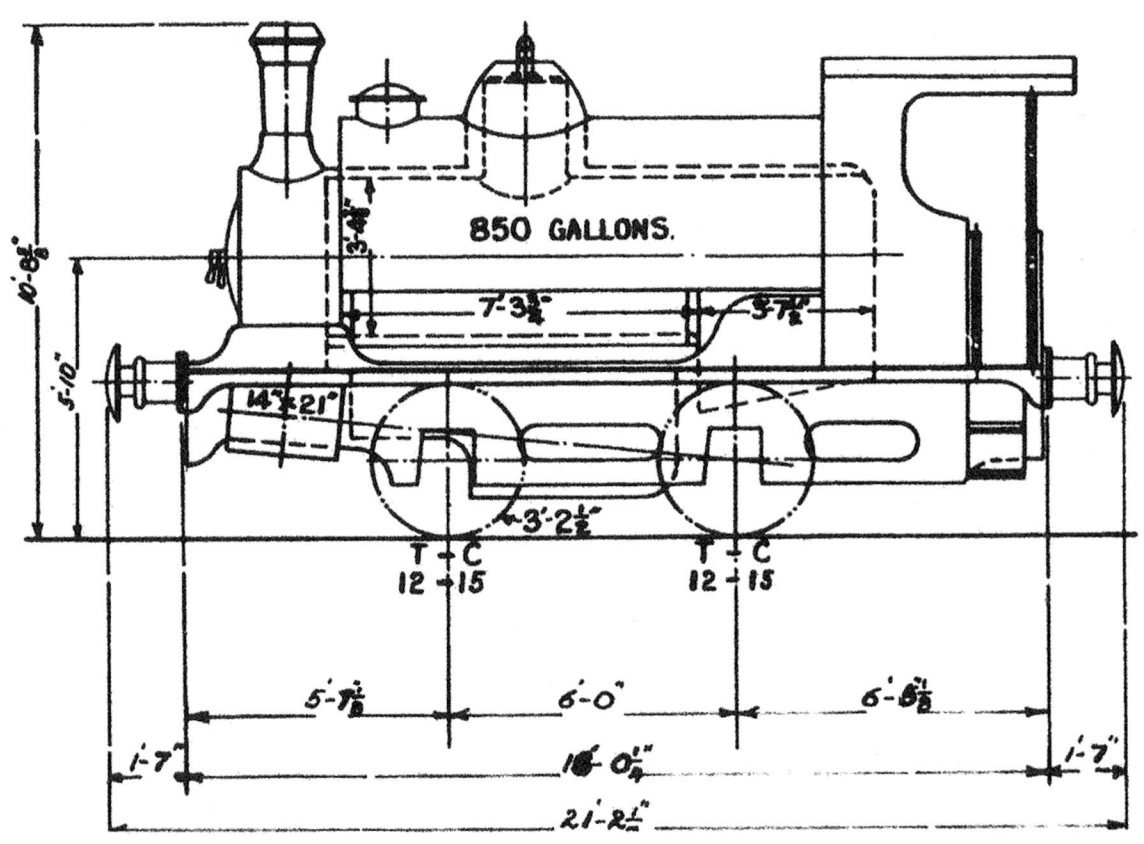

Statistics

Cdf Rly	Built	Maker	Rebuilt	GW No.	Withdrawn
5	1898	Kitson & Co	1/1918	1338	9/1963 (Preserved)
6	1899	Kitson & Co	12/1916	1339	5/1932

1-3 Steam Railmotors 0-4-0T, 1905
Statistics

Cdf Rly	Built	Maker	Withdrawn
1	2/1911	W. Sisson & Co	(kept as spare, withdrawal unknown)
2	1911	Gloucester C & W	1914 (converted to trailer vehicles for loco haulage)
3	1911	Gloucester C & W	1914 (converted to trailer vehicles for loco haulage)

36 (GW 1327) 2-4-2T LNWR, 1879, reb. 1898, acquired 1914
Weight diagram

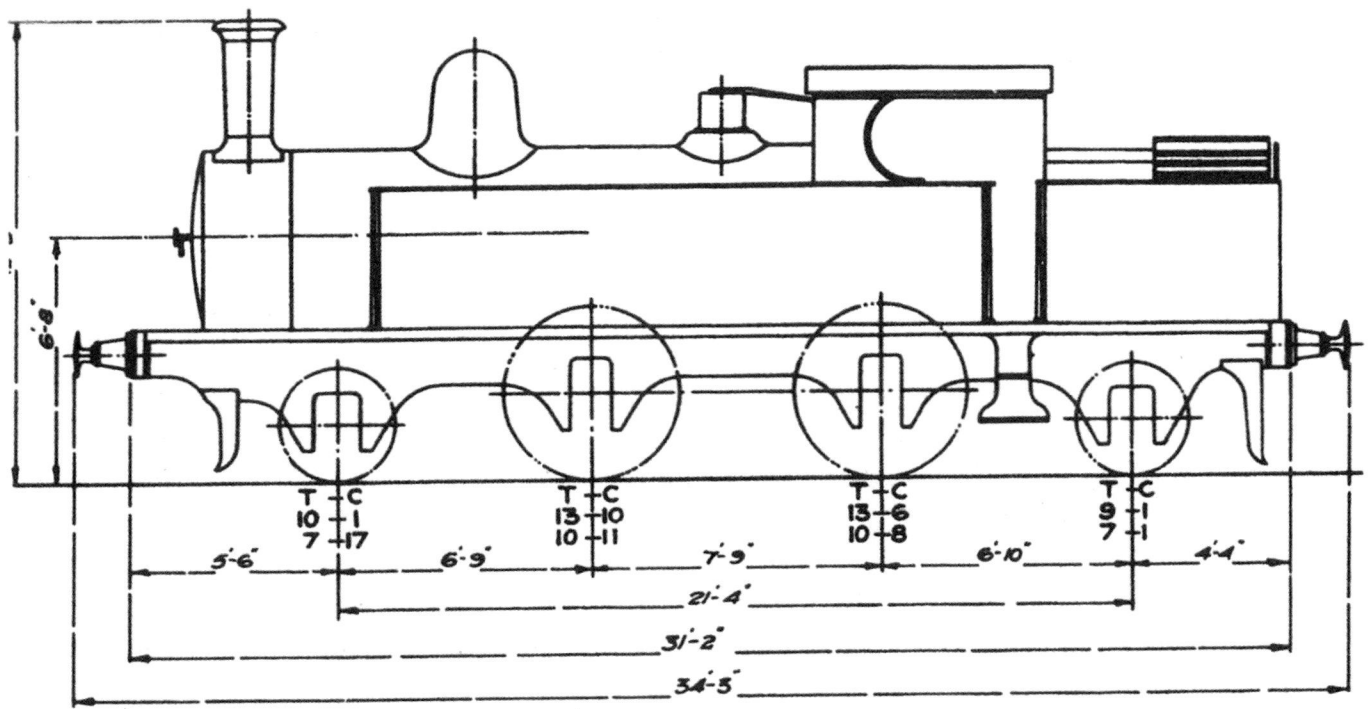

Statistics

Cdf Rly	Built	Maker	Rebuilt	Acquired	GW No.	Withdrawn
36 *The Earl of Dumfries*	1879	Crewe	1898	1914	1327	5/1922.

Midland & South Western Junction Railway
Swindon, Marlborough & Andover Rly
4, 0-4-4T Fairlie, 1878
5-8, 2-4-0T, 1882
Statistics

S & MR Rly	Built	Maker	Acquired	Renumbered	Withdrawn
4	1878	Avonside Engine Co	1882		1892 (stationary boiler)
5	1882	Beyer, Peacock			9/1912
6	1882	Beyer, Peacock			11/1906 (Sold)
7	1882	Beyer, Peacock			5/1910
8	1884	Beyer, Peacock		29 (1912)	1/1918 (Sold)

15 (GW 23) 0-4-4T, 1895
Weight diagram

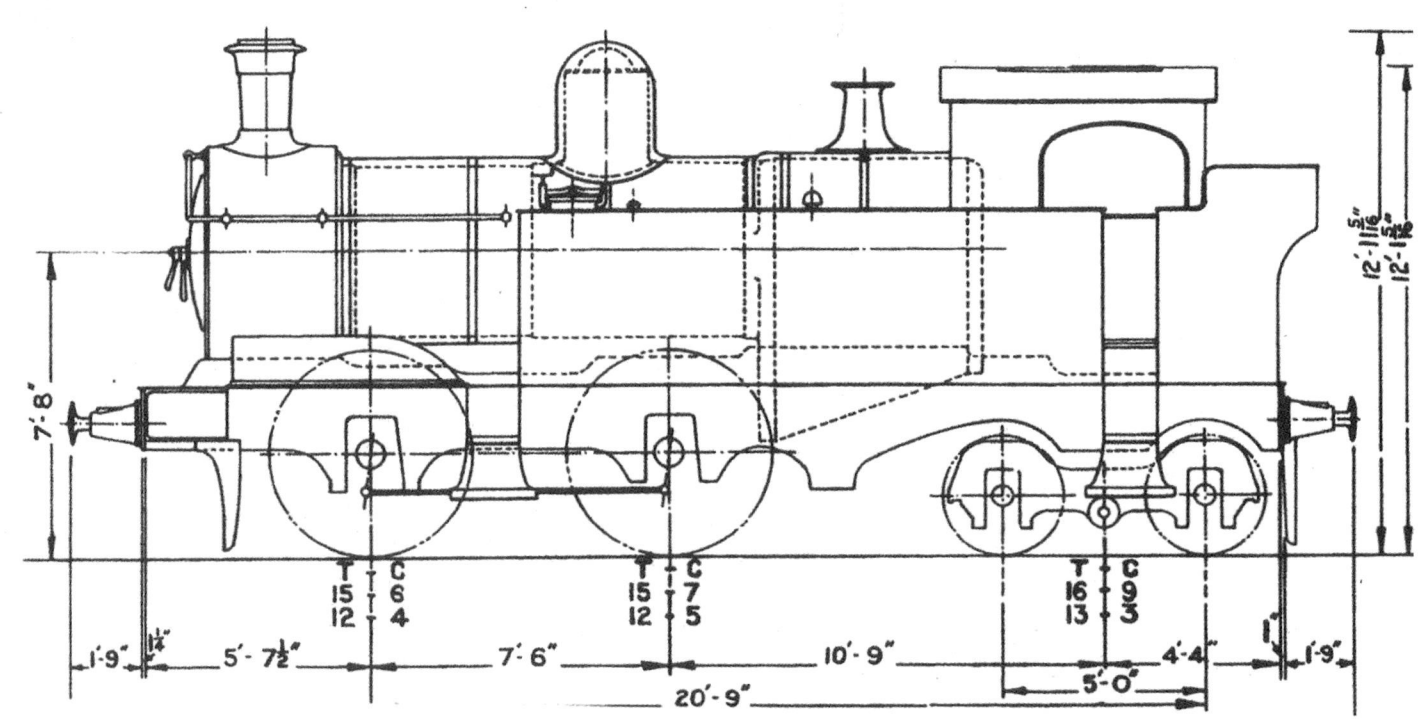

Appendix • 165

17, 18 (GW 25, 27) 4-4-4T, 1897
Weight diagrams

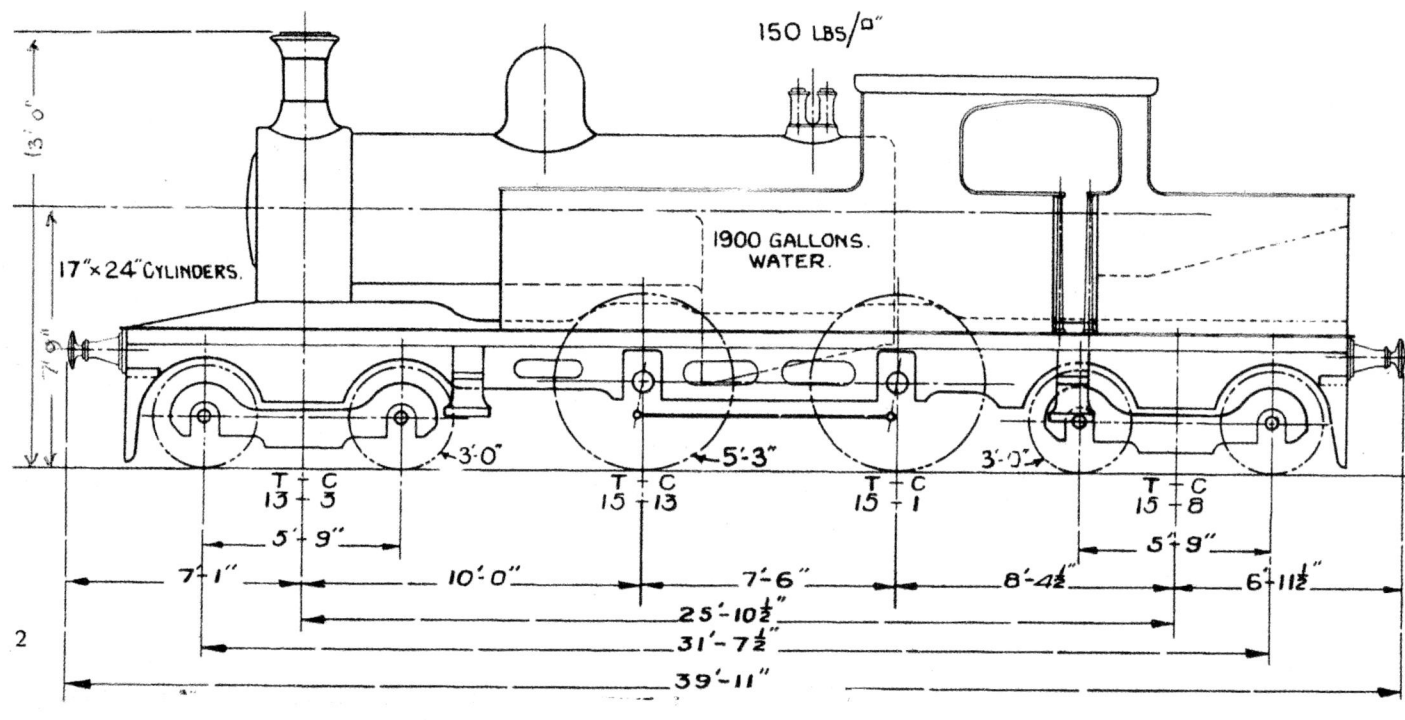

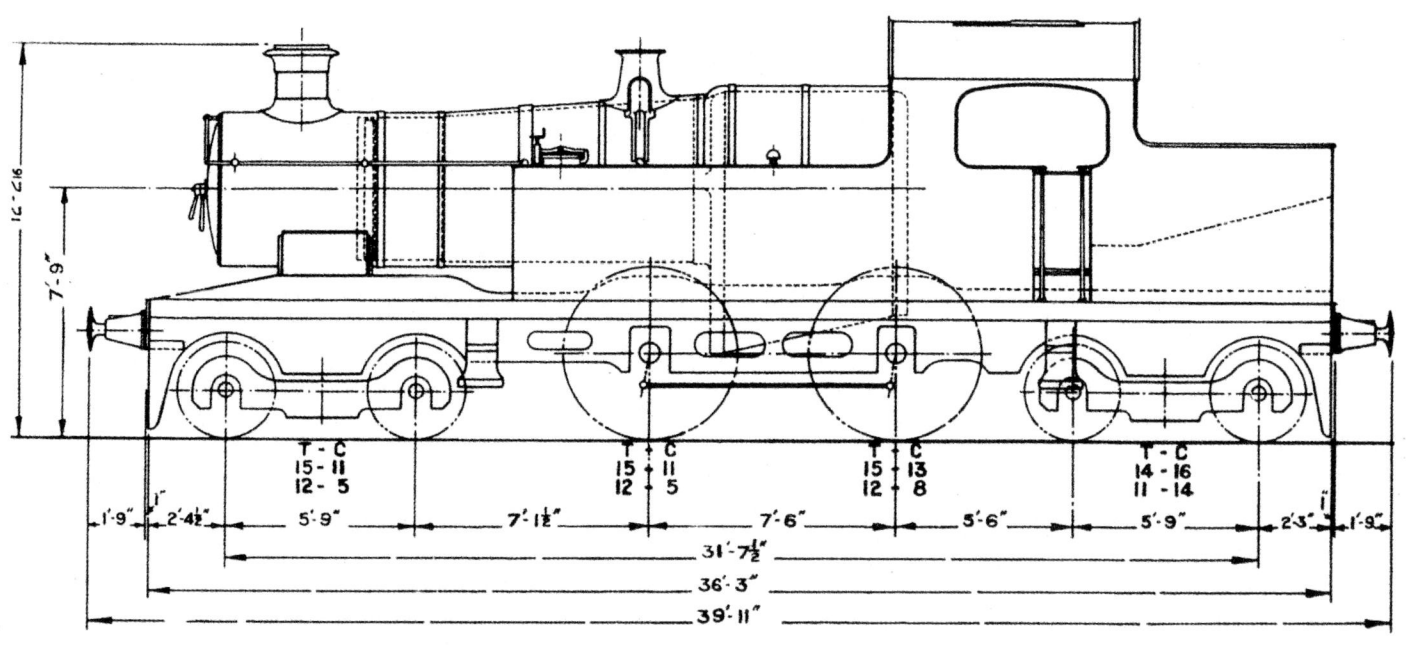

Statistics

M&SWJR	Built	Maker	GW No.	Rebuilt	Withdrawn
15	1895	Beyer, Peacock	23	1925	2/1930
17	1897	Sharp, Stewart	25	1925	10/1927
18	1897	Sharp, Stewart	27	1925	9/29

Neath & Brecon Railway
Progress Fairlie 0-4-4-0T, 1865
Mountaineer Fairlie 0-4-4-0T, 1866
4 (renumbered 5) (GW 1392) 4-4-0T, 1871
Weight Diagram

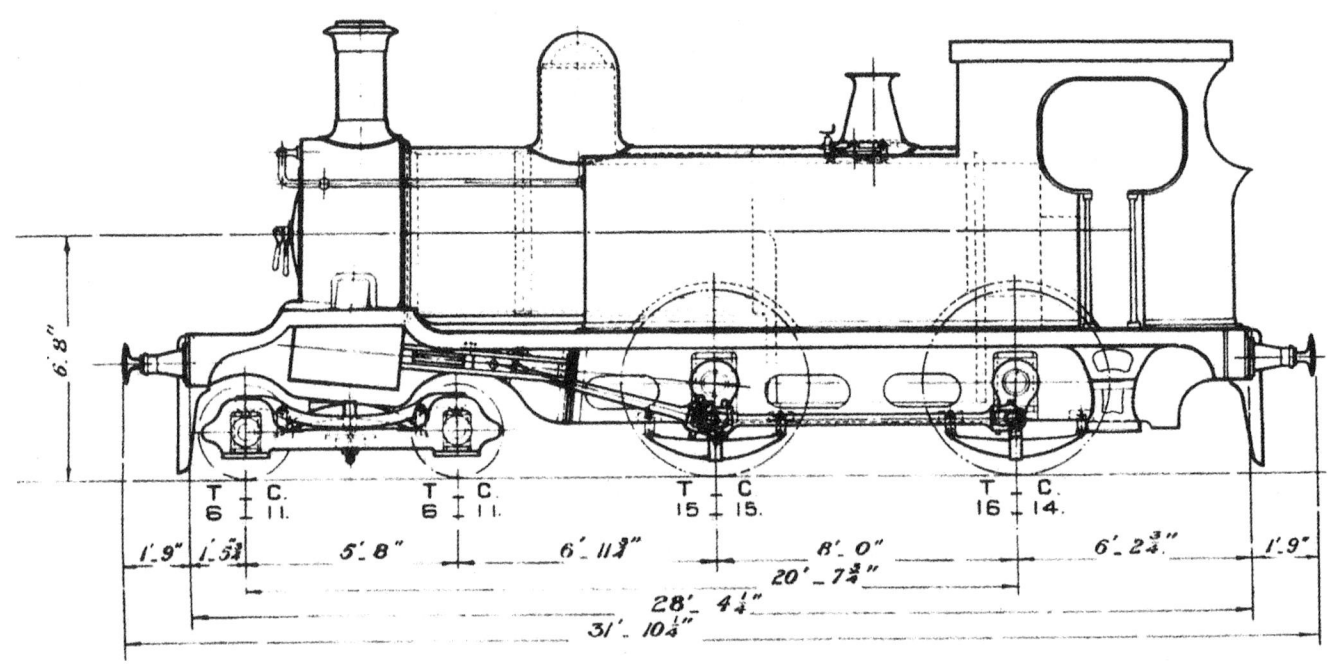

6 (GW 1400) 2-4-0T
Statistics

N & B	Built	Maker	Acquired	GW No.	Rebuilt	Withdrawn
Progress	12/1865	James Cross	1866 (leased)			9/1868 (lease terminated)
Mountaineer	8/1866	James Cross				2/1880 (Sold)
4 (later 5)	4/1871	Yorkshire Engine Co	1392	2/1898		4/1921, 1926
6	1892	Sharp, Stewart	1400	1908		10/1926

Port Talbot Railway
37 (GW 1189) ex-Barry Rly 'C' 2-4-0T, 1890
36 (GW 1326) ex-Barry Rly 'C' 52 2-4-2T, 1890
Weight diagrams

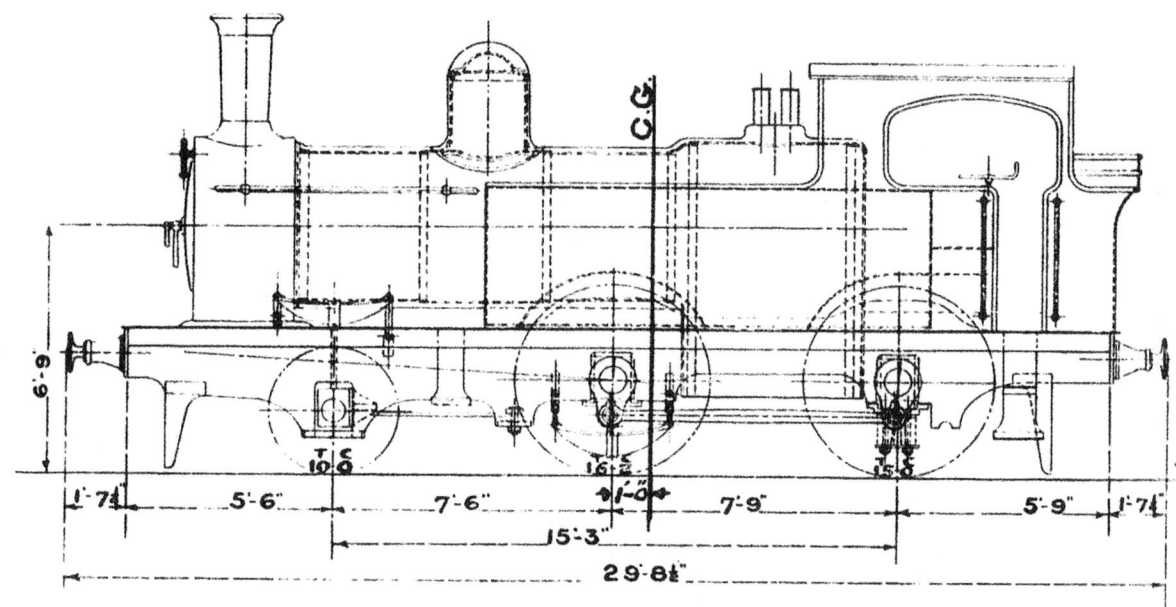

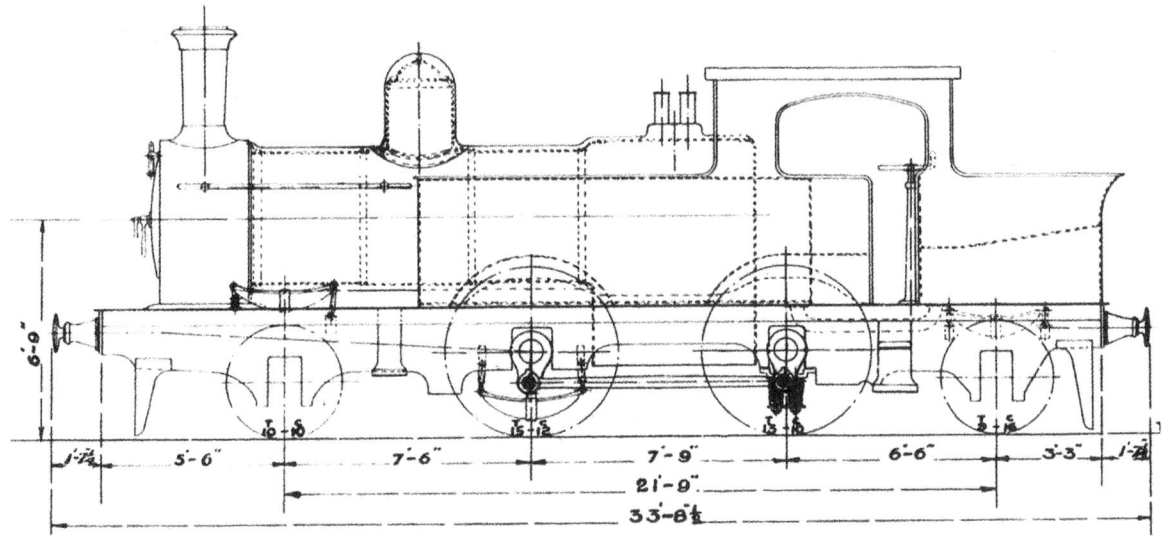

Statistics

PTR	Built	Maker	Acquired	GW No.	Rebuilt	Withdrawn
37	1890	Sharp, Stewart	1898	1189	1915	11/1926
36	1890	Sharp, Stewart	1898	1326	1925	8/1930

Rhondda & Swansea Bay Railway
17-19 (GW 1307, 1309-1310) 2-4-2T, 1895
Weight Diagrams
As Built

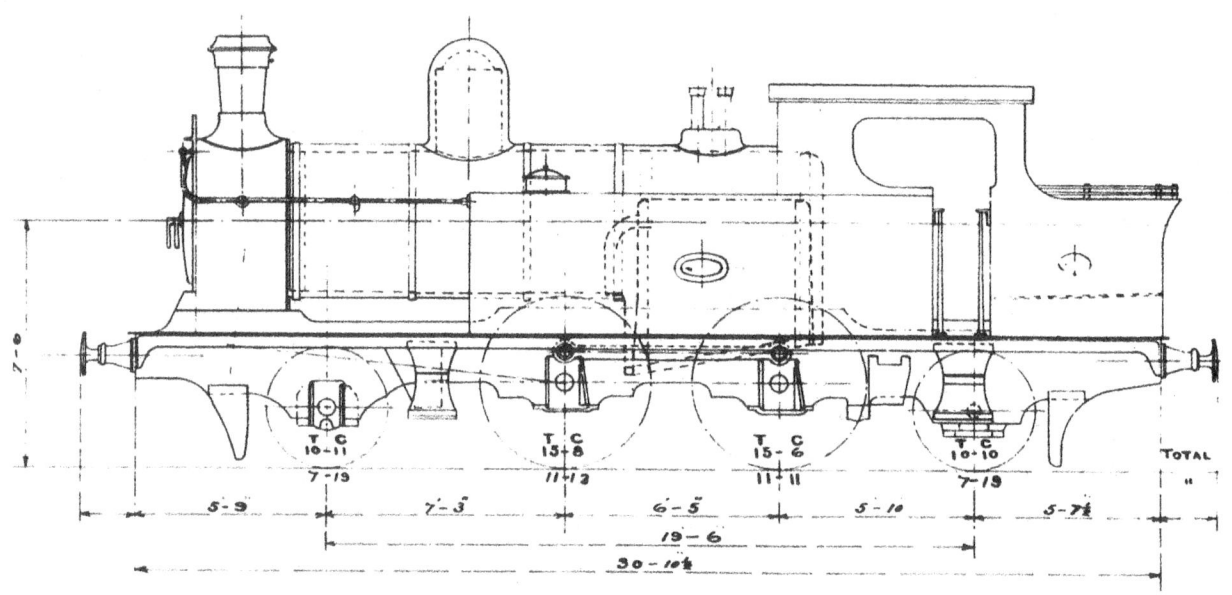

1310 as rebuilt in 1922

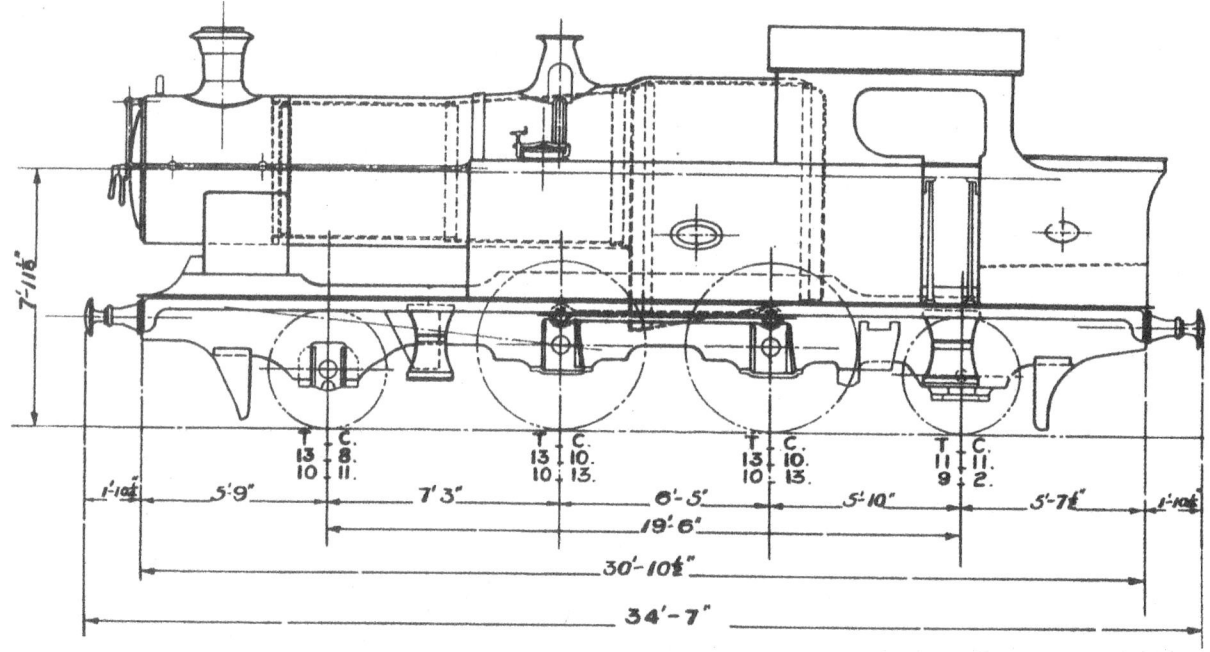

Statistics

R&SB	Built	Maker	GW No.	Rebuilt	Withdrawn
17	4/1895	Kitson	1307	2/1910	1926
18	4/1895	Kitson	1309	8/1907	1926
19	5/1895	Kitson	1310	4/1908, 2/1922	9/1928

Rhymney Railway
7-9 & 16, 2-4-0T, reb. from 1873
62-66 (GW 1324-1325) 2-4-2ST, 1891
Weight Diagram

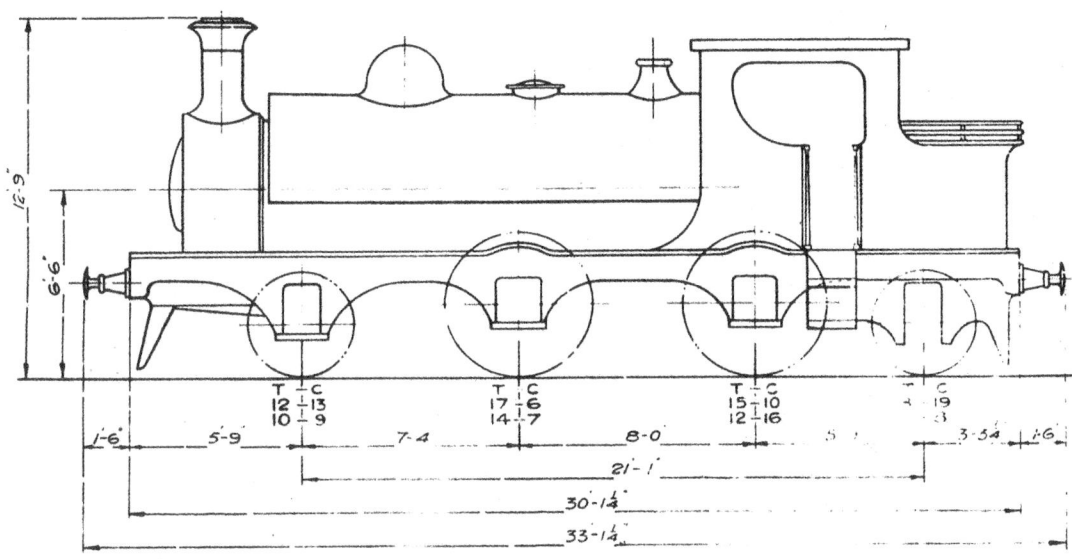

Statistics

RR	Built	Maker	Rebuilt	GW No.	Withdrawn
7	5/1858	Vulcan Foundry	1881		1895 (Sold 1902)
8	6/1858	Vulcan Foundry	1880		1895 (Sold 1902)
9	6/1858	Vulcan Foundry	1881		1895 (Sold 1902)
16	9/1861	Vulcan Foundry	1873 & 1881		1904
62	1891	Vulcan Foundry	1908 (as 0-6-2ST)		12/1921
63	1891	Vulcan Foundry	1908 (as 0-6-2ST)		10/1922
64	1891	Vulcan Foundry	1911 (as 0-6-2ST)		3/1923
65	1891	Vulcan Foundry		1324	10/1928
66	1891	Vulcan Foundry		1325	8/1928

1-2 Steam Railmotors 0-4-0T, 1907
Statistics

RR	Built	Maker	Rebuilt	RR No.	GW No.	Withdrawn
1	1907	Hudswell Clarke	1910 (as 0-6-0T)	120	661	1925
2	1907	Hudswell Clarke	1919 (as 0-6-0T)	121	662	1925

Swansea Harbour Trust Railway
1, 3-7 0-4-0ST Westlake, 1885
1-4, 7-10 (GW 886, 926, 930, 933) 0-4-0ST Peckett, 1891
1-3 (GW 150) 0-4-0ST, Hudswell Clarke, 1905
4-6 (SHT5, GW 701/1140), 0-4-0ST, 1905
11, 12, (GW, 929/1141, 968/1143, 1098/1145) 0-4-0ST, Peckett, 1906-18
Weight Diagram

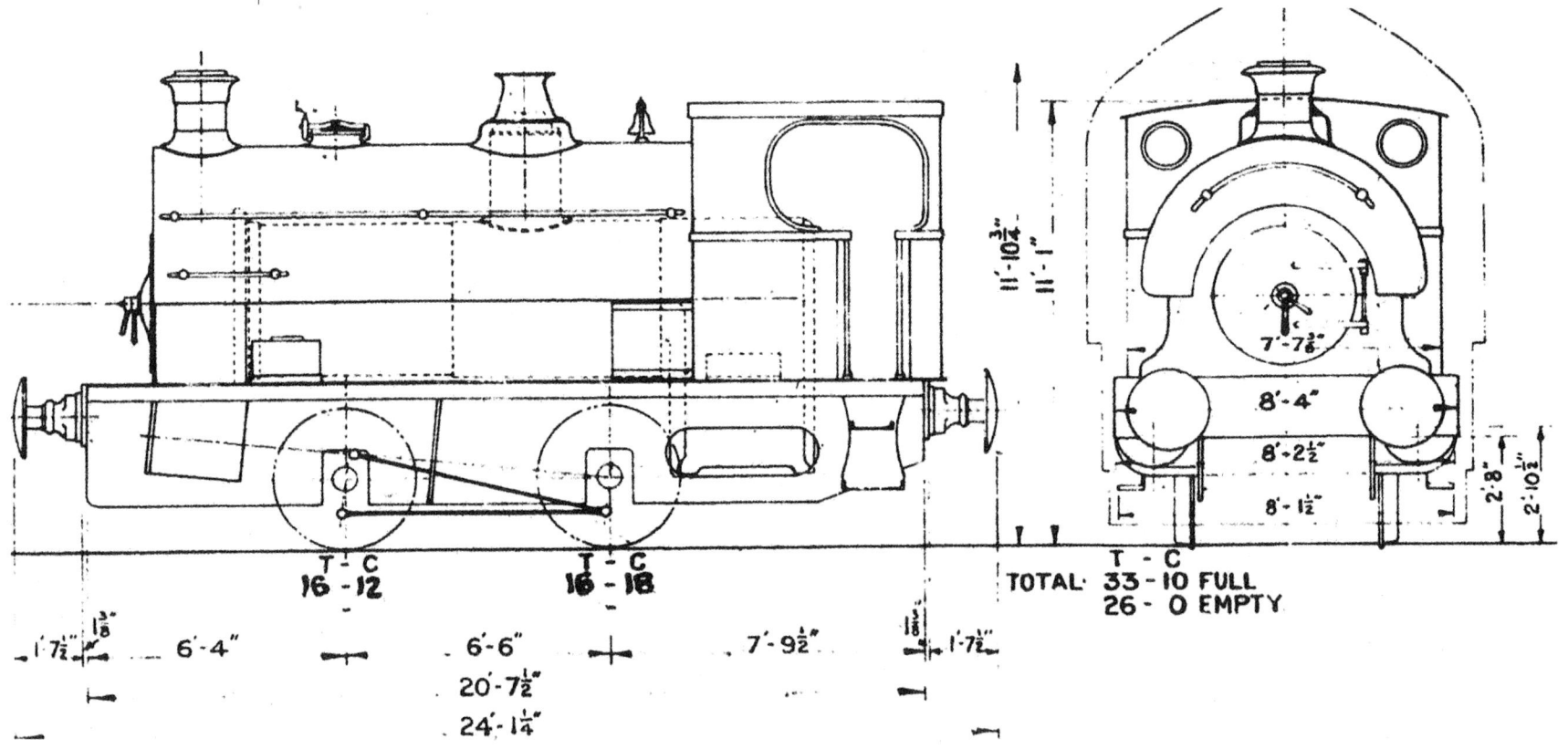

13 (GW 974/1144) Hawthorn Leslie, 0-4-0ST, 1909
Weight Diagram

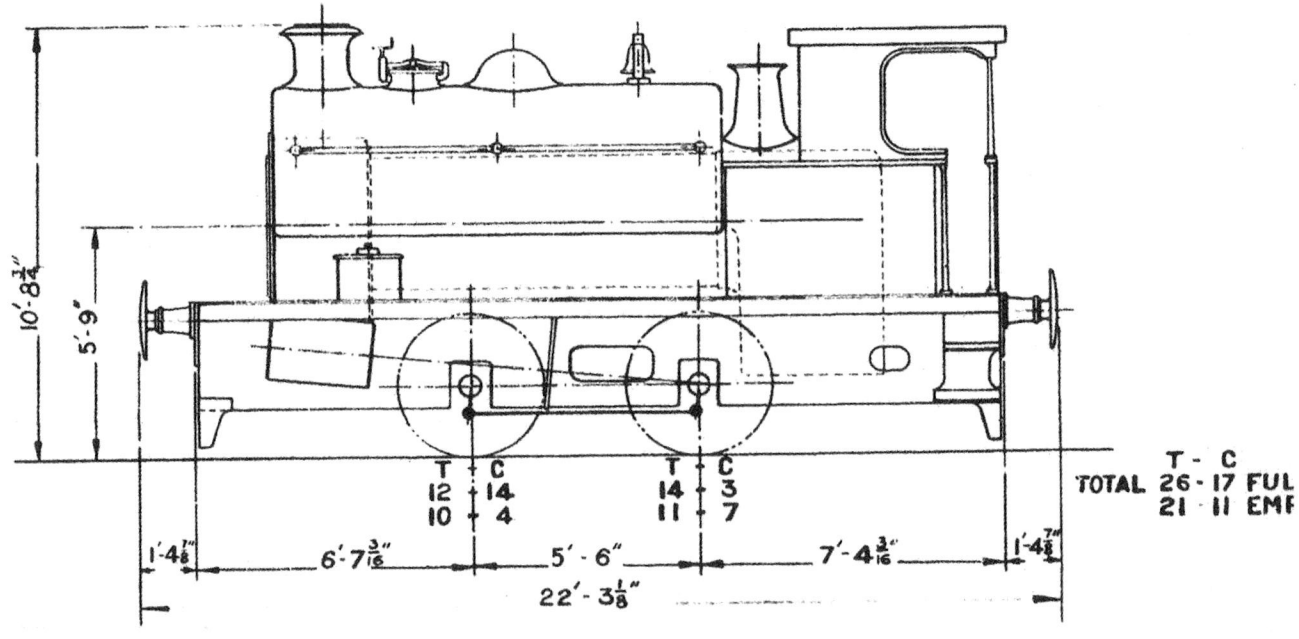

14 (GW 943/1142) Hudswell Clarke 0-4-0ST, 1911
Weight Diagram

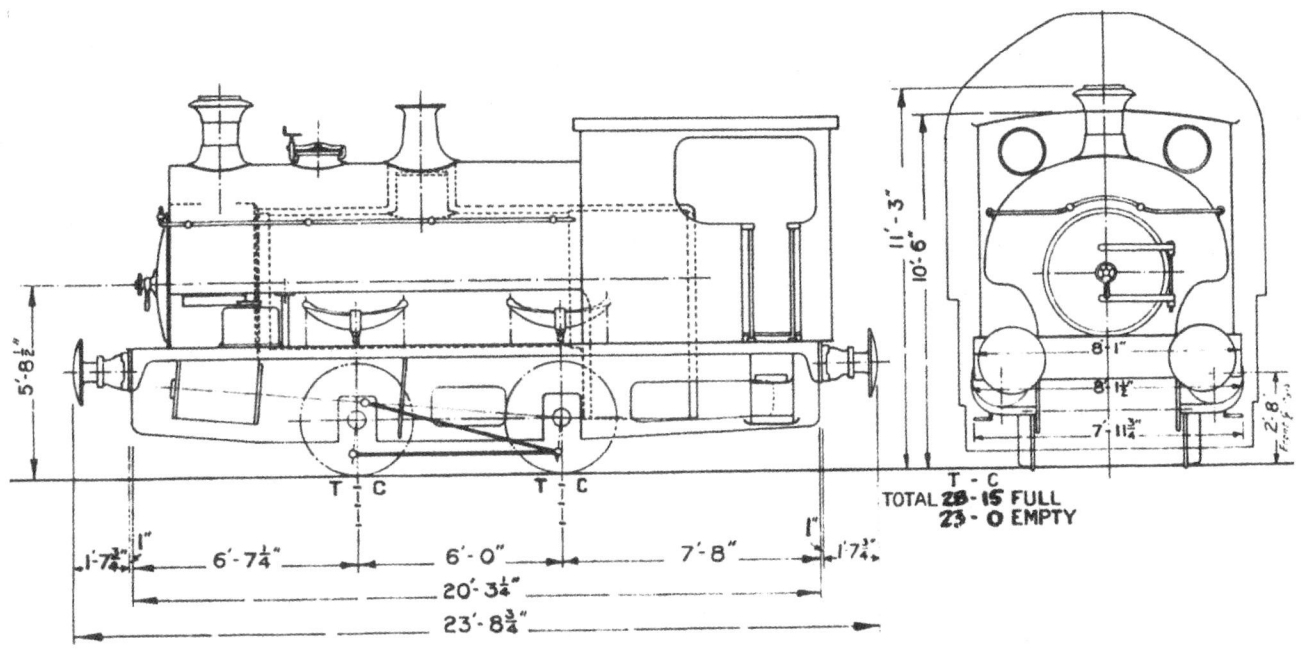

Statistics

Pre-SHT	SHT	Built	Maker	GW 1923 No.	GW 1946 No.	Withdrawn
1 Westlake		1885	Hawthorn, Leslie			1890s (Sold)
3 Westlake		N/A				1890s (Sold)
4 Westlake		1888	Hawthorn, Leslie			1890s (Sold)
5 Westlake		N/A				1890s (Sold)
6 Westlake		N/A				1890s (Sold)
7 Westlake		c1892	Manning, Wardle			1890s (Sold)
1 Rowland		7/1891	Peckett			1910 (Sold)
2 Rowland		8/1891	Peckett			1909 (Sold)
3 Rowland		9/1891	Peckett			1910 (Sold)
4 Rowland		5/1895	Peckett			1911 (Sold)
7 Rowland	7	8/1899	Peckett	886		2/1928
8 Rowland	8	10/1899	Peckett	926		7/1929 (Sold)
9 Rowland	9	4/1902	Peckett	930		2/1927
10 Rowland	10	4/1904	Peckett	933		12/1927 (Sold)
	1	4/1905	Hudswell, Clarke			1915 (Sold)
	2	4/1905	Hudswell, Clarke			1915 (Sold)
	3	4/1905	Hudswell, Clarke	150		5/1929
	4	4/1905	Barclay			1915 (Sold)
	5	4/1905	Barclay	701	1140	5/1958
	6	4/1905	Barclay			1915 (Sold)
	11	6/1906	Peckett	929	1141	7/1952
	12	5/1908	Peckett	968	1143	11/1960
	13	7/1909	Hawthorn, Leslie	974	1144	1/1960
	14	1911	Hudswell, Clarke	943	1142	11/1959
	18	10/1918	Peckett	1098	1145	7/1959

SHT - Powlesland & Mason Engines
5, 6 (GW 795, 921) Brush Electrical 0-4-0ST, 1903
Weight Diagrams

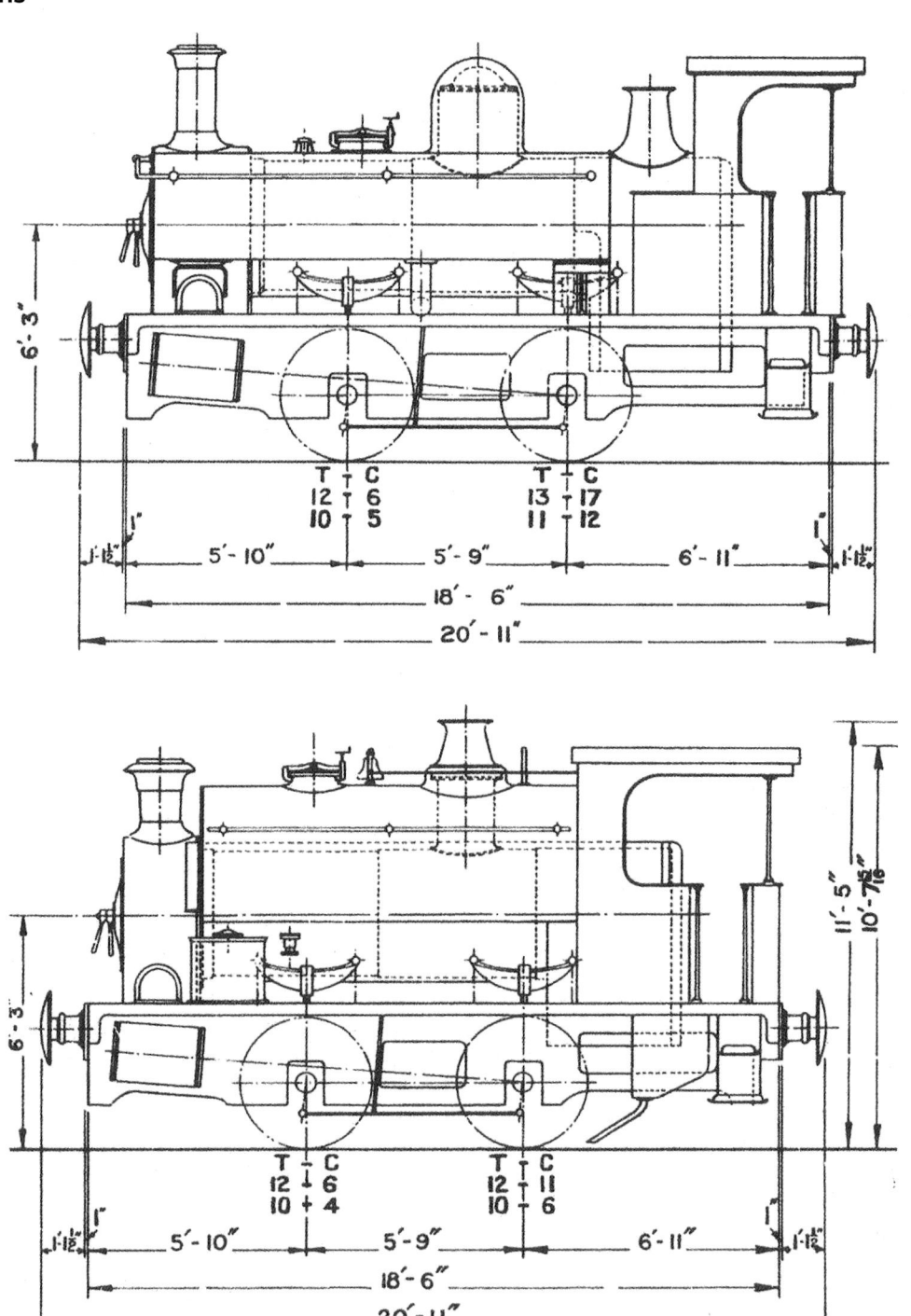

3, 4, 11, 12 (GW 696, 779, 927, 935/1150-1152), Peckett 0-4-0ST, 1907 7 (GW 925)
Avonside 0-4-0ST, 1874, acquired 1906-9
Weight Diagram

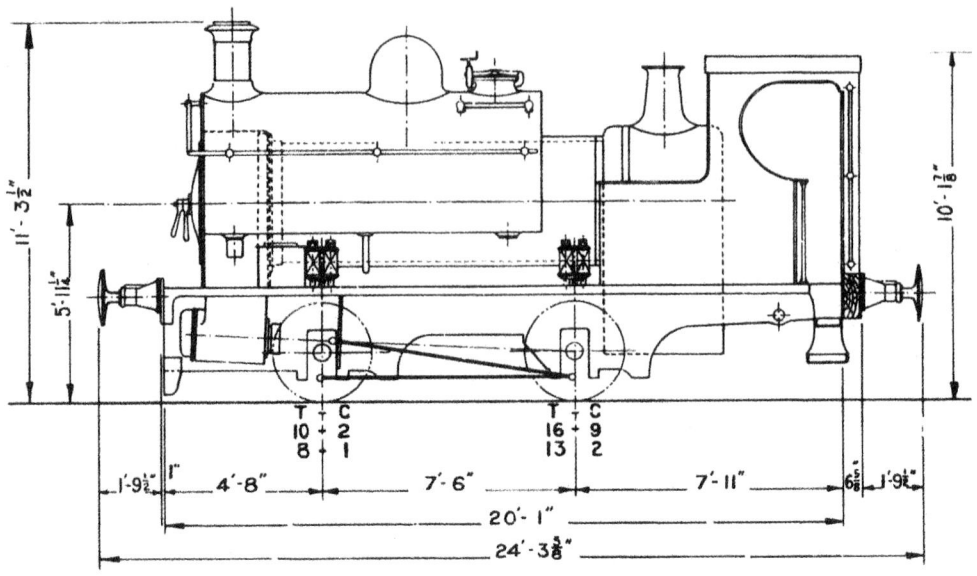

14 (GW 928) Barclay 0-4-0ST, 1912
***Dorothy* (GW 942/1153) Hawthorn Leslie 0-4-0ST, 1903, acquired 1919**
Weight Diagram

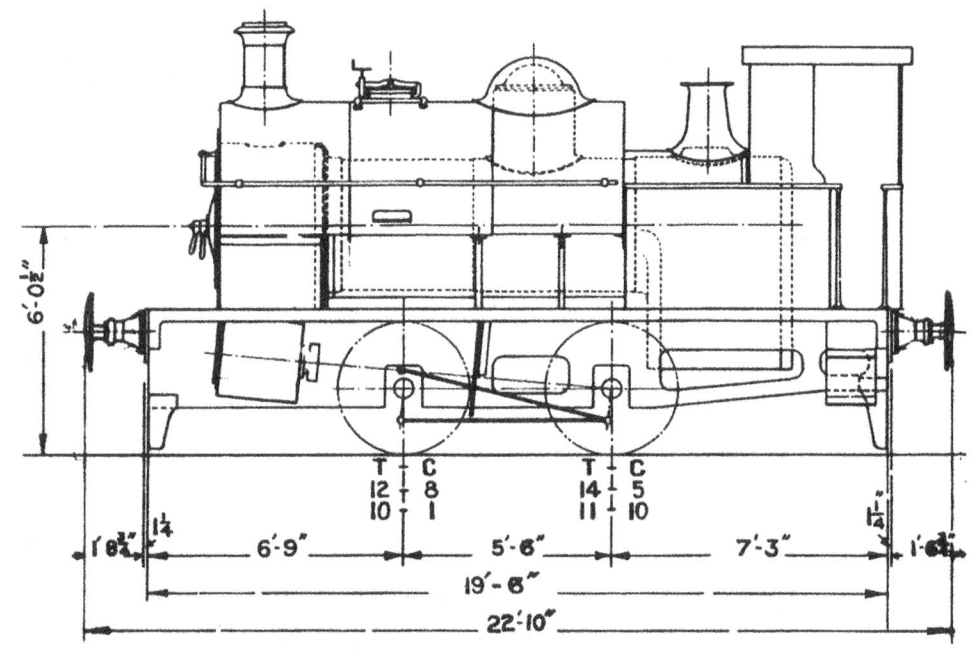

Statistics

P & M	Built	Maker	GW 1923 No.	GW 1946 No.	Withdrawn
3	7/1913	Peckett	696	1150	11/1952
4	9/1916	Peckett	779	1151	8/1963 (Sold)
5	1903	Brush Electrical Engineering	795 reb. 1926		6/1929 (Sold)
6	1906	Brush Electrical Engineering	921		9/1928 (Sold)
7	1874	Avonside Engine Co	925 reb. 1892		5/1929
8	1874	Avonside Engine Co	reb. 1892		1914 (Sold)
9	1874	Avonside Engine Co	reb. 1892		1914 (Sold)
10	1874	Avonside Engineering Co	reb. 1892		1914 (Sold)
11	11/1907	Peckett	927		11/1928
12	1/1912	Peckett	935	1152	12/1961
14	3/1912	A. Barclay	928		3/1927
	Dorothy 1903	Hawthorn Leslie	942	1153	10/1955

Taff Vale Railway
4, 5, 59, 66 'J' class 0-4-4T, 1876
67-69 (GW 999, 1133, 1184) 'I' class 4-4-0T, 1884
Weight diagram

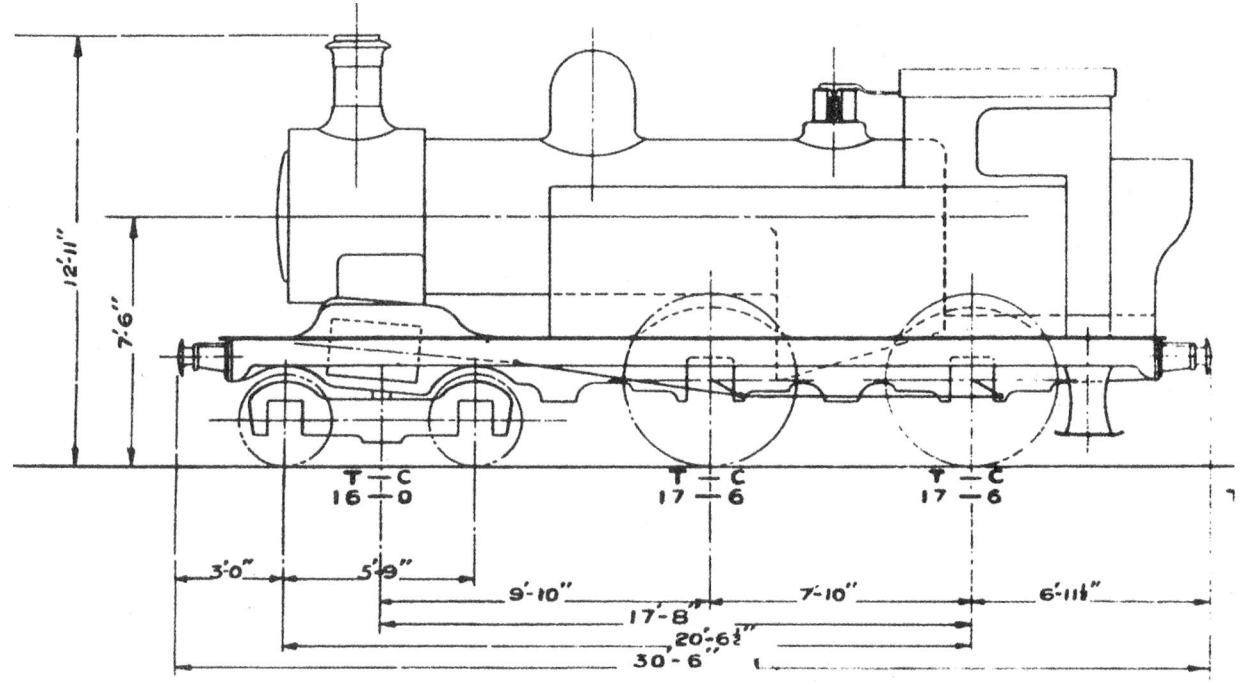

170-174 (GW 1301-1306) 'C' class 4-4-2T, 1888
Weight diagram

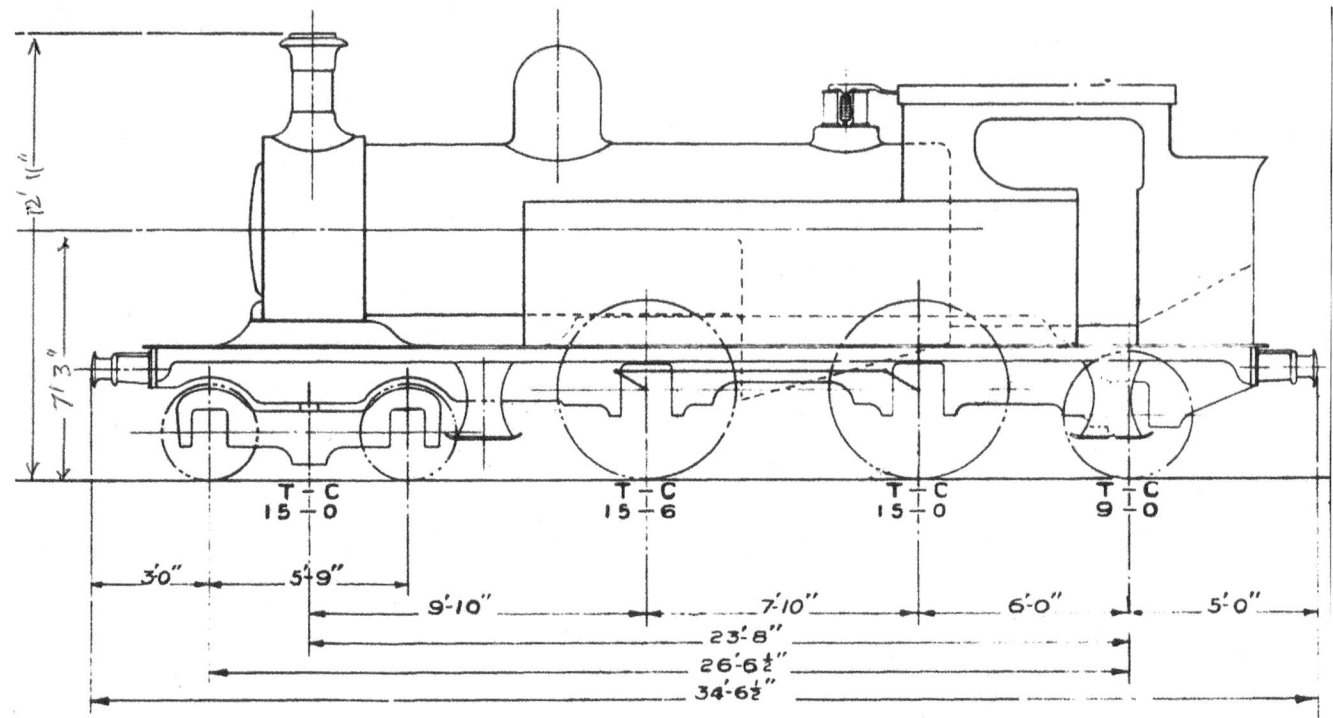

106, 107 (GW 1342-1343), 0-4-0ST, 1876
Statistics

TVR	Built	Maker	TVR Dupl No.	GW No.	Rebuilt	Withdrawn
4	1876 *	TVR	260			2/1893
5	1878 *	TVR	261			2/1893
59	1881 *	TVR	277			6/1906
66	1883 *	TVR	278			1902
67	7/1884	TVR	285	1133	1/1915	12/1925
68	5/1885	TVR	286	1184	6/1914	12/1925
69	9/1885	TVR	287	999	9/1914	12/1925
106	6/1876	Hudswell, Clarke	266	1343	1892	12/1925
107	9/1876	Hudswell, Clarke	267	1342	1895	8/1926
170	8/1888	Vulcan Foundry		1301	7/1911	8/1926
171	8/1888	Vulcan Foundry		1302	7/1910	8/1926
172	9/1888	Vulcan Foundry		1303	6/1913	10/1926

TVR	Built	Maker	TVR Dupl No.	GW No.	Rebuilt	Withdrawn
173	7/1891	Vulcan Foundry		1305	4/1911	10/1926
174	7/1891	Vulcan Foundry		1306	12/1918	6/1925
175	8/1891	Vulcan Foundry		1304	10/1913	11/1927

1-18 Steam Railmotors, 0-4-0T, 1903
Statistics

No.	Built	Maker	Withdrawn
1	1903	TVR	1919
2	1904	Avonside Engine Co	1919
3	1904	Avonside Engine Co	1920
4	1904	Avonside Engine Co	1919
5	1904	Avonside Engine Co	1920
6	1904	Avonside Engine Co	1920
7	1904	Avonside Engine Co	1920
8	1905	Kerr, Stuart & Co	1920
9	1905	Kerr, Stuart & Co	1920
10	1905	Kerr, Stuart & Co	1919
11	1905	Kerr, Stuart & Co	1920
12	1905	Kerr, Stuart & Co	1920
13	1905	Kerr, Stuart & Co	1919
14	1906	Manning, Wardle & Co	1919
15	1906	Manning, Wardle & Co	1920
16	1906	Manning, Wardle & Co	1919
17	1906	Manning, Wardle & Co	1919
18	1906	Manning, Wardle & Co	1919

Vale of Rheidol Railway
3 (GW 1198) 2-4-0T NG, 1896
Statistics

V of R	Built	Maker	Acquired	GW No.	Withdrawn
3 *Rheidol*	1896	Bagnall	1903	1198	7/1924

Weston, Cleveland & Portishead Railway
For details of 4 *Hesperus,* see GW 1384, page 46.

Ystalavera Tin Mine
For details of 1 *Hercules,* see page 131.

Corris Railway
Weight diagrams

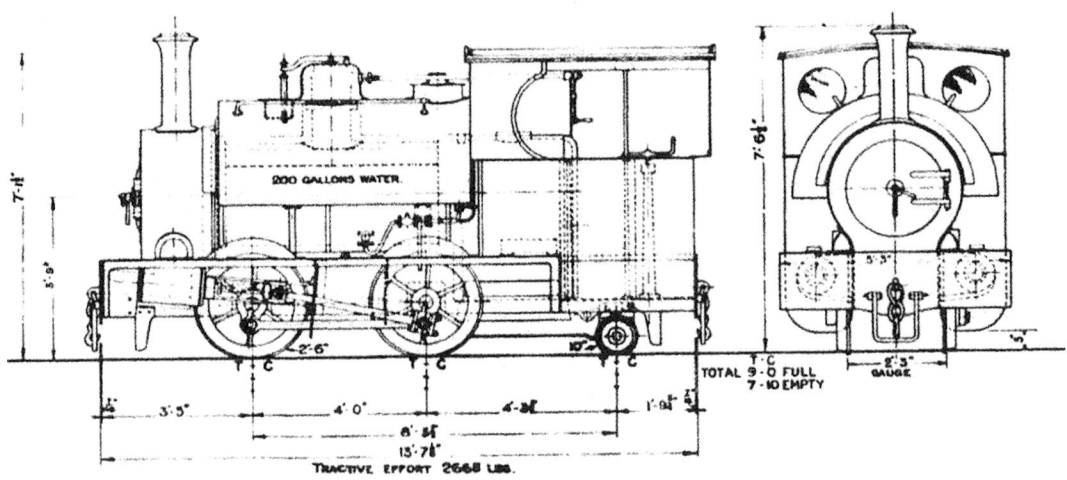

Corris Railway Falcon Engineering Co. No.3 0-4-2T

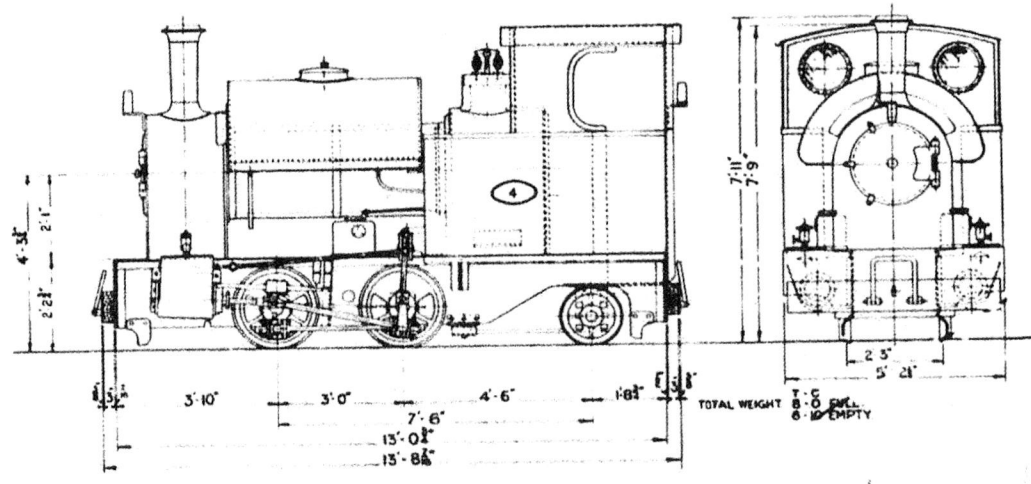

Corris Railway Kerr, Stewart No.4 0-4-2ST

For other details of Nos. 3 & 4, see pages 132 and 133.

Wantage Tramway
For details of No.5, see pages 134 and 139.

BIBLIOGRAPHY

Casserley, H.C., *Locomotives at the Grouping, No.4 Great Western Railway,* Ian Allan, 1966
Maidment, D.J., *Great Western Pannier Tank Classes,* Pen & Sword, 2019
Maidment, D.J. & Carpenter P., *Cambrian Railways Gallery,* Pen & Sword, 2020
Pritchard, Robert & Hall, Peter, *Preserved Locomotives of British Railways,* Platform 5, 2016
RCTS, *The Locomotives of the Great Western Railway, Parts 1-7,* RCTS, 1951
RCTS, *The Locomotives of the Great Western Railway, Parts 8-12,* RCTS, 1953
Russell, J.H., *A Pictorial Record of Great Western Absorbed Engines,* Oxford Publishing Co., 1978
Welsh Railways Research Circle, *The Welsh Railways Archive,* WRRC, November 2020

INDEX

Association of Railway Locomotive Engineers (ARLE), 50
Engineers,
  Auld, John, 13
  Cameron, John, 11
  Churchward, G.J., 50
  Dunbar, James, 12, 13
  Fowler, Sir Henry, 50
  Golding, Henry Frederick, 13
  Gooch, Sir Daniel, 10, 11, 14, 17
  Gregory, C.H., 14
  Gresley, Sir Nigel, 50
  Hosgood, J.H., 13
  Hurry Riches, C.T., 12
  Hurry Riches, Tom, 10, 11
  Long, Charles, 12
  Lundie, Cornelius, 10-12
  Maunsell, Richard, 50
  Owen, George, 12
  Pearson, James, 14
  Robinson, John G., 50
Geddes Committee, 50
Locomotive construction companies, 10
Locomotives, Broad Gauge, 14-23
  Bristol & Exeter Railway
  4-4-0ST (GW 2028-2053), 14-16
    Accident, 15
    Builders
      Avonside
        Construction, 14
        Dimensions, 14
        Statistics, 141
      Beyer Peacock
        Construction, 14
        Dimensions, 14
        Statistics, 140
      Rothwell
        Construction, 14
        Dimensions, 14
        Statistics, 140
    Operation, 15
    Withdrawal, 15
  0-4-2ST (GW 2058)
    Construction, 15
    Dimensions, 15
    Purchase, 15
    Statistics, 141
    Withdrawal, 15
  0-4-2WT (GW 2094-2095)
    Construction, 15
    Dimensions, 15
    Statistics, 141
    Withdrawal, 15
  Carmarthen & Cardigan Railway, 16-17
  4-4-0T, 1861
    Construction, 16
    Dimensions, 16
    Rebuilding, 16
    Sale, 16
    Statistics, 141
  4-4-0ST, 1864
    Construction, 16
    Dimensions, 16-17
    Rebuilding, 17
    Sale, 17
    Statistics, 141
    Withdrawal, 17
  Llynvi & Ogmore Railway, 17
  4-4-0ST *Rosa*
    Construction, 17
    Dimensions, 17
    Rebuilding, 17
    Statistics, 141, 144
    Withdrawal, 17
  South Devon Railway, 17-21
  4-4-0ST (GW 2096-2105)
    Construction, 17
    Dimensions, 18
    Drawing, 17
    Names, 17
    Operation, 18
    Statistics, 142
    Withdrawal, 18
  4-4-0ST (GW 2106-2121)
    Construction, 18
    Dimensions, 18
    Names, 18
    Operation, 18
    Statistics, 142
    Withdrawal, 18
  4-4-0ST (GW 2122-2127)
    Construction, 18
    Dimensions, 19
    Names, 18, 143
    Operation, 19
    Statistics, 143
    Withdrawal, 19
  4-4-0ST (GW 2128-2131)
    Construction, 19
    Names, 19
    Statistics, 143
    Withdrawal, 19
  4-4-0ST (GW 2132-2135)
    Acquisition, 19
    Names, 19, 143
    Statistics, 143
    Withdrawal, 20
  2-4-0ST (GW 2136)
    Acquisition, 20

Construction, 20
Drawing, 20
Name, 20
Operation, 20
Statistics, 143
Withdrawal, 20
2-4-0ST (GW 2137)
Construction, 20
Dimensions, 20
Name, 20
Rebuilding, 20
Statistics, 143
Withdrawal, 20
2-4-0T (GW 2171)
Construction, 20
Dimensions, 20
Name, 20
Rebuilding, 21
Sale, 21
Statistics, 144
0-4-0WT (GW 2172-2179)
Construction, 21
Dimensions, 21
Drawing, 21
Names, 21
Operation, 21
Rebuilding, 21
Sale, 21
Statistics, 144
Withdrawal, 21
0-4-0WT (GW 2180)
Dimensions, 21
Name, 21
Operation, 21
Preservation, 21, 138
Stationary boiler, 21
Statistics, 144
South Wales Mineral Railway, 21-22
0-4-0ST & 0-4-2ST (GW 2058)
Construction, 22
Dimensions, 22
Names, 22
Rebuilding, 22
Sale, 22
Statistics, 145
Torbay & Brixham Railway, 22-23

0-4-0WT *Queen*
Construction, 22
Dimensions, 22-23
Name, 22
Statistics, 145
Withdrawal, 23
0-4-0ST *Raven*
Construction, 23
Dimensions, 21
Name, 23
Sale, 23
Statistics, 145
Withdrawal, 21
Vale of Neath Railway, 23
4-4-0ST (1-6)
Construction, 23
Dimensions, 23
Livery, 23
Sale, 23
Statistics, 145
4-4-0ST (7-9)
Construction, 23
Dimensions, 23
Drawing, 23
Rebuilding, 23
Statistics, 145
Withdrawal, 23
Locomotives, Narrow Gauge
Corris Railway, 132-133
0-4-2ST Falcon & Co
Construction, 132
Dimensions, 133
Name, 133
Rebuilding, 133
Sale, 133
Talyllyn Railway, 133, 139
Weight diagram, 178
Withdrawal, 133
0-4-2ST Kerr Stewart
Construction, 133
Dimensions, 133-134
Name, 133
Sale, 133
Talyllyn Railway, 133, 139
Weight diagram, 178
Festiniog & Blaenau Railway, 29
0-4-2ST (1-2)

Construction, 29
Dimensions, 29
Sale, 29
Vale of Rheidol, 128-129
2-4-0T (GW 1198)
Dimensions, 128
Purchase, 128
Rebuilding, 128
Statistics, 177
Withdrawal, 128
Locomotives, Standard Gauge absorbed by 1914, 24-49
Birkenhead Railway, 24-26
2-4-0T (GW 97-98)
Construction, 24
Dimensions, 24
Names, 24
Operation, 24
Statistics, 146
Withdrawal, 24
0-4-0ST (GW 95-96)
Construction, 24
Dimensions, 24
Drawing, 25
Names, 24
Rebuilt, 26
Operations, 26
Statistics, 146
Withdrawal, 26
Bristol & Exeter Railway, 26-28
2-4-2T (GW 1353-1354)
Construction, 26
Dimensions, 26
Drawing, 27
Statistics, 146
Withdrawal, 26
2-4-0T (GW 1358-1359)
Construction, 26
Dimensions, 26
Operation, 26
Statistics, 146
Withdrawal, 26
0-4-0T (GW 1378-1380)
Construction, 26
Dimensions, 26
Statistics, 146
Withdrawal, 26

0-4-0WT (GW 1381-1382)
Construction, 28
Dimensions, 28
Operations, 28
Sale, 28
Statistics, 147
Bristol Port Railway, 28-29
0-4-2T (1-2)
Construction, 28
Dimensions, 28
Livery, 28
Sale, 29
Statistics, 147
Liskeard & Looe Railway, 29-31
2-4-0T (GW 1308)
Construction, 31
Dimensions, 31
Livery, 31
Name, 31
Rebuilt, 31
Operations, 31
Statistics, 147
Withdrawal, 31
Llanelly Railway & Dock Co., 31-32
2-4-0T *Lougher*
Construction, 32
Dimensions, 32
Names 32,
Statistics, 147
Withdrawal, 32
Llynvi & Ogmore Railway, 32
2-4-0ST (GW 915-918)
Construction, 32
Dimensions, 32
Names 32,
Statistics, 148
Withdrawal, 32
Manchester & Milford Railway, 32-34
2-4-2T (GW 1304, 1306)
Construction, 32
Dimensions, 32, 34
Names, 32
Statistics, 148
Withdrawal, 34
Monmouthshire Canal Co., 34-37

2-4-0T, (GW 1301-1302)
Construction, 34
Dimensions, 34
Rebuilding, 34
Statistics, 148
Withdrawal, 34
4-4-0ST (GW 1303)
Construction, 34
Dimensions, 35
Statistics, 148
Withdrawal, 35
4-4-0T (GW 1304-1307)
Construction, 35
Dimensions, 35
Operations, 35
Rebuilding, 35
Statistics, 148-149
Withdrawal, 35
0-4-4T (GW 1345-1352)
Construction, 36
Dimensions, 36
Operations, 36
Rebuilding, 36
Statistics, 149
Withdrawal, 36
0-4-4T (GW 1308-1310)
Construction, 36
Dimensions, 37
Operations, 37
Rebuilding, 37
Statistics, 149
Withdrawal, 37
Newport, Abergavenny & Hereford Railway, 37-38
0-4-2T, 0-4-0T, (GW 194, 195, 227)
Construction, 37
Dimensions, 37-38
Drawings, 37-38
Operations, 38
Rebuilding, 38
Sale, 38
Statistics, 149
Withdrawal, 38
Oxford, Worcester & Wolverhampton Railway, 38-39
0-4-2ST (GW 221, 222)

Construction, 39
Dimensions, 39
Drawing, 39
Rebuilding, 39
Sale, 39
Statistics, 149
Withdrawal, 39
Severn & Wye and Severn Bridge Railway, 39
0-4-0T (GW 1359) *Wye*
Construction, 39
Dimensions, 39
Operations, 39
Statistics, 150
Withdrawal, 39
South Devon Railway, 40-42
2-4-0T *King*
Construction, 20
Rebuilding, 40
Renumbering, 40
Sale, 40
Statistics, 150
2-4-0ST *Prince* **(GW 1316)**
Construction, 20
Rebuilding, 40
Renumbering, 40
Stationary boiler, 40
2-4-0T (GW 1298-1300)
Construction, 40
Crane engine, 41
Dimensions, 40
Operations, 41
Rebuilding, 41
Statistics, 150
Withdrawal, 41
Shrewsbury & Chester Railway, 43-44
2-4-0T (GW 2)
Construction, 43
Dimensions, 43
Drawing, 43
Statistics, 150
Withdrawal, 43
0-4-0ST (GW 15)
Construction, 43
Dimensions, 43-44
Rebuilding, 44

Statistics, 150
Withdrawal, 44
0-4-0WT (GW 16)
Construction, 44
Dimensions, 44
Drawing, 44
Rebuilding, 44
Statistics, 150
Withdrawal, 44
Shrewsbury & Birmingham Railway, 44-45
0-4-2T (GW 40)
Construction, 44
Dimensions, 44
Operations, 44
Rebuilding, 44
Statistics, 150
Withdrawal, 44
0-4-0WT (GW 45)
Construction, 44
Dimensions, 44
Drawing, 45
Rebuilding, 44-45
Statistics, 150
Withdrawal, 45
Shrewsbury, Hereford & Tenbury Railways, 45-46
2-4-0WT (GW 121, 130, 131)
Construction, 46
Dimensions, 46
Drawing, 46
Operations, 46
Statistics, 151
Withdrawal, 46
Watlington & Princes Risborough Railway, 46-48
0-4-2T (GW 1384)
Construction, 46
Dimensions, 46
Operations, 48
Rebuilding, 46
Sale, 48
Statistics, 151
Weight diagram, 151
Withdrawal, 48
West Cornwell Railway, 48
0-4-0T (GW 1391)
Construction, 48
Dimensions, 48
Operations, 48
Sale, 48
Statistics, 152
Withdrawal, 48
West Midland Railway, 48-49
2-4-0T (GW 225, 226)
Construction, 48
Dimensions, 49
Drawing, 49
Operations, 49
Statistics, 152
Withdrawal, 49
2-4-0T (GW 197, 199, 201)
Construction, 49
Dimensions, 49
Drawing, 49
Rebuilding, 49
Statistics, 152
Withdrawal, 49
Locomotives, Standard Gauge absorbed after 1914, 50-128
Alexandra Dock Company, 50-54
0-4-0ST (GW 1340, 1341)
Dimensions, 51
Names, 51
Operations, 51, 53
Preservation, 136
Purchase, 51
Sale, 53
Statistics, 153
Weight diagram, 152, 153
Withdrawal, 51, 53
0-4-0T Steam Railmotor
Construction, 53
Dimensions, 53
Operations, 53
Statistics, 153
Withdrawal, 53
0-4-2T (GW 517 class)
Dimensions, 54
Purchase, 53
Return to GWR, 54
Statistics, 153
Withdrawal, 54
Barry Railway, 54-61
0-4-2T 'E' class
Acquistion, 54
Dimensions, 54
Livery, 54
Operation, 54
Rebuilding, 54
Statistics, 153
Withdrawal, 54
2-4-0T 'C' class
Construction, 55
Dimensions, 55
Operations, 55
Rebuilding, 55
Statistics, 154
Withdrawal, 55
0-4-4T, 'G' class
Construction, 57
Dimensions, 57
Operations, 57
Statistics, 154
Weight diagram, 154
Withdrawal, 57
2-4-2T 'J' class
Construction, 58
Dimensions, 58
Operations, 58
Rebuilding, 58
Statistics, 156
Weight diagrams, 155
Withdrawal, 58
0-4-0T Steam Railmotor
Construction, 61
Dimensions, 61
Operations, 61
Statistics, 156
Withdrawal, 61
Brecon & Merthyr Railway, 61-65
0-4-0ST *Tiny*
Construction, 62
Dimensions, 62
Operations, 62
Sale, 62
Statistics, 156
2-4-0T *Usk*
Construction, 62
Dimensions, 62

Operations, 62
Rebuilding, 62
Statistics, 156
Withdrawal, 62
4-4-2T (ex LSWR)
Dimensions, 62
Livery, 63
Operations, 62
Purchase, 62
Statistics, 157
Weight diagram, 157
Withdrawal, 63
2-4-0T (Met Tank)
Construction, 63
Dimensions, 63
Livery, 63
Operations, 63
Statistics, 157
Withdrawal, 63
Burry Port & Gwendraeth Valley Railway, 66-67
0-4-0ST *Lizzie& Gwendraeth*
Construction, 66
Dimensions, 66
Operations, 67
Rebuilding, 67
Statistics, 157
0-4-4-0T Fairlie class
Construction, 67
Dimensions, 67
Names, 67
Statistics, 157
Withdrawal, 67
Cambrian Railways, 67-79
0-4-2ST *Milford*
Construction, 68
Dimensions, 68
Operations, 68
Statistics, 157
Withdrawal, 68
0-4-0ST *Lilleshall*
Construction, 68
Dimensions, 68
Drawing, 69
Sale, 68
Statistics, 157
0-4-0ST *Plasfynnon* etc

Construction, 69
Dimensions, 69
Names, 69
Operations, 69
Statistics, 157
Withdrawal, 69
4-4-0T ex-Metropolitan
Dimensions, 71
Livery, 71
Operations, 71
Purchase, 71
Statistics, 158
Weight diagram,, 158
Withdrawal, 71
2-4-0T (GW 1190-1191)
Construction, 71
Dimensions, 73
Names, 73
Operations, 73
Rebuilding, 73
Statistics, 160
Weight diagram, 160
Withdrawal, 73
2-4-0T (GW 1192, 1196, 1197)
Construction, 73
Dimensions, 73
Names, 73
Operations, 75
Rebuilding, 75
Statistics, 161
Weight diagram, 160
Withdrawal, 75
0-4-4T (GW 10-21)
Construction, 75
Dimensions, 75
Operations, 77
Statistics, 161
Weight diagram, 161
Withdrawal, 77
0-4-0ST *Coel*
Dimensions, 79
Operations, 79
Purchase, 79
Sale, 79
Statistics, 161
Cardiff Railway, 79-83
0-4-0T Marquis of Bute 5

Acquisition, 80
Dimensions, 80
Statistics, 162
0-4-0T Marquis of Bute 17
Acquisition, 80
Dimensions, 80
Sale, 80
Statistics, 162
0-4-2T Marquis of Bute 24
Acquisition, 80
Rebuilding, 80
Statistics, 162
Withdrawal, 80
4-4-0T Marquis of Bute ex-NLR
Construction, 80
Dimensions, 80
Drawing, 81
Purchase, 80
Statistics, 162
Withdrawal, 80
0-4-0ST (GW 1338-1339)
Acquisition, 80
Dimensions, 80
Operation, 80
Preservation, 80, 82, 136
Rebuilding, 80
Statistics,, 163
Weight diagram, 162
Withdrawal, 80
0-4-0T Steam Railmotor
Construction, 82
Conversion, 83
Dimensions, 83
Operation, 82
Statistics, 163
2-4-2T ex-LNWR
Acquisition, 83
Dimensions, 83
Livery, 83
Name, 83
Operation, 80
Statistics, 163
Weight diagram, 163
Withdrawal, 83
Midland & South Western Junction Railway, 83-90
0-4-4T Fairlie SM&AR

Dimensions, 84
Purchase, 84
Stationary boiler, 84
Statistics, 164
Withdrawal, 84
2-4-0T SM&AR
Construction, 84
Dimensions, 84
Operations, 84
Sale, 84
Statistics, 164
0-4-4T M&SWJR
Construction, 86
Dimensions, 86
Operations, 86
Statistics, 16
Weight diagram, 164
Withdrawal, 86
4-4-4T M&SWJR
Construction, 87
Dimensions, 87
Operations, 87
Rebuilding, 87
Statistics, 166
Weight diagrams, 165
Withdrawal, 87
Neath & Brecon Railway, 91-94
0-4-4-0T Fairlie
Construction, 91
Dimensions, 91
Names, 91
Operations, 91
Sale, 91
Statistics, 166
4-4-0T (GW 1392)
Dimensions, 92-93
Operations, 92
Purchase, 92
Statistics, 166
Weight diagram, 166
Withdrawal, 93
2-4-0T (GW 1400)
Acquisition, 93
Dimensions, 93-94
Operations, 92
Statistics, 166
Withdrawal, 94

Port Talbot Railway, 94-95
2-4-0T (GW 1189)
Acquisition, 94
Dimensions, 94
Operations, 95
Statistics, 167
Weight diagram, 167
Withdrawal, 95
2-4-2T (GW 1326)
Dimensions, 95
Operations, 95
Purchase, 95
Statistics, 167
Weight diagram, 167
Withdrawal, 95
Rhondda & Swansea Bay Railway, 95-97
2-4-2T (GW 1307-1310)
Construction, 95
Dimensions, 95
Operations, 97
Rebuilding, 97
Statistics, 169
Weight diagrams, 168
Withdrawal, 97
Rhymney Railway, 97-103
2-4-0ST Vulcan
Construction, 98
Dimensions, 98
Operations, 98
Rebuilding, 98
Sale, 98
Statistics, 169
Withdrawal, 98
2-4-2ST (GW 1324, 1325)
Construction, 100
Dimensions, 100
Operations, 100
Statistics, 169
Weight diagram, 169
Withdrawal, 100
0-4-0T Steam Railmotor
Construction, 102
Dimensions, 102
Statistics, 170
Withdrawal, 103
Swansea Harbour Trust, 103-110

0-4-0ST Westlake (1, 3-7)
Acquisition, 103
Dimensions, 103
Sale, 104
Statistics, 172
0-4-0ST (GW 886, 926, 930, 933)
Acquisition, 104
Dimensions, 104
Sale, 104-105
Statistics, 172
Withdrawal, 104-105
0-4-0ST (GW 150) Hudswell Clarke
Construction, 105
Dimensions, 105
Sale, 105
Statistics, 172
Withdrawal, 105
0-4-0ST (GW 1140) Barclay
Construction, 105
Dimensions, 105
Sale, 107
Statistics, 172
Withdrawal, 107
0-4-0ST (GW 1141, 1143) Peckett
Acquisition, 107
Dimensions, 107
Sale, 107
Statistics, 172
Weight diagram, 170
Withdrawal, 107
0-4-0ST (GW 1144) Hawthorn Leslie
Acquisition, 108
Dimensions, 108
Statistics, 172
Weight diagram, 171
Withdrawal, 108
0-4-0ST (GW 1142) Hudswell Clarke)
Construction, 108
Dimensions, 108
Statistics, 172
Weight diagram, 171
Withdrawal, 108
0-4-0ST (GW 1145) Peckett
Acquisition, 110

Dimensions, 107
Statistics 172
Withdrawal, 172
Powlesland & Mason (for SHT) 110-117
0-4-0ST 1-3, Brush Electrical Co.
Acquisition, 110
Sale, 110
Statistics,, 175
0-4-0ST GW 795, 921, Brush Electrical Co.
Construction, 111
Dimensions, 111
Preservation, 112, 135
Sale, 111-112
Statistics, 175
Weight diagrams, 173
0-4-0ST (GW 1150-1152) Peckett
Acquisition, 112
Dimensions, 112
Statistics, 175
Weight diagram, 174
Withdrawal, 112
0-4-0ST (GW 925) Avonside
Conversion from Broad Gauge, 115
Dimensions, 115
Renumbering ex-1330-1333, 115
Statistics, 175
Withdrawal, 115
0-4-0ST (GW 928) Barclay
Dimensions, 116
Purchase, 115
Statistics, 175
Withdrawal, 116
0-4-0St (GW 1153) Hawthorn Leslie
Acquisition, 116
Dimensions, 117
Name, 116
Statistics, 175
Weight diagram, 174
Withdrawal, 117
Taff Vale Railway, 117-128
0-4-4T ('J' class)
Construction, 118
Dimensions, 118

Livery, 118
Names, 118
Operation, 118
Rebuilding, 118, 120
Statistics, 176
Withdrawal, 120
4-4-0T, 'I' class
Auto-fitting, 120
Construction, 120
Dimensions, 120
Livery, 120
Operation, 120, 122
Statistics, 176
Weight diagram, 175
Withdrawal, 122
4-4-2T 'C' class
Auto-fitting, 122
Construction, 122
Dimensions, 122
Operation, 122, 125
Statistics, 176-177
Weight diagram, 176
Withdrawal, 125
0-4-0ST (GW 1342, 1343)
Dimensions, 125
Operation, 125-126
Purchase, 125
Statistics, 176
Withdrawal, 126
0-4-0T Steam Railmotor
Construction, 127
Dimensions, 127
Operation, 128
Statistics, 177
Withdrawal, 128
Locomotives acquired by the GWR after 1923, 130-134
Weston, Cleveland & Portishead Railway, 130-131
2-4-0T Dübs
Name, 131
Purchase, 131
Sale, 131
2-4-0T Sharp Stewart
Dimensions, 46
Name, 131
Operation, 131

Purchase, 131
Statistics, 151
Withdrawal, 131
Ystalevera Tinplate Company, 131
0-4-0ST (BRWR 1)
Acquisition, 131
Dimensions, 131
Name, 131
Operation, 131
Withdrawal, 131
Wantage Tramway, 134
0-4-0WT *Shannon*
Dimensions, 131
Earlier locomotives, 21, 39, 134
Preservation, 134, 138-139
Purchase, 134
Photographs, Locations
Aberystwyth, 77, 78, 129
Alexandra Dock Junction, 51
Barmouth, 72
Barry Town, 55-57, 59, 124
Birkenhead Docks, 103
Blagdon, 47
Blodwell Junction, 74
Cardiff Bute Dock, 122, 127
Cardiff Cathays, 121, 125, 126
Cardiff Riverside, 60
Cheltenham, 88, 89
Corris, 132, 133
Cwmfelin RTB, 116
Danygraig, 107, 110, 113, 117, 132
Didcot GW Railway Centre, 137-139
Exeter, 41, 42
Gloucester, 35
Gloucester C&W Works, 48
Handsworth Junction, 90
Hemyock, 42, 47
Kerry, 70
Kidwelly Junction, 67
Llangynog, 75
Machen, 65
Machynlleth, 71
Maespoeth, 133
Marlborough, 88
Merthyr, 65

Newcastle Emlyn, 33
Newton Abbot Works, 22, 139
Oswestry, 69, 72, 74, 76
Oswestry Works, 30
Pontardawe RTB, 111
Swansea East Dock, 81, 106, 107, 112-114, 116
Swansea King's Dock, 104
Swansea South Dock, 82, 108, 114
Swindon station, 86
Swindon Town, 86, 87
Swindon Works, 36, 40, 41, 51, 57, 94, 95, 106
Tamworth, Alders Ltd., 52, 138
Truro, 35
Van Railway, 78
Watchet Docks, 15
Westleigh Quarry, 28

Photographs, Locomotives (GW numbers unless otherwise stated)

Broad Gauge
Heron, 16
71 (Bristol & Exeter Rly), 15
74 (Bristol & Exeter Rly), 15
2122, 18
2125, 19
2132, 20
2180, 22, 139

Narrow Gauge
2 (Festiniog & Blaenau Rly), 29
3 (Corris Rly), 132, 133
3 (Vale of Rheidol), 129
4 (Corris Rly), 133

Standard Gauge
1, 132
1 (Bristol Port Rly), 28
1 (Westlake, SHT), 103
1 (Weston, Cleveland & Portishead Rly), 130
2 (Cambrian Rlys), 71
2 (Manchester & Milford Rly), 32
4, 57
4 (Swindon, Marlboro' & Andover Rly), 84
4 later 5 (Neath & Brecon Rly), 92, 93
4 (Taff Vale Rly), 118
5 (Cambrian Rlys), 76
6 (Neath & Brecon Rly), 93
7 (Cambrian Rlys), 76
7 (Swindon, Marlboro' & Andover Rly), 85
7 (Rhymney Rly), 98
8 (Cambrian Rlys), 77
8 (Swindon, Marlboro' & Andover Rly), 86
9 (B & M), 64, 65
9 (Rhymney Rly), 99
10, 78
10 (renumbered 5) (Swindon, Marlboro' & Andover Rly), 85
10 (Westlake), 104
12 (B & M), 63
12 (Cambrian Rlys), 72
14 (Powlesland & Mason), 115
15, 43
15 (Midland & South Western Junction Rly), 86
16 (Rhymney Rly), 99
17 (Midland & South Western Junction Rly), 87
17 (Rhondda & Swansea Bay Rly), 96
18 (Midland & South Western Junction Rly), 88, 89
19 (Rhondda & Swansea Bay Rly), 96
20, 77
22 (Barry Rly), 56
27, 89, 90
33 (Barry Rly), 55
40, 45
44 (B & M Rly), 63
44 (Cambrian Rlys), 72
58 (Cambrian Rlys), 74
59 (Taff Vale Rly), 119
64 (Rhymney Rly), 101
65 (Rhymney Rly), 100, 101
67 (Taff Vale Rly), 120, 121
68 (Barry Rly), 57
68 (Taff Vale Rly), 121
86 (Barry Rly), 60
88 (Barry Rly), 59
90 (Barry Rly), 58
96, 25-26
97 (Barry Rly), 60
150, 105
170 (Taff Vale Rly), 122
171 (Taff Vale Rly), 123
267 (Taff Vale Rly), 126
696, 112
779, 113
795, 111
921, 111, 135
930, 105
942, 116
943, 109
1104, 107
1140, 106, 107
1142, 109
1143, 107
1144, 108
1145, 110
1151, 107, 113
1152, 114
1153, 113, 116, 117
1189, 94
1196, 74
1197, 75
1299, 41
1300, 41, 42
1302, 34
1304, (Monmouthshire Canal Co) 4-4-0T, 35
1304, (Taff Vale Rly), 124
1305, (Taff Vale Rly), 124
1306, 33
1307, 4-4-0T, 35
1308, 30, 31
1308, 0-4-4T, 36
1310, 97
1313, 59
1316, 40
1324, 102
1326, 95
1338, 81, 82, 136, 137
1339, 51
1340, 51, 52, 138
1341, 51
1342, 126

1343, 125
1351, 36
1358, 27
1381, 28
1384, 46, 47
1391, 48
1460, 65
4666, 109
5029, 137
ADR Steam Railmotor No.1, 53
ADR Steam Railmotor No.2, 54
Barry Rly Steam Railmotor No.2, 61
Cardiff Rly Steam Railmotor No.3, 82
Rhymney Rly Steam Railmotor, No.1, 102
Taff Vale Rly Steam Railmotor No.6, 127
Taff Vale Rly Steam Railmotor No.11, 128
Coel (Cambrian Rlys), 78
Earl of Dumfries (Cardiff Rly), 83
Hesperus (Weston, Cleveland & Portishead Rly), 131
Lizzie (BP&GVR), 66
Milford (Cambrian Rlys), 68
Mountaineer (BP&GVR), 67
Mountaineer (N & B Rly), 92
Pioneer (BP&GVR) 67
Plasfynnon (Cambrian Rlys), 70
Progress (N & B Rly), 91
Prometheus (Cambrian Rlys), 69
Shannon (Wantage Tramway), 139